Madness in Cold War America

This book tells the story of how madness came to play a prominent part in America's political and cultural debates. It argues that metaphors of madness rise to unprecedented popularity amidst the domestic struggles of the early Cold War and become a preeminent way of understanding the relationship between politics and culture in the United States. In linking the individual psyche to society, psychopathology contributes to issues central to post-World War II society: a dramatic extension of state power, the fate of the individual in bureaucratic society, the political function of emotions, and the limits to admissible dissent. Such vocabulary may accuse opponents of being crazy. Yet at stake is a fundamental error of judgment, for which madness provides welcome metaphors across US diplomacy and psychiatry, social movements and criticism, literature and film. In the process, major parties and whole historical eras, literary movements and social groups are declared insane. Reacting against violence at home and war abroad, countercultural authors oppose a sane madness to irrational reason—romanticizing the wisdom of the schizophrenic and paranoia's superior insight. As the Sixties give way to a plurality of lifestyles an alternative vision arrives: of a madness now become so widespread and ordinary that it may, finally, escape pathology.

Alexander Dunst is Assistant Professor of American Studies at the University of Paderborn.

Routledge Studies in Cultural History

For a full list of titles in this series, please visit www.routledge.com

Madness in Cold War America

Alexander Dunst

Routledge
Taylor & Francis Group

NEW YORK AND LONDON

First published 2017
by Routledge
711 Third Avenue, New York, NY 10017

and by Routledge
2 Park Square, Milton Park, Abingdon, Oxon OX14 4RN

Routledge is an imprint of the Taylor & Francis Group, an informa business

Library of Congress Cataloging in Publication Data
Names: Dunst, Alexander, 1980– author.
Title: Madness in Cold War America / by Alexander Dunst.
Description: New York : Routledge, 2017. | Includes bibliographical
   references and index.
Identifiers: LCCN 2016017510 (print) | LCCN 2016019711 (ebook) |
   ISBN 9781138951242 (hardback : alkaline paper) | ISBN
   9781315668338 (ebook) | ISBN 9781315668338
Subjects: LCSH: United States—Politics and government—1945–1989. |
   Cold War—Political aspects—United States—History—20th century. |
   Psychoses—Political aspects—United States—History—20th century. |
   Metaphor—Political aspects—United States—History—20th century. |
   Politics and culture—United States—History—20th century. | Cold War—
   Social aspects—United States. | Psychoses—Social aspects—United States—
   History—20th century. | Popular culture—United States—History—
   20th century. | Counterculture—United States—History—20th century. |
   United States—Social conditions—1945–
Classification: LCC E839.5 .D79 2017 (print) | LCC E839.5 (ebook) |
   DDC 973.92—dc23
LC record available at https://lccn.loc.gov/2016017510

ISBN: 978-1-138-95124-2 (hbk)
ISBN: 978-1-315-66833-8 (ebk)

Typeset in Sabon
by Apex CoVantage, LLC

MIX
Paper from
responsible sources
FSC
www.fsc.org FSC® C013056

Printed and bound in Great Britain by
TJ International Ltd, Padstow, Cornwall

Contents

Figures

Acknowledgments

The first idea for this book came almost ten years ago with the observation that US literature in the 1960s and '70s was fascinated by madness in ways that are, in comparison, lacking in the writing of contemporary American authors. Why was this so, and how did it come to be? Turning questions such as these into a monograph is not the work of one individual. Throughout my PhD at the University of Nottingham, my supervisor Peter Brooker was a role model of generosity and erudition, and I find it difficult to imagine myself as an academic without remembering the friendly guidance and support he provided.

During the writing of this book, a number of people have shared their time and knowledge and provided criticism and encouragement. This book would be unthinkable without them. The errors of judgment or fact that remain are wholly mine, but I would like to show my appreciation to: Fabienne Collignon, Neal Curtis, Erik Davis, Mark Fenster, Philip Goodchild, Martin Halliwell, Peter Knight, Roger Luckhurst, Matthew Mead, Alexander Pavlovic, Christoph Ribbat, Adity Singh, Matthew Smith, Luke Thurston, Véronique Voruz, and Colin Wright. I'm also grateful to the Rare Book and Manuscript Library at Columbia University, the Tamiment Library at New York University, the Berg Collection of English and American Literature at New York Public Library, and the Science Fiction Collection at Pollak Library, California State University, Fullerton, for providing access to their collections; as well as to Routledge's anonymous reviewers for their incisive feedback. Andrea Wilhelmi compiled the index with her customary intelligence and diligence. Finally, I want to thank my friends and family. Their love made every minute of this worthwhile.

1 Introduction

Cold War Madness

Introducing a new edition of *The Paranoid Style in American Politics*, historian Sean Wilentz returned to essays penned half a century earlier to intervene in a presidential contest. Wilentz, an advisor to Hillary Clinton, lashed out both against liberals within the Democratic Party and conservative Republicans. The former he accused, simply, of "left-wing paranoia." As for Republicans, they fell prey to a simplistic moralism and suffered from what he described as a "Manichean political psychology."[1] Wilentz's use of psychiatric terminology for political ends rehashed debates originally conducted at the height of the Cold War. His fellow historian Richard Hofstadter wrote his essay on the paranoid style shortly after the assassination of John F. Kennedy and aimed his ire at Barry Goldwater, Lyndon B. Johnson's contender for the presidency. Such vocabulary may, in effect, accuse opponents of being crazy. Yet at stake is a fundamental failure or error of judgment, for which these terms provide welcome metaphors in America's news media, or in everyday conversation. Thus, not only individuals may be accused of madness: political parties and whole historical eras, literary movements and entire social groups, are routinely demonized as paranoid, or their behavior dismissed as schizophrenic.

This study tells the story of how madness came to play such a prominent part in political and cultural debates. Although individual illness or clinical psychosis feature at length, what follows is not a history of psychiatry, or a medical account of madness. Rather what interests me are cases where madness becomes social and, therefore, political. What seems remarkable about the political deployment of psychiatric concepts is their description of both friend *and* foe—their equal application to self and other. The casual usage of this terminology does not imply vagueness of meaning, or an absence of ideological import. Describing a film or an artistic style, a group or persuasion as mad participates in a precise political, cultural, and intellectual history. One of the central arguments of this book is that today's culture of madness in the United States can be understood only in the context of the Cold War. Social pathology gains its rhetorical force amid the violent confrontation between communism and capitalism and functions as an intellectual weapon in the internal power struggles that ensue. As Martin Halliwell suggests, Cold War anti-communism was characterized by a "rhetoric of disease."[2] Its long-standing association with immorality meant that insanity lent itself to attacks like not other illness.

Since the 1990s, revisionist research within historiography and literary studies has transformed our understanding of postwar social science, psychiatry and anti-psychiatry, the 1950s and '60s counterculture, as well as postmodern literature, film, and criticism.[3] Even where the focus lies on madness—whether in a paranoid conspiracy culture or antipsychiatry's romance with schizophrenia—a tendency to read these registers in separation means that the force field of dialogue and debate that connects them goes unnoticed. To read countercultural madness at a remove from liberal pathologies of the left and right deprives it of its immediate adversaries and gives rise to simplistic caricatures. The fundamental ambivalence of countercultural celebrations becomes visible only as a reaction to what surrounds it. Novelists like Marge Piercy and Leslie Marmon Silko, the psychologist Phyllis Chesler, and a social movement like mental patients' liberation, seek respite from the dismissal of alternative selves. At the same time, they return to psychopathology at every juncture, or oppose demonization with facile romanticism.[4]

The application of psychopathology beyond the individual mind does not begin in the United States, nor does it first appear after World War II. At least since Sigmund Freud, who famously based his understanding of paranoia on the autobiography of a judge instead of a case study, and who analyzed literature, the masses, and religion with equal gusto, have such uses become widespread.[5] It is with the popular adaptation of this thought in mid-century America, in which European influences combine with a diverse US tradition, that psychology establishes itself as a privileged framework for understanding all aspects of modern life. Psychopathology breaks free from its ties to the medical profession and social elites. Mad vocabulary seeps into everyday life. In the process, the boundaries between neurosis and psychosis, between unconscious motivations and surface manifestations, blur. Pathological symptoms no longer express individual illness but may now refer to social types or even to the arts and rhetoric. The Cold War gives birth to the paranoid style and pronounces itself mad. I will say more about diagnosing communists and conservatives later on but begin by explaining my insistence on madness—a notion some may find outdated. Before turning to psychiatry in detail, I summarize the evolution of cultural pathology throughout the Cold War, then take a brief look at developments after the fall of the Berlin Wall.

1.1 More than Mental Illness

An understanding of madness as illness dominated mainstream accounts during the Cold War. Madness appeared as a form of thought and behavior partially or wholly devoid of reason, or lacking the subjective agency seen to result from the exercise of reason. Adapted from clinical psychiatry as it developed from the work of Emil Kraepelin and others, the notion of madness as pathology functions as a central cultural and intellectual resource in the popular imagination. This holds true across the political spectrum and includes postwar liberals, leftists of different persuasions, and moderate to right-wing Republicans. The actual terminology varies and is, in fact, used quite interchangeably. Even highly educated observers like the critic Leslie Fielder or the diplomat George Kennan, who inspired the containment doctrine in the late 1940s, wildly mixed their metaphors. With Kennan's "Long Telegram," sent from Moscow during his stint at the US embassy, and the psychological assessment of negotiators in Korea, Cold War madness influenced decision-making at the highest level and entered the world stage. Communist leaders found themselves diagnosed as schizoid, paranoid, hysterical, or plain crazy—often all at once.[6]

Despite rhetorical variation, two conceptions dominate. Schizophrenia and paranoia constitute two of the three psychoses identified by Kraepelin and function as shorthand for different aspects of madness. Yet, the third psychosis, mania—or what became subsumed under manic depression and today goes as bipolar disorder—appears in postwar literature as well. The characteristic pendulum swing between depressive and manic episodes and the habit of over-diagnosing schizophrenia often led to the identification with either the former or depression. Mary Jane Ward's *The Snake Pit* (1946) and Sylvia Plath's only novel, *The Bell Jar* (1963), provide two examples analyzed here. Due to these symptoms, mania frequently remains absent from the popular use and academic appropriation that characterize the two others. In popular and academic usage, schizophrenia signifies reason's disintegration, which reflects the origin of the term as a splitting of the psychic functions in the writing of Swiss psychiatrist, Eugen Bleuler.[7] This understanding of madness is then appropriated for a perceived disintegration of social order. John Frankenheimer's satire *The Manchurian Candidate* (1962), for instance, repeatedly invokes the threat of madness, and the infiltration of the political establishment in the film denotes a failure of ideological cohesion.

A related yet distinct understanding of madness sees it as a partial impairment of rational insight. Motivated by an attempt to understand mass democracy, powerful social scientists and historians like Hofstadter, Harold Lasswell, and Arthur Schlesinger, Jr., accused the left at home and abroad of irresponsible paranoia. Their work built on mid-century psychology, particularly *The Authoritarian Personality*, co-authored by Frankfurt School sociologist Theodor Adorno. This insanity stems from an excess of emotion: anger or suspicion warping a correct understanding of reality. More rarely, paranoia results from exaggerated and abstract thought processes that become disconnected from basic facts. Hofstadter leveled the same accusations against the rising tide of conservatism that threatened the liberal consensus during the 1950s and '60s. Deprecating political adversaries as irrational depends, of course, on a positive valuation of reason. Here lies one of the central fault lines separating postwar liberalism from the emerging counterculture and social movements of the Sixties. Authors who doubt reason itself and reject postwar society for an emphasis on emotion and authenticity, endorse and celebrate its absence.

Driven by scientific optimism and large increases in funding, postwar America saw a steady expansion in mental health care, epitomized by Kennedy becoming the first US president to address Congress on the topic.[8] Psychiatry's radical critics, most influentially Thomas S. Szasz, exploited the growing disconnection between biological medicine and psychoanalytic treatment, and accused it of an ideologically driven repression of dissent. Chapter 3 discusses and other polemical attacks contributed to a self-help psychology that provided non-medical alternatives, and sometimes direct contestation. At the outer reaches of the movement, the question that animated liberal reformers, namely how to better care for the mentally ill, was transformed into something entirely different: a conception of madness that sought healing in a liberation *from* psychiatry and proclaimed madness the only true sanity in an insane world. Such criticism also contributed to the drastic reorientation of institutional psychiatry in the United States. Turning their back on depth psychology, psychiatrists began to pursue a biochemical and genetic research program that, ironically, shares much with Szasz's conservative libertarianism.

The literary counterculture posed a second challenge to psychiatry. Chapter 4 documents how these writers supplemented attacks on state power with biting satire and an aesthetics of rebellion. Paranoia held special appeal in this respect. Ishmael Reed and Thomas Pynchon are two of many authors who envisioned paranoia as a subversive epistemology that countered the Cold War politics of secrecy, lies, and psychological warfare. Tobin Siebers and Ann Douglas contend that postmodern literature responds to the increasing gap between available and necessary knowledge brought about by the national security state.[9] In the absence of political change, the paranoid belief in conspiracy holds the only hope for Oedipa Maas, the female protagonist of Pynchon's *The Crying of Lot 49* (1966): either as a desire for knowledge or as a diversion from its impossibility. The analysis of Cold War thrillers in chapter 5 moves from Pynchon's novel to the extraordinary series of conspiracy films that flowered in the early 1970s, including Alan J. Pakula's *Klute* (1971) and *The Parallax View* (1974), and Francis Ford Coppola's *The Conversation* (1974). Throughout my reading, I argue that many Sixties reversals remain fundamentally ambivalent. Celebrations of paranoia and schizophrenia coexist with dominant pathologies of madness.

In contrast to some countercultural authors, I do not conceive of madness as necessarily progressive—the marker of a positive freedom or individual authenticity. My discussion of paranoia equally steers clear of simplistic condemnation and celebration. If paranoia amounts to partial impairment, it also provides a measure of insight. Paranoia's detection of a structure of authority or oppression, I contend, speaks the truth of society—its structural responsibility, or the unbroken interrelation between all constituents of the symbolic universe—and transforms it into the existence of conspiracy. But in the meaning instituted by their portraits of power, conspiracy theories also strengthen the belief in an authority whose potential disintegration is announced in the need for paranoid certainty. Paradoxically, paranoid narratives simultaneously expose social antagonism and reinforce the status quo. Over the last two decades, scholars of America's conspiracy culture have challenged its conflation with a dangerous insanity and radically altered the way we look at these narratives. Yet these studies balance their reassessment of conspiracy theories with the continued abnegation of paranoia. In so doing, they follow in the footsteps of a political and intellectual tradition that discredited opponents by associating them with madness.

Szasz famously declared mental illness a myth.[10] My insistence on the term madness does not deny the existence of mental illness, which continues to wreak havoc on the lives of millions of people, but refuses the reduction of the former to the latter. The perspective adopted throughout this study owes much to the French psychiatrist Jacques Lacan who wrote: "Not only can man's being not be understood without madness, but it would not be man's being if it did not bear madness within itself as the limit of his freedom."[11] So accepted has the identification of madness as disease become that any other perspective seems almost beyond the pale. However, it is contradicted by some relatively well-known facts: in most countries, a stable proportion of the population, around one percent, receive a diagnosis of schizophrenia. About ten times as many experience hallucinations, without feeling ill or seeking treatment. Diagnosed schizophrenics often view their hallucinations as a valuable part of their lives and don't want them suppressed by antipsychotic drugs. Other studies have failed to distinguish the delusional beliefs of mental patients from those held by followers of new age religions, who do not consider themselves ill either.[12]

A strictly medical perspective ignores many practical aspects of madness. The first concerns the success or failure of biological psychiatry, measured not in small or large scientific breakthroughs but in its effect on the US population. At the end of the Cold War, a report estimated that only one in five Americans with serious mental illness was receiving adequate care. Twice as many people suffering from schizophrenia and bipolar disorder were homeless or imprisoned than in mental hospitals. The nation spent only $ 515 million, a fraction of the money reserved for cancer or heart disease, on mental health.[13] Recent studies showing that the life expectancy of the mentally ill actually has declined over the last twenty-five years indicate that not much has changed for the better.[14] The second aspect has to do with the economics of mental health care in the United States today—as well as its class, racial, and gender divisions. The emphasis on outpatient services and private insurance ignores those too ill to receive adequate care in community centers, or without coverage. These two categories frequently overlap. Many of those who suffer the most are poor, female, and black or Hispanic. Strikingly, the term neoliberalism does not feature in the index of some of the most prominent recent histories of psychiatry.[15] Nor does Michel Foucault's concept of biopower. In the 1980s, Szasz's utopia of "the freely contracting individual" became true for a middle class who could pay for mental health—a process begun during Ronald Reagan's tenure as governor of California.[16] Szasz's right-wing libertarianism, often criticized by scholars, is closer to the reality of mental health care in the United States today than some of the very same critics care to admit. In the meantime, charity and underfunded public services will have to do for less fortunate Americans. This dire situation showcases biopower in its stark complexity: life is extended through prevention and aftercare for those subject to mild forms of unease or able to afford quality care; and life is abridged through neglect and imprisonment for those who cannot.

1.2 The Cold War Culture of Madness

One of the stories that Cold War madness can tell us concerns the split between humanistic and medical conceptions. If much psychoanalysis after World War II stressed the acquiescence to a reality shadowed by nuclear bombs, mental health professionals also questioned the prerogatives of a docile psychiatry. A writer like Philip K. Dick—whose novels build on a lifelong reading of psychiatry—understood very well that depth psychology could be an instrument of oppression *and* a guide to emancipatory critique. Few would make the second claim about today's psychiatric orthodoxy. There can be little doubt that drug treatments have helped a huge number of mental patients since the first antipsychotic, chlorpromazine, was introduced to hospitals in 1954. Important medical research has led to insights into brain function and genetic predispositions to illness. Yet many of those who were interested in the workings of the mind sought understanding in a psychology that paid heed to basic wisdom: that body and mind cannot be understood without taking society into consideration.

In *The Liberal Imagination* (1950), a tour de force of postwar literary criticism, Lionel Trilling remarked on a recent reversal in attitudes to madness. Increasingly, it was becoming a condition for speaking the truth, especially for artists and writers.[17] More and more people refused to see madness as a mere pathology—or, indeed, to value reason above all when logic seemed to dictate a murderous arms race, or reducing Southeast Asia to rubble. Observing the world around him, even a liberal thinker like Trilling could not help but propose an alternative view: *"[w]e are all ill."*[18] Over the next three decades, critical mental health workers, former psychiatric patients, artists and authors of all persuasions, shook to the core an institution of immense power and direct relevance to millions of Americans. For many, madness became an epidemic that threatened the health of the entire country; Kennedy declared it the nation's most pressing medical issue. Trilling's comments should be understood in this context. So can statements like R.D. Laing's who questioned who was crazier: a 17-year-old female patient who believed that she carried nuclear weapons inside of her or the statesmen who threatened to drop them on the Soviet Union, Korea, and Vietnam.[19]

Radical critique found a niche within postwar psychiatry. So did Frieda Fromm-Reichmann's refusal to pathologize madness. One of several clinicians to develop psychotherapy for psychotics, she insisted that schizophrenia should not be seen as an illness but a different way of living that would never conform to standard expectations.[20] Admittedly, these views were never widespread. Whereas Sixties movements from civil rights to feminism lambasted the social roots of psychological malaise, psychiatry moved toward drug treatments.[21] Despite the efforts of a small group of progressive reformers within the American Psychiatric Association, this rift only widened during the 1970s.[22] The turn-around was completed with the third edition of the Diagnostic and Statistical Manual of Mental Disorders (DSM-III), published in 1980 under the direction of Robert Spitzer. Many mental health workers continue to explore a scientific integration of social and physiological perspectives today but they remain a minority. To the detriment of both, this development often leaves psychiatry and the humanities unable to find a common language.

This historical rupture has overshadowed ideological commonalities. Others may be increasingly on the horizon. Before returning to the split between humanistic and medical madness, I want to comment briefly on the issue of periodization. Two questions loom large. The first concerns my preference for the Cold War over other descriptors of the historical period in question. The second relates to the evolution of cultural pathology over four decades, a topic that may benefit from further elaboration. The temporal boundaries of the Cold War are somewhat imprecise but usually do not elicit much debate. Whether one considers 1946 or a later year of that decade as a starting point may depend on one's disciplinary and thematic focus. The same goes for the demise of the Cold War in the period from 1989 to 1991.[23] I have argued that US conceptions of madness emerge against the background of domestic Cold War struggles, where they act as important intellectual resources in the definition of the self and the demonization of ideological adversaries. In this historical context, the mad metaphors of establishment and counterculture reveal themselves as interventions in debates central to post-World War II America: the extension of and potential limits to state power, the fate of the individual subject in bureaucratic societies, the political function of emotions, and the question of admissible opposition in populist democracy. As Georg Lukács wrote, madness constitutes the final dramatization of the modern subject in mass society. Only in the theater of the psyche, he writes, do the abstract processes of contemporary capitalism achieve a truly symbolic quality.[24] The imaginative process described by Lukács moves from the level of the social to the individual mind. Collective processes appear as the fate of insanity.

Metaphors of madness link the individual psyche to society: in the process they become a dominant way of thinking the relationship between politics and culture in the Cold War period. In this sense, my book contributes to what Alan Nadel has called a "tropology of the American Cold War" that connects disparate aspects of US society within a network of everyday meanings and practices.[25]

The movement between politics and culture may count as a distinctive feature of the Cold War as a periodizing concept. No other historical descriptor of the mid- and late twentieth century quite connects these two strata in the same way: globalization, neoliberalism, the post-industrial age, or postmodernism tend to privilege the economy over politics, or the cultural sphere over both. One reason why cultural historians have embraced the term Cold War is its capacity to suggest a wide variety of cultural expression within the boundaries of its constitutive conflict. Earlier research at times portrayed a homogeneous society dominated by political and sexual repression. In contrast to such a negative understanding of power, the Cold War may be seen as a partial and productive framework. These limitations are of particular importance for this study when it comes to the decisive impact of the interwar period and World War II, which transformed attitudes to psychotherapy and led to the forced emigration of European thinkers, many of them Jewish, to the United States.

I have emphasized the importance of postwar liberalism and the countercultural movements that extend from the 1950s to the '70s up to this point. To put forward an analogy, the latter may be taken as the détente of Cold War psychopathology: at times repealing the persecution of political and personal alternatives and exploring the psychological extremes of the human mind. An aspect that cannot be underestimated is the personal experience of many cultural figures with psychotic states, or approximations thereof. Poets such as Plath and Anne Sexton wrote at length about their time in hospital, Allen Ginsberg drew on his own and his mother's time in mental institutions, and many psychiatrists experimented with psychedelic substances. The author Ken Kesey, who took LSD as part of the secret MK-Ultra program run by the CIA to test its viability for interrogation, later promoted the drug as a recreational activity. A substance that was said to mimic madness, and sometimes caused it, turned into entertainment and spawned the psychedelic Sixties. Like Kesey, William Burroughs found himself in uncomfortably close quarters with dubious medical practice when his homosexuality played a part in his admission to a psychiatric ward.

Kesey and Burroughs gave accounts of their experiments, hoping they might make eccentric behavior more acceptable. More often, excess provided ground for moral indignation as the country began to shift to the right. It would be simplistic to oppose an essentially libertarian counterculture to the United States that emerged from the 1960s, however. Left-wing radicalism self-destructed under intense pressure from the authorities, but cultural transformation included a pluralistic acceptance of progressive lifestyles. As a consequence, the political pathology of the early Cold War did not return in full force. In some cases, it was the left that mourned its defeat in the language of madness. In the 1950s, Richard Wright portrayed the Communist Party as a potential escape from the madness of a racist society and, ultimately, insanity's identical twin. Three decades later, Fredric Jameson's essays on a schizophrenic postmodernity allowed him to reflect on the disintegration of Marxism. Others, such as Kathy Acker, celebrate an ecstatic schizophrenia as a liberation from repressive gender identity. These opposing valuations of madness were a feature of America's intellectual culture during the renewed Cold War of the 1980s, which is discussed in chapter 6. These writers' infatuation with French theory and distance from political movements stands in marked contrast to the speed of economic reform under Ronald Reagan and the rapid consolidation of conservative hegemony.

Adopting an individualist model of insanity, a rejuvenated biological psychiatry reinforced reductions of madness to mental illness. During the early 1970s, patients had begun to speak in their own voice—countering assumptions that madness meant an absence of reason and an inability to act. Under the banner of mental patients' liberation, activists demanded a say in their own treatment. Amidst federal budget cuts a decade later, they were overtaken by reformers who defined themselves as consumers. Founded in 1979, the National Alliance for the Mentally Ill (NAMI) quickly became the largest advocacy group of its kind. The name was telling in itself: where earlier ex-patients spoke for themselves, the new group consisted of parents and relatives who spoke *for* them. Radical groups had a hand in their own downfall, however. The refusal to build alliances with progressive health workers did immeasurable harm to a group with few natural allies. In addition, their fervent belief in patient autonomy and wholesale subscription to Szasz's myth of mental illness meant that they applauded neoliberal reforms that masked as an appeal to freedom.

1.3 After Madness?

Two terms—paranoia and schizophrenia—dominate Cold War debates around madness. This study traces their adoption in a variety of different fields, ranging from political science to social psychology, from historiography to social movements, across literature and film. This does not mean that paranoia and schizophrenia alone feature in US politics and culture during that period. Bipolar disorder is one example. With the publication of DSM-III, multiple personality disorder (MPD) and post-traumatic stress disorder (PTSD) joined the roster of serious mental illnesses. These syndromes contribute to the further conflation of neurosis and psychosis, always a porous boundary. New diagnoses allow for new ways of being a person. They also respond to lived experience, so it is no surprise that descriptions resembling MPD and PTSD surface with increasing regularity in the 1970s and '80s. A full appraisal of these phenomena would have necessitated a separate book.[26] However, I offer interpretations of Flora Rheta Schreiber's *Sybil* (1973) and Marmon Silko's *Ceremony* (1977) in chapters 2 and 4 to situate MPD and PTSD within the historical account provided here.

Newer editions of the DSM have added even more diagnoses.[27] Today, one can suffer from innumerable addictions, or from undue resistance to authority. These additions enforce a constant need to medicalize supposed deviance. Ironically, this logic—driven by the need to classify and treat, usually in the form of highly profitable pharmaceuticals—parallels the very different efforts of Lacanian psychoanalysts. As Jacques-Alain Miller has written, "[e]veryone is crazy. It is only then that it becomes interesting to make distinctions."[28] Unlike mainstream psychiatry, Lacanians do not seek to pathologize. For them so-called normality and madness are simply different impositions of meaning on a baffling world. Both are delusions in the strict sense but neurosis is a shared delusion, as it institutes a socially accepted limit to thought and behavior. In contrast, psychotics must construct this limit individually and often fail at it. Lacanian psychoanalysis seeks to expose the supposed epistemological privilege of sanity as a form of shared belief: precisely the conviction in the inherent logical difference of a supposedly sane organization of reality. Such a conception of psychosis leads not, as one might assume, to conceptual indistinction. Sanity is not denied existence as a category but defined as a sub-category of madness distinguished by its hegemonic status: the one madness accepted as rational. It is thus that Miller can pronounce everyone crazy. If all of us are mad—and the constant increase in diagnosis indicates as much—then no one is.

This perspective isn't new. Frieda Fromm-Reichmann said as much in 1948 when she described schizophrenia as a different way of life that need not conform to expectations. Nor is another proposal: In the book that introduced the term schizophrenia, Bleuler noted what he called its latent form. Those afflicted were withdrawn and odd, moody, and prey to obsessive ticks.[29] Lacanians summarize these symptoms as ordinary psychosis and describe it as the dominant structure of subjective organization today. Ordinary, in the sense of quotidian and banal, describes many contemporary subjects, whose sense of normality derives from holding on to the clutter of everyday life—a boring job, the bric à brac of a room or apartment, small obsessions, minor addictions. Until he finds himself in the crosshairs of rogue CIA agents, the same may be said of Lee Harvey Oswald, as portrayed by Don DeLillo in *Libra* (1988). In its recent manifestations, paranoia can be similarly understood: a paranoia at once ubiquitous and near-invisible, not antagonistic but deeply wedded to irony and world-weary cynicism, a pragmatic crutch supporting today's subjects in their daily acts of reality-construction. The United States since the Sixties has been characterized by the withdrawal of frequently opposed microcommunities from collective solidarity. Such a breakdown of universal values may be described as madness. This is the logic of Cold War psychopathology. Mistaking scientific autonomy for political neutrality, much psychiatry continues to play this game. Yet, surely liberal plurality disarms normative judgment and normalizes a madness that, finally, may become ordinary.

Notes

1 Sean Wilentz, introduction to *The Paranoid Style in American Politics and Other Essays*, by Richard Hofstadter (New York: Vintage, 2008), xxv and xxviii.
2 Martin Halliwell, *Therapeutic Revolutions: Medicine, Psychiatry, and American Culture, 1945–1970* (New Brunswick, NJ: Rutgers University Press 2013), 181.
3 Among the best results of this research are: Ron Robin, *The Making of the Cold War Enemy: Culture and Politics in the Military-Industrial Complex* (Princeton, NJ: Princeton University Press, 2001); Michael E. Staub, *Madness Is Civilization: When the Diagnosis was Social, 1948–1980* (Chicago: University of Chicago Press, 2011); Peter Knight, *Conspiracy Culture: From the Kennedy Assassination to "The X-Files"* (London: Routledge, 2000); and Mark Fenster, *Conspiracy Theories: Secrecy and Power in American Culture* (Minneapolis: University of Minnesota Press, 2008).
4 See chapters 3 and 4 for my discussion of countercultural movements and authors.
5 Sigmund Freud, "Psycho-Analytical Notes on an Autobiographical Account of a Case of Paranoia (Dementia Paranoides)," in *The Standard Edition of the Complete Psychological Works of Sigmund Freud*, vol. 12, trans. and ed. James Strachey (London: Hogarth, 1958), 9–82; Sigmund Freud, *Group Psychology and the Analysis of the Ego*, in *SE* 18 (London: Hogarth, 1955), 69–143; and Sigmund Freud, "The Future of an Illusion," in *SE* 21 (London: Hogarth, 1961), 5–56.
6 George Kennan, "Long Telegram," accessed April 15, 2010, http://www.trumanlibrary.org/whistlestop/study_collections/coldwar/do-cuments-/index.php?-documentdate=19460222&documentid=66&study-collectionid=&page-number=1; Nathan Leites, *The Operational Code of the Politburo* (Westport, CT: Greenwood, 1972).
7 Eugen Bleuler, *Dementia Praecox or the Group of Schizophrenias*, trans. Joseph Zifkin (New York: International Universities Press, 1950), 8. This psychological fragmentation is at times transformed into the appearance of separate identities, or multiple personalities. Kieran McNally has argued that such conceptions should not be seen as a misunderstanding but build directly on Bleuler and mid-century US psychiatry. Kieran McNally, "Schizophrenia as Split Personality/Jekyll and Hyde: The Origins of the Informal Usage in the English Language," *Journal of the History of the Behavioral Sciences* 43, no. 1 (Winter 2007): 69–79; and see also my analysis of Flora Rheta Schreiber's *Sybil* in chapter 2.
8 John F. Kennedy, "Special Message to the Congress on Mental Illness and Mental Retardation," accessed November 18, 2010, http://www.arcmass.org/Portals/0/JFK%20Message%20to%20the%20Congress.pdf.
9 Tobin Siebers, *Cold War Criticism and the Politics of Skepticism* (New York: Oxford University Press, 1993); and Ann Douglas, "Periodizing the American Century: Modernism, Postmodernism, and Postcolonialism in the Cold War Context," *Modernism/Modernity* 5, no. 3 (1998): 71–98.
10 Thomas S. Szasz, *The Myth of Mental Illness: Foundations of a Theory of Personal Conduct*, rev. ed. (New York: Harper & Row, 1974).
11 Jacques Lacan, "Presentation on Psychical Causality," in *Ecrits: The First Complete Edition in English*, trans. Bruce Fink (New York: Norton, 2002), 144.

12 Richard Bentall, *Madness Explained: Psychosis and Human Nature* (London: Penguin, 2004), 98–100 and 352.

13 Cited in Olga Loraine Kofman, "Deinstitutionalization and Its Discontents: American Mental Health Policy Reform," 39, accessed September 26, 2015, http://scholarship.claremont.edu-/cgi/viewcontent.cgi?article=1348&-context=cmc_theses.

14 Andrew Scull, *Madness in Civilization: A Cultural History of Insanity from the Bible to Freud, from the Madhouse to Modern Medicine* (London: Thames & Hudson, 2015), 14.

15 See, for instance: Edward Shorter, *A History of Psychiatry: From the Era of the Asylum to the Age of Prozac* (New York: Wiley, 1997).

16 Thomas S. Szasz, *The Manufacture of Madness: A Comparative Study of the Inquisition and the Mental Health Movement* (New York: Harper & Row, 1977), 37.

17 Lionel Trilling, "Art and Neurosis," in *The Liberal Imagination: Essays on Literature and Society* (Oxford: Oxford University Press, 1981), 152–71.

18 Trilling, "Art and Neurosis," 167. Italics in the original.

19 R.D. Laing, "Preface to the Pelican Edition," in *The Divided Self* (London: Penguin, 1990), 12.

20 Frieda Fromm-Reichmann, "Notes on the Development of Treatment of Schizophrenics by Psychoanalytic Psychotherapy," *Psychiatry* 11 (1948): 273.

21 For a brief discussion of the civil rights and Black Power movements, and its recourse to psychopathology, see chapter 2.3. I talk about the feminist psychology of Phyllis Chesler in chapter 3.1.

22 See my discussion in chapter 3; and for a more detailed account: Lucas Richert, "'Therapy Means Change, Not Peanut Butter': American Radical Psychiatry, 1968–1975," *Social History of Medicine* 27 (2013): 104–21.

23 Although I sympathize with Anders Stephanson's and other interventions that declare the Cold War effectively over after the Cuban Missile Crisis in 1962, this focus on diplomatic history excludes precisely the historical evolution this study seeks to analyze. Anders Stephanson, "Cold War Degree Zero," in *Uncertain Empire: American History and the Idea of the Cold War*, ed. Joel Isaac and Duncan Bell (Oxford: Oxford University Press, 2012), 19–49. Recently, some scholars have emphasized the continuities between the Cold War and the so-called 'war on terror.' With regard to madness, it can be observed that evil frequently replaces madness in describing Islamic Jihadis as the ideological enemy, an indicator that any attempt at understanding is herewith abandoned.

24 Georg Lukács, *Entwicklungsgeschichte des modernen Dramas*, ed. Frank Benseler (Darmstadt, Germany: Luchterhand, 1981), 118–119. Fredric Jameson comments on this passage in *The Geopolitical Aesthetic: Cinema and Space in the World System* (Bloomington, IN: Indiana University Press, 1992), 57.

25 Alan Nadel, *Containment Culture: American Narratives, Postmodernism, and the Atomic Age* (Durham, NC: Duke University Press, 1995), 12.

26 For a wonderful example see: Ian Hacking, *Rewriting the Soul: Multiple Personality and the Sciences of Memory* (Princeton, NJ: Princeton University Press, 1995).

27 Most recently with the fifth edition in 2013.

28 Jacques-Alain Miller, "A Contribution of the Schizophrenic to the Psychoanalytic Clinic," trans. Ellie Ragland and Anne Pulis, accessed April 9, 2015, http://www.lacan.com/contributionf.htm.

29 Bleuler, *Dementia Praecox or The Group of Schizophrenias*, 236.

2 The Pathologies of Dissent

Constructing the Cold War Psyche

"Psychology has burst out of the consulting room and clinic," announced *Time* magazine in a cover story on Carl Jung in 1955, "spreading all through life and leaving nothing untouched—neither love nor the machine, war nor politics, neither art nor morals nor God."[1] For once the journalistic hyperbole was justified. Therapy for the masses combined with a newly prominent behavioral science and a popular fascination with introspection and mental growth to make psychology America's preferred lens to view self and society. In the process, Freud and Jung became pop stars, the federal government turned to social scientists for advice, and politicians and academics alike used paranoia or schizophrenia to denigrate those with whom they disagreed. This postwar boom reached its apotheosis on February 5, 1963. Identifying mental illness as "one of our most critical health problems," John F. Kennedy became the first president in the history of the United States to address Congress on the topic.[2] Kennedy said nothing of his personal experience in the matter—his younger sister Rosemary had been diagnosed as mildly 'retarded' and undergone lobotomy—but claimed that:

> mental illnesses and mental retardation occur more frequently, affect more people, require more prolonged treatment, cause more suffering by the families of the afflicted, waste more of our human resources, and constitute more financial drain upon both the public treasury and the personal finances of the individual families than any other single condition.[3]

Such high-level attention may have been new, but psychology's prominence had been a long time coming. Building on nineteenth-century conceptions of nervous minds and bodies, by the 1920s it had become chic, a measure of individual worth, to be seen as neurotic.[4] As would be the case after World War II, the psychiatric help received by veterans of the Great War legitimized therapy in the eyes of the wider public and weakened its association with insanity.[5] A possessive individualism threatened by the rise of mass society could now be bolstered by the discovery of psychological depth that promised personal significance and stimulating party talk alike. As industrial psychiatry screened applicants and sought to increase productivity, social control could be matched by self-control. For middle-class Americans unconscious thoughts and urges remained tantalizingly hidden but reassuringly within reach. Thus, the glamour of a divided psyche matched the fragility of social bonds.

Psychology promised even more. Its historical roots in philosophy and physiology and its practical application to medicine and social work allowed psychological experts to stake claims to an immensely broad arena

Figure 2.1 President John F. Kennedy signs the Mental Retardation Facilities and Community Mental Health Center Construction Act in the White House on October 31, 1963. Next to him are Senator George A. Smathers (left) and Representative Paul G. Rogers, both of Florida. Photo by Abbie Rowe, courtesy of the John F. Kennedy Presidential Library and Museum, Boston.

of social life: "They possessed, in turn, a technology of behavior, a science of social relations, a theory of society, and a theology of emotional healing," writes Ellen Herman.[6] All these elements were present in the early decades of the twentieth century, but the terrible cataclysm of World War II brought about a qualitative leap. By 1963, Kennedy's assertion that mental illness affected more Americans than any other family of diseases raised few eyebrows. Throughout the war, a total of 2.5 million men were deemed unfit for military service due to psychological malfunction, so that the initial emphasis on psychiatric screening gave way to intensive treatment programs, overcoming the military's skepticism of psychotherapy. When the fighting ceased, 60 percent of all patients cared for by the Veterans Administration were psychiatric cases. A decade later, the second Hoover Commission reported that the mentally ill occupied half of all hospital beds.

In the writings of intellectuals and literary authors, madness became an epidemic. Psychiatrists found themselves in the spotlight like never before. Some authors, like Sylvia Plath, declared the profession "the God of our age."[7] Others accused them, more simply, of quackery. In 1946, Mary Jane Ward's best-selling novel *The Snake Pit* looked forward to a time when the number of mentally ill might overtake those who remained sane. The title of Erich Fromm's *The Sane Society* (1955) was similarly ironic: for the German emigré cited the findings of the Hoover Commission to suggest that America might not be in good health after all. Barbara O'Brien's *Operators and Things* (1958), a celebrated autobiography of schizophrenic breakdown, connected the perceived epidemic of mental illness to the fear that arguably lay behind it. "At the rate at which schizophrenia is increasing, there is a reasonable chance that if the intercontinental missile doesn't get you, schizophrenia will."[8] Here lay the foundation for making madness a dominant metaphor of postwar America. Not just individuals but the whole country was routinely diagnosed insane. *Society as the Patient* had been the title of a well-received essay collection published in 1948, and Martin Luther King was one of countless public figures to couch his critique in psychiatric language when he claimed that "America has [. . .] a schizophrenic personality."[9] The popularity of madness as metaphor owed not only to the spread of psychiatric vocabulary, or the perceived increase in cases of insanity. Had mental illness seemed a hopeless cause, it is unlikely that it would have suffused postwar culture the way it did, applied equally to the denunciation of the radical left and right and fantasized as the only true sanity in a mad world.

A new optimism pervaded postwar psychiatry. Its message of hope combined with Kennedy's trademark rhetoric when he promised Congress "a bold new approach" that would "make it possible for most of the mentally ill to be successfully and quickly treated in their own communities and returned to a useful place in society."[10] Alarmed by the number of army rejects, William Menninger, director of the Neuropsychiatry Consultants Division, had emphasized therapy over initial screening during the war and instituted a policy of prompt intervention. Quick professional attention could stem the development of more serious disturbances in almost all cases, he believed. Therapeutic innovations and the introduction of the anti-psychotic drug chlorpromazine fed a scientific optimism that was inseparable from the belief in progress that men like Menninger and Kennedy symbolized. Hidden underneath the harshest critique, it subtended most cultural diagnoses of America. Even in the radical psychiatry of William Grier and Price Cobbs's *Black Rage* to call a racist America "a sick nation" held out the promise of cure.[11] At a time when neuroses found a sympathetic hearing on the analyst's couch and at dinner parties, when even the most serious cases could be subdued with pharmaceuticals or hidden away in state institutions, psychopathology left behind the walls of the insane asylum to enter middle America.

Emotional healing constituted only one growth market for psychiatry. Prominent practitioners like Menninger, Harry Stack Sullivan, or Frieda Fromm-Reichmann were increasingly joined by a new breed of professionals. The war effort, first in the confrontation with Germany and Japan, then in a Cold War against the Soviet Union, called for understanding troubled soldiers and the manipulation of enemy morale. 'Psychological warfare,' as it was called, depended on expert analysis of foreign cultures. Above all, studies of German and Russian national character owed to political scientist Harold Lasswell, who almost single-handedly introduced psychoanalytic concepts into political science. In *Psychopathology and Politics* (1930), Lasswell presented case studies of community organizers and bureaucrats to understand politics as "the process by which the irrational bases of society are brought out in the open."[12] This definition underlay all of Lasswell's efforts and formed the basis of influential attempts to understand national socialism, and later communism. The shift from the former to the latter was almost seamless. Roger Money-Kyrle's *Psychoanalysis and Politics* modeled its title and method on Lasswell. Describing national socialism as "a collective flight into madness," the following sentence shifted to America's new arch enemy: "In much the same way, though we know much less about it, [. . .] the communist tyranny has created an environment in which it is almost impossible for anyone deeply embedded in the system to stay quite sane."[13] Money-Kyrle's rhetoric exemplified the psychoanalytical behaviorism of the early Cold War: a disregard for hard facts leveled the economic and political differences between fascism and communism, powerful ideologies were summarily dismissed as the rationalization of unconscious desires. A lack of empirical evidence was initially acknowledged, then followed up by sweeping conclusions. For writers like Money-Kyrle psychopathology's greatest advantage lay in its ability to clothe value judgments in pseudo-scientific objectivity. Performing a thought experiment that would also be applied to US citizens, he wrote:

> Now suppose we were asked to put aside whatever personal predilections we may have and, solely on the basis of our analytic knowledge, to adjudicate in a dispute between a supporter of this liberal-welfare state,

and an opponent who favours some alternative. The first thing to notice is the personality of this opponent.[14]

Ever the objective scientist, Money-Kyrle characterized the personality of any such opponent as an "elaborate defense against [. . .] irrational anxieties."[15] In similar fashion, Lasswell had already denied the validity of left-wing protest during the Great Depression in Chicago.[16] Behavioralists made very much the same claims about communism in Asia as psychocultural analyses entered the world stage with the War in Korea. At the armistice talks in Panmunjom the brief treatise *The Operational Code of the Politburo*, authored by Nathan Leites, an analyst for the army's think tank Rand Corporation and a former student of Lasswell, became the chief guide to the enemy psyche.[17] Communist elites all over the world were divorced from reality and driven by persecutory fantasies, he claimed.[18] The implication was clear, but aware of Washington's distrust of psychoanalysis, Leites omitted openly psychological language. When writing for an academic audience, he was less cagey, stressing the "importance of fantasies about passive homosexuality" for the understanding of the Bolsheviks and asserting their fabrication of enemies as "defenses against inner rather than outer dangers."[19] This difference in tone was replicated elsewhere. Politicians, diplomats, and academics who freely referenced psychological terms in their private correspondence or scholarly texts avoided frank diagnoses in policy documents. The taint of mental illness still shone through.

   The most famous study of national character, *The Authoritarian Personality*, followed in 1955 and marked a decisive change of direction. The volume was at once the culmination of a particular research tradition and distinct from it. Co-authored by German emigré thinker Theodor Adorno, it epitomized the impact of European academics in the creation of an interdisciplinary social science in the United States. The combination of philosophical questioning and complex research design was so extraordinary at the time, and perhaps remains so to this day, that an essay collection dedicated to it was titled *Studies in the Scope and Method of 'The Authoritarian Personality.'* The Freudian Marxism that informed the volume caused numerous misunderstandings upon its publication, but more important proved who was thus analyzed. Turning to a home-grown anti-Semitism, *The Authoritarian Personality* examined the psychological motivations of every-day Americans, and initiated a new view of US politics. Sections two and three of this chapter will trace its evolution in the work of Cold War historians and social scientists, among them Richard Hofstadter, a writer who owed two of his best-known concepts, the 'paranoid style' and 'pseudo-conservatism,' to *The Authoritarian Personality*. Hofstadter's work was equally indebted to Lasswell, who he credited as "one of the first in the country to be dissatisfied with the rationalistic assumptions" of his profession.[20]

Lasswell's intellectual project went beyond establishing the importance of the unconscious in politics or even the insanity of unwelcome ideologies. Arguing that most individuals could not be trusted to act in their best interest given their inherent irrationality, he explicitly contrasted his own viewpoint with "the premise of democracy." To restrict politics to solving social conflicts was too little, too late: "The problem of politics is less to [. . .] serve as a safety valve for social protest than to apply social energy to the abolition of recurrent sources of strain in society."[21] Lasswell named his approach "preventive politics" but aimed at the prevention *of* politics. If the common man was not to be trusted with the organization of society because "the discovery of truth is an object of specialized research," politics had to be replaced by expert administration.[22] In psychological warfare, the extension of psychiatric help to communities, a booming psychotherapy, or the marketing of psycho-pharmaceuticals: at stake was the comprehensive control of entire populations. In linking psychology and social control, behavioral scientists carved a niche for themselves in the burgeoning nexus of state administration and academic research. And a lucrative niche it turned out to be. After World War II the military quickly became the biggest sponsor of psychological research. Medical funding for mental health surpassed the money spent on heart disease. In return, psychological experts in fields as diverse as military strategy, medicine, and social work extended the reach of government control into the country's every corner, and beyond.

As psychiatry entered every-day lives, so did a new and effective way of manipulating human emotions. Or so at least its advocates promised. Yet it was in the family home that psychiatry came up short most dramatically. Postwar models of domestic life advocated a retreat into early marriage and suburban affluence after the social ruptures caused by the Great Depression and World War II. As such, domesticity constituted a dominant framework of gender and sexual identities at the time.[23] This ideal of the nuclear family in a nuclear age tended to exclude African Americans, and poor people unable to afford suburban housing developments. For many white middle-class women, as well, privacy spelled frustration, and sometimes mental illness, rather than marital bliss and self-realization in motherhood. For their part, American men were expected to conform to an ideal of forceful masculinity. If the expansion of large-scale bureaucracies and the multinational corporation made a mockery of individual autonomy, the deadly rivalry with the Soviet Union still bred the "anti-Communist machismo" of politicians like McCarthy, or Kennedy.[24] Popular films like Stanley Kubrick's *Dr. Strangelove*, or John Frankenheimer's *The Manchurian Candidate*, satirized such posturing and exposed the fears that subtended ideologies of the individual self. These anxieties regularly focused on so-called sexual deviance and combined the pathologization of left-wing thought, mental illness, and homosexuality. George Kennan's seminal "Long Telegram," to which I return repeatedly in this chapter, was one of many texts to link homosexual desire to madness, and to tie both to moral weakness. The reorientation of US foreign policy around national security in the late 1940s explicitly politicized gender, sexuality, and mental health in an effort to narrow permissible behavior and opinion to a liberal consensus. Despite the Kinsey Report's insistence that sexual relations between members of the same sex were neither rare, unnatural, nor "evidence of neuroses or even psychoses," anti-communist repression combined with the persecution of those suspected of homosexuality.[25] Not coincidentally, some of the writers who broke most forcefully with the dominant model of postwar masculinity, among them William Burroughs and Allen Ginsberg, spent time in psychiatric institutions at least partly due to their sexual orientation.

Dissent was never absent, but sometimes it took a particularly forceful voice to change the debate. Betty Friedan's *The Feminine Mystique* (1963) wasn't the first book to notice the hollowness of women's lives in the postwar era, but she attacked the "mystique of feminine fulfillment" in the home with a vehemence that resonated with readers.[26] As the introduction emphasized, the discrepancy between such promises and postwar reality amounted to a "schizophrenic split."[27] Friedan's use of the term was metaphorical but derived its force from a perceived increase in actual cases of depression and psychosis. It was the "cheap Freudian sophistication" of the media that renewed old prejudices about female inferiority and kept women from facing the changing reality outside of their suburban homes.[28] Friedan's account remained narrowly focused on the white middle class, dismissing economic problems and mentioning African American women only as servants and nannies. But her interviews revealed that even privileged women were at a loss to fulfill their role as lovers, mothers, and housewives, and sought help in psychotherapy or relief in tranquillizers. Unsurprisingly, then, the postwar years witnessed a boom in literary accounts of female depression and schizophrenia. Often thinly veiled memoirs of the author's own mental trouble, these novels, films, and poetry collections exposed Cold War domesticity as male oppression, and mental illness as its outcome. By admitting their own illness these mad heroines also questioned the health of the nation. Psychiatry appeared both as patriarchy's stooge, punishing women for voicing their unhappiness, and as offering liberation from repressive gender norms in nurturing relationships with other women.

A focus on suburban domesticity means that other aspects of women's lives at the time have often received less attention than they deserve. Thus, it is sometimes forgotten that the number of women in employment continued to climb alongside marriage and birth rates. Indeed, novels like Ward's *The Snake Pit* and Plath's *The Bell Jar* (1963) are concerned as much with career paths and economic independence as they are with more stereotypical facets of Cold War femininity. *The Snake Pit*, in particular, provided an influential model for later fictions of female madness. As Plath wrote in her journal in June 1959: "Read *Cosmopolitan* from cover to cover. Two mental-health articles. I *must* write one about a college girl suicide [. . .] a story, a novel even. Must get out *Snake Pit*. There is an increasing market for mental-hospital stuff."[29] Told from the perspective of the young writer Virginia Cunningham, the novel questioned the distinction between sanity and insanity, sought to debunk romantic myths about mental hospitals, and highlighted the lack of funding for state institutions. In the end, the protagonist regains her sanity more out of sheer will than any effort by the staff of Juniper Hill Hospital—a fictionalized version of New York's Rockland State where Ward spent time—after she is thrown into the 'snake pit' of the chronic ward. An immediate best-seller upon publication, a film adaptation reached cinemas two years later. Despite a screenplay co-written by the left-wing playwright Arthur Laurents, soon to be blacklisted, the film adaptation illustrates the narrowing of female gender roles in the early Cold War. The book describes Virginia as an ambitious young novelist and journalist, as well as a socialist. Thus, she experiences her first electro-convulsive treatment (ECT) as a case of anti-communist repression. Referring to the perennial presidential candidate for the Socialist Party, she asks herself: "Could they electrocute you for having voted for Norman Thomas?"[30] Its generous use of voice-over notwithstanding, these passages are absent from the film. The same is true of Ward's gentle satire of Trotskyism, or the references to Virginia and her husband's dire financial situation, which understand mental illness as more than simply a personal crisis: a threat to female independence and economic survival as opportunities for skilled work dried up with the return of war veterans.

In contrast, Anatole Litvak's adaptation turns *The Snake Pit* into an advertisement for psychoanalysis. The pipe-smoking psychiatrist Dr. Kik receives Virginia in an office adorned with Freud's portrait, and her cure results from Virginia gaining insight into the childhood trauma of her father's early death. In the novel, Kik is explicitly described by Virginia as silly.[31] "Well, the hell with my subconscious," she declares, as her husband expedites her release by promising to take her to Illinois, where another state will pick up the bill in case of a relapse.[32] The final scene of the film most clearly marks the departure from the greater freedom that many American women experienced during the war years. Virginia is released from the mental hospital, but only into the arms of her husband and marriage, as the two symbolically renew their wedding vows on its front steps.

Like *The Snake Pit*, Plath's only novel tells the story of a young ambitious heroine battling mental illness and conservative gender norms. First published under the pseudonym Victoria Lucas, the book became a staple of college reading lists newly shaped by women's liberation upon its re-release in 1971. Set in the early years of the Eisenhower presidency, Esther Greenwood's depression reacts to the pressures of postwar society. Already the first page fuses the imagery of psychiatric treatment and political repression—an

Figure 2.2 Psychiatrist Dr. Kik (Leo Genn) receives the hospitalized author Virginia Cunningham (Olivia de Havilland) in an office adorned with the image of Sigmund Freud in *The Snake Pit* (1948), directed by Anatole Litvak.

association that would be given memorable expression by antipsychiatric writings and the counterculture throughout the 1960s and '70s. In Esther's as in Virginia Cunningham's imagination, electro-shock treatment turns into electrocution: specifically here that of Julius and Ethel Rosenberg, who are about to be put to death for treason. In *The Bell Jar*, Esther perceives ECT as a punishment for failing to live up to feminine ideals, which seek to contain her career ambitions and sexuality in motherhood and marriage. Unlike in Ward's novel, written in the final days of the Soviet-American alliance, Esther's escape from sexual containment remains bound to a Cold War imaginary. Reacting against her college boyfriend's conviction that a man is "an arrow into the future" and a woman "the place the arrow shoots from," Esther envisions herself as a rocket instead.[33] Marriage is compared to brainwashing and life in a totalitarian state, and a Russian interpreter at the UN remains inaccessible to American minds by fiat of "her own unknow-able tongue."[34]

In Plath's writing insanity figures as debilitating mental illness, rarely as the escape of madness. In retrospect, Plath's mental problems, leading to several suicide attempts and ultimately her death in February of 1963, weigh heavily on her oeuvre. Yet a systematic critique of psychiatry is absent from *The Bell Jar*, as it is from Plath's poems and journals. In 1958, Plath took part in Robert Lowell's writing workshop at Boston University along-side Anne Sexton. All three were for some time patients at McLean Hospital in Massachusetts, and the personal revelations contained in Lowell's *Life Studies* (1959), Sexton's *To Bedlam and Part Way Back* (1960), and *The Colossus* (1960) saw them summarized as confessional poets. While each of their poetic endeavors reaches far beyond the confessional mode, Plath and Sexton shared the struggle with severe depression and its literary expression. In their poetry, mental illness, made public, rewrites personal breakdown as social malaise, and in the insistence on self-exposure domesticity appears as obliteration, not liberation, of the self. In Sexton, in particular, depression is joined by hallucinations, and the value of madness lies in the insight it provides into the destruction of women's lives and minds: creative powers that need to be defended from overpowering psychoanalysts, and their subversion of poetic language. Plath, in comparison, enjoyed an amiable relationship with her psychoanalyst Ruth Beuscher. In *The Bell Jar*, a fictionalized Beuscher cures Esther Greenwood's depression. In the journals, Plath records feeling like a new person after the analyst gives her permission, as she notes, "to hate your mother," from whom she had been unable to establish any distance.[35]

The relationship of female patient to psychiatrist also stands at the center of Joanne Greenberg's *I Never Promised You a Rose Garden* (1964). The novel portrays Greenberg's treatment by the prominent psychoanalyst Fromm-Reichmann, or Dr. Fried as she is called in the book. A German immigrant, and one-time wife of Erich Fromm, she is best known for the concept of the "schizophrenogenic mother." The term described schizophrenia as the outcome of a lack of nurturing care during early childhood and formed part of the postwar emphasis on pathological family dynamics.[36] The theme runs through the work of several postwar thinkers of madness, from anthropologist Gregory Bateson and psychiatrist R.D. Laing, to Claude Steiner, founder of the Berkeley Radical Psychiatry center. Given the pressure to stay at home with their children it is difficult not to feel that many housewives were punished twice over: first, by limiting their existence to their families; second, by then accusing them of rearing schizophrenics. Fromm-Reichmann's essay was also notable for another intervention in psychiatric debates. At the private mental hospital Chestnut Lodge, Fromm-Reichmann had pioneered psychoanalysis for psychotics, inspired in part by her colleague Sullivan. Fromm-Reichmann's view of schizophrenia differed markedly from its understanding as an illness whose cure, if at all possible, involved a return to normality. Psychiatrists should not force social conventions on schizophrenics but help them find "their own sources of satisfaction and security," irrespective of the approval of others: "Schizophrenia, in this sense, is not an illness but a specific state of personality with its own ways of living."[37]

The impact of Fromm-Reichmann's views on schizophrenia are on display throughout Greenberg's account. The protagonist, Deborah Blau, is a bright sixteen-year-old girl, a model case of what Fromm-Reichmann described as "the introspectively gifted schizophrenic" amenable to psychoanalysis. Her madness is understood as a defensive reaction to "a world of anarchy and terror."[38] In contrast to the novels by Ward and Plath, *I Never Promised You a Rose Garden* repeatedly switches narrative perspective between Deborah and her psychiatrist. Greenberg describes at length Deborah's schizophrenic imagination of an alternative world. These sections borrow from fantastic literature. However, their emphasis on the subjective experience of the schizophrenic and a mad imagination also show the influence of existential psychiatry. In turn, the passages focusing on Dr. Fried reiterate her belief that madness provides insight into sanity, rather than being a mere aberration from it. Such perspectives were rare during the first decades of the Cold War. As I will show in chapter 3, they became more prominent with the rise of a literary counterculture but mostly remain absent from establishment thought in the United States, to which the next section turns in more detail. Even more so, Fromm-Reichmann's refusal to pathologize madness, her insistence that schizophrenia should not be seen as an illness but a specific way of living, will prove almost completely alien to American Cold War culture, voiced only by European emigré thinkers, or US thinkers heavily influenced by them.

2.1 In Defense of the Liberal Center

Richard Hofstadter bridged the gap between historiography, political science, psychology, and cultural analysis like few others in postwar academia, yet this "archetypal intellectual of his times" is still read along disciplinary lines.[39] Whereas fellow historians have focused on his analyses of the US political system, cultural critics examine its 'paranoid style' without showing interest in the term's intellectual origins. Both, however, acknowledge Hofstadter's importance for their respective fields, seeing him as the greatest postwar historian, or as setting a "crucial precedence for current cultural studies."[40] In what follows, I take Hofstadter's famous diagnosis of a paranoid style in American politics as a lens with which to focus on a wider movement running through the postwar era: the attempt at preserving an increasingly exhausted and elitist New Deal liberalism, afraid of mass culture and political action, doubtful of the efficacy of reason, yet fearful of the forces that are imagined to lurk underneath it. This is the thought of a political class on the retreat, its faith in progress, social change, and education spent, but unable, unlike the generation after it, to embrace the affective dimensions of society—what Hofstadter will consistently label as a dangerous irrationality. The partial successes and ultimate failure of this defense set the stage for the contradictory strands of thought that have sometimes been understood as an American, or even global, postmodernity: the rise of a fragile mass democracy and neo-conservative reaction, the culture industry, and media society. Within this broader context, Hofstadter's recourse to psychopathology functions as a defense against a wide swath of political opposition. His writing also reveals the links between an earlier European intellectual tradition and the emergence of an interdisciplinary study of culture, what Hofstadter envisioned "as a sort of literary anthropology."[41] Hofstadter's popularization of the Frankfurt School's social psychology, in its omissions as much as its additions, provides unique insight into Cold War psychopathology. The metaphorical psychosis of the left and right, of communists and McCarthyites, remains a diagnosis of political opponents in Hofstadter's and other establishment uses, and never amounts to self-critique. Yet this rejection of radical opposition sets the stage for a conception of the mad self that will occupy us for the rest of this study.

The American Political Tradition, Hofstadter's second book, established him as a leading intellectual and understood US history as unified by a central consensus. Hofstadter seemed to be aware of the ideological production of this consensus, the fact that the "range of ideas [. . .] which practical politicians can conveniently believe in is normally limited by the climate of opinion that sustains their culture."[42] Hofstadter's tendency to dissolve ideology into "climates of opinion" foreshadowed the loss of this critical mindset as he moved inside the consensus. Around the same time, Hofstadter began to show interest in the social sources of opinions. Moving away from the materialism of a preceding generation of Progressivist historians, he found them in "individual and social character types, in social mythologies and styles of thought [. . .], and in politics as a sphere of behaviour into which personal and private motives are projected."[43] Hofstadter positions himself at the forefront of an interdisciplinary social science. At Columbia University, where the Frankfurt School of Social Research had sought refuge and C. Wright Mills led the sociology department, he entered what he called "the high and dangerous ground of social psychology."[44] In the process, Hofstadter gained access to what became known as the New York Intellectuals, among them the sociologist Seymour Martin Lipset, political scientist Irving Kristol, and the literary critics Irving Howe and Lionel Trilling.[45]

In 1954, Columbia hosted a seminar on McCarthyism, then already on the wane. Although Theodor Adorno and Max Horkheimer, the two leading exponents of the Frankfurt School, had left, their influence was still keenly felt. As Hofstadter described it: "We began by talking about the movement in terms set by the study of *The Authoritarian Personality* [. . .] we found ourselves moving quite spontaneously back and forth between social-psychological categories and historical events."[46] It was from these discussions that Hofstadter's conception of paranoid politics emerged. The first major outcome, his essay "The Pseudo-Conservative Revolt," attacked McCarthyism as an irrational and pathological movement. Hofstadter also derived the term 'status politics' from the seminar, which would launch his best-known work. Status politics allowed Hofstadter to combine his interests in political and intellectual history, his colleague Arthur Schlesinger said later, opening the way for an investigation of non-economic factors—from social aspirations to party traditions, from religion to morals and emotions.[47] Hofstadter's analyses distinguished between two central building blocks: on the one hand, interest politics, the struggle for material gain between different social groups, on the other, "projective rationalization arising from status aspirations and other personal motives."[48] Status politics was an entirely negative concept, and a double standard emerged in its application. If mainstream politicians appealed to irrational motives, then populism was necessary. Elected officials, in other words, were exempt from status anxiety. Hofstadter had already found this to be true of Franklin D. Roosevelt. Now he praised mainstream politicians for their sober response to the Cold War, a welcome respite from the unfounded panic expressed by everyday Americans. Thankfully, the general "irrationality of the public" was balanced by the superior reason of liberal intellectuals.[49] From this lay diagnosis of public irrationality, it was only a small step to its characterization as paranoid.

The concept of status politics exposed any number of ideological prejudices: from a late modernist intelligentsia that looked down on the common man, to a centrist liberalism that praised its own realism while attacking the supposed utopianism of the left. The outcome was an intellectual position that understood the consensus, of which it formed so comfortably a part, as non-ideological. Defending this position against the right-wing politics of Barry Goldwater, the Republican candidate for the 1964 presidential elections, Hofstadter wrote: "In the past, the American political party has always been a consensual, accommodating, non-ideological instrument run by experienced and practical men [. . .] to make effective government possible."[50] Implicit in this understanding of status was an equally negative concept of ideology. As Hofstadter acknowledged, the main impetus had been provided by Karl Mannheim, whose *Ideology and Utopia* established the necessary link between ideas and social situations.[51] Mannheim defined ideology as that which forestalled objective knowledge, but he opened a loophole through which it could be attained after all. As in Marx, the solution lay in a classless element capable of synthesis. Unlike in Marx, this unanchored social class was the intelligentsia.[52] Objective knowledge was not given to intellectuals per se but depended on them rejecting any affiliation with either the bourgeoisie or the proletariat. Not the lack of political affiliation betrayed a deficiency of character, Mannheim held, but its presence. "We merely wish to point out that the fanaticism of radicalized intellectuals [. . .] bespeaks a psychic compensation for the lack of a more fundamental integration into a class."[53] Mannheim's insistence upon the unique role of the intellectual, what Hofstadter and others came to theorize as an "office of spiritual leadership," provided an influential sanction of their ambitions.[54] The emphasis on social non-attachment and the association of political engagement with psychopathology was transformed into an attack on unwelcome political contenders. The true intellectual lived for ideas, Hofstadter wrote, and his independent viewpoint was secured by his single-minded dedication to them.[55] In contrast, the politically committed intellectual, what Hofstadter came to call the "zealot"—and here his favorite example was Lenin—was not really an intellectual at all, as his capacity for thought was compromised by his political ideals.[56] The ease with which morality and reason were transformed into the moralism and irrationality of one's opponents highlighted Hofstadter's retreat onto the high ground of intellectual purity.

In stark contrast to liberal thinkers, McCarthy and Goldwater stood "psychologically outside the frame of normal democratic politics."[57] Hofstadter was not the only one to think so. In 1964, the magazine *Fact* portrayed Goldwater as a clinical paranoiac and sent questionnaires about his mental health to all 12,356 registered psychiatrists in the country.[58] Of the 2,417 that responded, about half declared Goldwater psychologically unfit for the presidency. The diagnoses they offered from afar ranged from paranoia to schizophrenia, and megalomania to sadomasochism. In response, the American Psychiatric Association instituted regulations—known as the Goldwater rule—prohibiting psychiatrists to publicly comment on the mental health of individuals they had not personally examined.[59] For Hofstadter, as for others, McCarthy and Goldwater had violated the consensus by replacing the pursuit of interests with a moralistic populism. But expelling right-wing Republicans from reasonable debate proved a complex endeavor. As leading representatives of one of America's two mainstream parties, McCarthy and Goldwater seemed to belong squarely *inside* this frame. Goldwater laid bare liberalism's increasingly narrow understanding of democracy. Criticizing definitions of democracy that "reinforced the spirit of egalitarianism," Hofstadter restricted it to universal suffrage and access to political office.[60] This had not always been his opinion. Twenty years earlier he had defended popular government as the only political system that gave the common man a chance in life.[61] With an egalitarian ethics banished from liberal thought, US democracy was wide open to attacks from those who did not relinquish political values so easily.

In this situation, Hofstadter took to social psychology once more to demonize the right. What masqueraded as appeals to freedom were simply rationalizations of impulsive tendencies in the unconscious, surface manifestations that hid, and here Hofstadter quoted Adorno, " 'violence, anarchic impulses, and chaotic destructiveness in the unconscious sphere'."[62] The New Right jeopardized not only the hegemony of New Deal liberalism. On a more personal level, McCarthyism endangered the social position as spiritual guides to the establishment that intellectuals like Hofstadter aspired to. Besieged for their past associations with the left, these thinkers had to protect their brand of moderate welfare politics against the onslaught of the anti-communist right and portray themselves as patriots in the intensifying Cold War. The dangers inherent in such a strategy could not be underestimated: too liberal a position risked being seen as unreliable by an increasingly conservative political establishment, but moving too far to the right entailed the loss of the values, from civil rights to free speech, that liberalism stood for. In the end, postwar liberalism chose to burn its bridges with the left. A decisive step in this direction was the theory of totalitarianism.[63] Drawing on surface phenomena that disregarded economic, political, and ideological differences between communism and fascism, liberal intellectuals proclaimed the shared irrationality of old and new foe. Basing his insights on Fromm's *Escape from Freedom* (1941), whose earlier writings had established the concept of the authoritarian personality, Arthur Schlesinger, Jr.'s, *The Vital Center* (1949) described totalitarianism psychologically. The politics of fascism and communism could not explain their allure. Rather, communism had bred a "psychology of conspiracy." As a consequence, "conspiratorial paranoia has become the conditioned reflex of communism," and this "totalitarian psychosis sickens the whole society."[64]

Liberals could count on a thinker even closer to power at the time. In 1946, the diplomat George Kennan, then stationed at the Embassy in Moscow, had replied to a request by the State Department for an explanation of recent Soviet politics with what become known as the "Long Telegram." Kennan decisively shaped US policy toward the Soviet Union and contributed to the deterioration of an uneasy alliance into a long-lasting confrontation. Throughout the Long Telegram, Kennan assumed the authority of a psychiatrist diagnosing a patient, who was robbed of any legitimate response.[65] Kennan's stance, implicit in much cultural pathology but rarely presented with such certitude, opposed his own professionalism with the infantility of the enemy. Political analysis turned medical expertise, dissent became a symptom of disease. In the burgeoning Cold War of the late 1940s and early '50s, America's politics of madness was transformed into a core element of intellectual culture. What seems significant is not that these and many other authors base their writings entirely or exclusively on madness, or that they provide elaborate or accurate diagnoses, but that they draw on psychopathology for a wide variety of different disciplines outside of psychiatry.[66] As Martin Halliwell has written, Cold War anti-communism was characterized by a "rhetoric of disease."[67] Its association with immorality meant that insanity lent itself to political attacks like no other illness.

Kennan began the Long Telegram by describing the Kremlin as neurotic, but his analysis painted a psychological portrait more akin to psychosis, collapsing the distinction between them. In educated lay understandings, psychosis implied a loss of reality and the domination of a weak or splintered ego by the irrational forces of the id.[68] Kennan's account of Soviet leadership followed such conceptions closely. Soviet power was "seemingly inaccessible to considerations of reality in its basic reactions" and "[i]mpervious to [the] logic of reason."[69] A year later, he extended his argument in an article originally written for Secretary of the Navy, James Forrestal, and published anonymously as "The Sources of Soviet Conduct."[70] Communism was not a rational worldview. Rather, it based itself on convenient rationalizations that masked hidden desires. Given its sources in the unconscious, the Soviet conception of truth "is [. . .] nothing which flows from objective reality."[71] Kennan's description of Soviet politics as psychotic predetermined his conclusion that the U.S.S.R. could no longer be seen as an ally. If the Soviets were figuratively, or perhaps literally, mad, negotiations were in vain. Here, a cultural politics of madness came to shape a global confrontation that would dominate the remainder of the twentieth century. This understanding of opponents as irredeemably irrational and therefore dangerous in a manner that did not allow for dialogue remained influential even where psychological metaphors disappeared from the surface of Cold War rhetoric. In the highly influential National Security Council report known as NSC 68, or Albert Wohlstetter's essays on Cold War strategy, the Soviet Union was assumed irrational und deceitful from the outset.[72] Despite its protestations of detachment, a sense of betrayal emanated from Kennan's discourse of a mad Soviet elite. At pains to express his admiration for the Russian 'national character,' Kennan implied that its people had been led astray by communism. The recourse to psychological vocabulary was grounded in an attempt at understanding, even when the conclusion was that none was possible. Where such basic empathy was missing, the language of evil often replaced metaphors of madness.

The identification of communism as a conspiracy gained its best-known expression in a polemic by Sidney Hook. Programmatically titled *Heresy, Yes—Conspiracy, No*, (1952), its author had once been America's foremost Marxist theorist and was to become one of the philosophers of neoconservatism. For Hook, not only the Communist Party but communism itself was a conspiracy, since it took inspiration from Lenin. The line to be drawn between permissible pursuit and dangerous expression could be defined as an excessive commitment to ideas. The communist was "a dedicated person working with fanatical zeal and prepared to make great personal sacrifices while in the grip of his belief."[73] It followed that communism was a "cancerous growth" and curtailing the rights of its adherents a matter of "ethical hygiene." In an argument that was recycled after 9/11 with the exemption of so-called enemy combatants from the Geneva Convention, Hook distinguished between the exercise of human rights in war and peace.[74] Step by step, the political commitment of dissenters was likened to madness. Madness, in turn, was defined by the excess of the irrational. As with Hofstadter's conception of status politics, the deeper causes of psychological developments, their origins in social structures, receded. What was blocked from view was the question—on which Adorno insisted in his contemporary writings on paranoia—whether the material basis of society, the supposedly rational construction of capitalism, was not in itself irrational. Neither left nor right presented a viable alternative. "Conservatism in its crisis of despair turns to fascism: so progressivism in its crisis of despair turns to Communism," Schlesinger wrote.[75] The only place to turn was a liberalism that behaved distinctively illiberal toward those who disagreed with it.

2.2 The Frankfurt School and Richard Hofstadter's 'Paranoid Style'

Historians have long noted, albeit rather casually, that Hofstadter drew on *The Authoritarian Personality* for his work on right-wing politics, a fact he readily acknowledged.[76] In contrast, studies in cultural pathology have focused on the 1965 essay that gave *The Paranoid Style* its title and ignored the term's intellectual roots. Neither has paid attention to the contradictions and omissions in Hofstadter's adaptation, which tell us as much about this thinker as the concepts he popularized. Written by Adorno and three associates, *The Authoritarian Personality* appeared in the "Studies in Prejudice" series edited by Max Horkheimer as Director of the Institute for Social Research. The project was initially based on a conference on racism and anti-Semitism held in 1944 and used quantitative and qualitative methods to establish a connection between character and prejudice. As Horkheimer explained in his preface, the book analyzed the rise of a new authoritarian type of man who combined the ideas and skills typical of industrial capitalism with "irrational [. . .] beliefs."[77] The main theorist of the Frankfurt School's adaptation of Freudian psychoanalysis had been Erich Fromm, and it was with him that the concept of the authoritarian personality originated.[78] We have already seen that a liberal thinker like Schlesinger drew on Fromm's 1941 *Escape from Freedom* for his pathologization of left politics. Fromm's impact on Adorno and Horkheimer stemmed from his earlier work and most clearly from the chapter on social psychology in the 1936 *Studien über Autorität und Familie*.[79] In contrast to *The Authoritarian Personality* and their work published in the United States, the "Studies on Authority and Family" did not hide their Marxist bent. Contemporary society was "for immanent reasons a structure doomed for destruction," but revolution depended on a political vanguard free from the submissiveness typical of the average man.[80] The concept of the "authoritarian character," which Fromm advanced in his contribution to the volume, encapsulated this submissiveness.[81]

Fromm based his arguments on Freud, Wilhelm Reich, and Karen Horney's work on sadomasochism, but also criticized the founder of psychoanalysis. Freud had overlooked that the family's function in society was not primarily the transmission of opinions but the production of a psychological structure, and more particularly a super-ego, suitable to a capitalist economy.[82] Contemporary Western society—Horkheimer had spoken of a shift from liberal to totalitarian state—could have no interest in a strong ego, as this only encouraged resistance to its structural oppression.[83] Instead, an irrational society—and by this Fromm meant a social order that was not organized according to the interests of the collective good, intensified in its irrationality but not completely transformed with the rise of fascism—remained chaotic and inscrutable to its members.[84] In such a society, authority, which Fromm equated with Freud's super-ego, appeared threatening in its unpredictability and yet potentially benevolent. Without a structural outlet for their feelings, the masses transformed their aggressive impulses into a servile adoration of power, and violence directed against society's weakest. This paradoxical mixture of hate and love Fromm described as sadomasochistic, "and this in turn makes authoritarian hierarchies necessary."[85]

According to Fromm, this dynamic only attained dominance if the individual under its sway also profited. A blind faith in authority provided sadomasochistic personalities, caught in a society they could neither understand nor control, with a measure of reassurance, what he called a "sort of prosthetic security."[86] Here, he was closest to Adorno's reflections in *The Authoritarian Personality*. Fromm never spoke of paranoia in his essay, although he mentioned narcissism and homosexual impulses, both central components of Freud's thoughts on the topic.[87] But sadomasochism's provision of reassurance closely resembles Adorno's later description of political stereotypes, and by implication paranoia, as "signposts of orientation."[88] It also foreshadows the phrase Fromm would use five years later to describe the political implications of the authoritarian personality—as an escape from freedom. Equipped with Fromm's concept, *The Authoritarian Personality* found close links between intolerance and unconscious frustrations, which were then projected onto a substitute object. Thus, the authoritarian type averted "more radical manifestations of a blocking of the subject's relationship to reality, e.g., psychosis."[89] Although authoritarian personalities were not clinical psychotics, they showed "some measure of psychotic mechanisms."[90] Adorno's analogy between psychosis and prejudice showed a clear pattern. There was no one-to-one equation, but the authoritarian personality as it had revealed itself in interviews manifested symptoms of paranoia. Interviewees showed "a mildly paranoid touch," "somewhat paranoid ideas," and "strong paranoid traits." A 26-year-old woman who had been assigned the number 5004 to safeguard her identity merged "semi-psychotic idiosyncrasies" with "wild anti-Jewish imagery" and expressed herself in "authentic paranoid style."[91]

This blurring of borders between neurosis and psychosis, psychological mechanisms and symptoms, transformed paranoia into a surface phenomenon. Limited to interviews rather than sustained analysis, Adorno and his collaborators, among them the psychoanalyst Else Frenkel-Brunswick and the psychologist Daniel Levinson, detected traces of underlying psychological structures—ideas, traits, and touches of paranoia. As a social type, authoritarian man exhibited symptoms of psychosis that manifested themselves in his discourse: the paranoid style was born. Once again, the volume was exemplary of a wider trend. As postwar academia and the wider culture absorbed Freudian and post-Freudian thought, references to mental illness became briefer, simple terms stood in for complex concepts and the structural distinction between neurosis and psychosis was de-emphasized. Writers often used psychological labels indiscriminately. Individuals as well as groups could be hysteric, beset by mania, or suffer from paranoia from one page to the next. At times, they deemed a general diagnosis of madness, insanity, or psychosis sufficient. These different conditions offered intellectuals and literary authors alike a rich vocabulary with which to dramatize their personal unease or critique Cold War America.

Another central element of authoritarian man was what Adorno named his pseudo-conservatism. The true American conservative, the authors held, supported not only capitalism and liberal individualism but also stood for the democratic traditions of the United States. In contrast, the pseudo-conservative, under a veil of conventionality, betrayed, as Hofstadter would quote five years later: "authoritarian submissiveness on the ego level, with violence, anarchic impulses, and chaotic destructiveness in the unconscious sphere."[92] *The Authoritarian Personality* contains any number of concepts and associations that find an echo in Hofstadter. The authoritarian sub-type of "the crank" approached paranoid delusion and was a self-aggrandizing fanatic. Highly prejudiced personalities showed a "general anti-intellectual attitude" and provided the "ideal breeding ground for the modern type of a reactionary mass movement." The authors also linked authoritarian character traits to social status. "The feelings of marginality" experienced by many of these subjects, Frenkel-Brunswick noted, "do not seem to be related to the gross economic conditions of the families in question but rather to those more subtle factors which determine the relationship between social aspiration and effective social status."[93] A casual reader could be forgiven for seeing in the volume a wholeheartedly psychologizing take on politics. Many did. Horkheimer was aware of this danger and stressed that "the cause of irrational hostility is in the last instance to be found in social frustration and injustice."[94] Fragments of such critique remained present throughout. Psychological determinants had to be relativized in a cultural climate that showed an anti-Semitic bias, was potentially fascist, and kept the people ignorant. American capitalism, in its purely formal democratic quality, did not satisfy the elementary needs of the population. The psychological types that Adorno and his colleagues postulated ultimately reflected a society that itself reified its members into types. These pointers were of little avail. In a review of *The Authoritarian Personality* referred to by Hofstadter, the sociologist Edward Shils complained that its discussion of authoritarianism was so ambiguous that there was no point in repeating it.[95] The book's readers were only partly to blame for such misunderstandings. The Frankfurt School's diminishing revolutionary enthusiasm and its precarious welcome had led to a mixture of ideological refashioning and self-censorship. *The Authoritarian Personality* provided an example even in its title, originally meant to be *The Fascist Character*. This was changed into *The Potential Fascist* and, shortly before publication, softened even further—after all, the book studied a population that had just defeated Nazi Germany. These changes came so late that only Horkheimer's preface referred to the authoritarian personality, and the book still spoke of the fascist and potential fascist.[96]

Although the analysis of the fascist character was published in English, its philosophical basis remained inaccessible to most Anglo-American readers. Ironically, the unavailability of *Dialectic of Enlightenment*, the Institute's major statement on fascism and anti-Semitism, may have eased the volume's initial reception. In contemporary references to *The Authoritarian Personality*, it was almost exclusively the few remaining indicators of Adorno's true politics that met with criticism, whereas the book's psychological theses were praised. Hofstadter voiced vague disagreement and ignored the rest. Paranoid symptoms in prejudiced persons were intimately connected to modern society, argued Adorno; in effect, they were a reaction to the complexities of capitalist modernity. Political stereotypes should be understood as a device for overcoming these complexities and seen, Adorno wrote in a suggestive phrase, as "signposts of orientation." In their conclusion, the contributors emphasized an aspect that would come to dominate the work of Herbert Marcuse. If fascism sowed fear and destruction, then at least eros belonged to democracy.[97]

Returning to Hofstadter, continuities with and differences from *The Authoritarian Personality* become apparent. Hofstadter and the book's co-authors shared a number of broad ideological suppositions and theoretical interests. These were not so much convergences of individual beliefs as consequences of a shared cultural formation: with national socialism and the Holocaust an immediate presence, Western intellectuals felt called upon to defend a modernity seemingly under threat. For Hofstadter as for Adorno, the defense of reason could be accomplished only with the help of the singular individual, an individual that often took the form of the artist or intellectual. Neither turned to psychology because of an interest in subjective experience, the decisive factor for countercultural authors and a younger generation of thinkers. What drew them to Freud and his successors was the political development of the common man, whether their initial disappointment lay in the failure of workers as a revolutionary class or their support for the extreme right. What they shared was a dissatisfaction with Marxist accounts of collective behavior. Hofstadter writes: "I do not wish to appear to deny the presence of important economic and political causes. [. . .] But none of these things seems to explain the broad appeal of pseudo-conservatism, its emotional intensity, its dense and massive irrationality."[98] These overlaps and the American reception of *The Authoritarian Personality* formed the basis of Hofstadter's reading. Yet these shared concerns could not hide clear differences. In the opening pages of "The

Pseudo-Conservative Revolt" Hofstadter quotes Adorno's study at length, but notes "reservations about its methods and conclusions."[99] These were spelled out in an essay written for a think tank, The Fund for the Republic, and titled "The Contemporary Right Wing in the United States: A Memorandum." There were many things wrong with the book, Hofstadter wrote, naming its failure to identify authoritarian personalities on the left and to distinguish them from the European fascist.[100] In a paper he described as a confidential document among friends, Hofstadter offered his most outspoken definition of supporters of the American right wing: "I would say that he is a poorly educated paranoid, whose paranoid delusions are, to a very large degree, vented against authority."[101] Hofstadter notes the importance of political issues such as inflation and heavy taxation, and acknowledges the role of conservative donors and pressure groups. But the main emphasis, as has been the case in recent discussions of the Tea Party, is on the popular origins of pseudo-conservatism. Similarly, Hofstadter insists on the anti-modern character of the right. About Goldwater, he writes: "The rhetoric of these speeches [. . .] resounds with the fundamentalist revolt against the conditions of modernity."[102]

This understanding of pseudo-conservatism as a revolt against modernity can be traced to an additional motivation. In *The Authoritarian Personality*, the rise of a potentially fascist character clearly functions as an indictment of industrial capitalism. Authoritarianism is the malady of our modernity. Hofstadter concurs that the postwar right is a dangerous disease. Yet for him the disease threatens from outside a narrowly defined consensus: not the inherent contradictions of capitalism but the populism of America's political culture presents an imminent danger. For Hofstadter, pseudo-conservatism originates with the people, and more specifically, with the uneducated and the poor, with religious believers and the inhabitants of the American village. Rising from below, reactionary dissent then affects irresponsible parts of the elite. Ten years later, Hofstadter will stress the support McCarthy received from "the ill-educated, [. . .] the lower classes" and distinguish between a deeply religious wing solely concerned with moral issues and more affluent conservatives.[103]

The advances of the right seemed to reach new heights with Goldwater's nomination for the 1964 presidential election. Hofstadter closely observed the candidate's fortunes. Initially, he appeared baffled. Yet Goldwater could be fitted neatly into the category of the pseudo-conservative. He was uneducated but showed evidence of "a dangerous impulsiveness." He was an ideologue and religious believer hoping to "weld together a mass of grievances and delusions large enough to win office."[104] In his first two commentaries, Hofstadter had sensed immediate danger, reiterating his belief that a well-organized minority could threaten American democracy. His later articles lacked such shrill rhetoric. Goldwater, if representative of a long-term threat, would not be able to secure the presidency. Despite his ultimate failure at the presidential polls, Goldwater exposed the fragile nature of the liberal consensus. Hofstadter's analysis, in its initial fear and later arrogance, displayed a fundamental misunderstanding of the far right. In an essay published two months after the election, he reacted to Goldwater's post-election statement that "[t]wenty-five million votes are a lot of votes and a lot of people dedicated to the concept of conservatism."[105] Such a statement, Hofstadter argued, reflected an amateur understanding of politics. Driven by the aim to popularize ideological doxa, it was concerned with doctrine rather than practical consequences. Once again, Hofstadter stuck to the distinction between interest and status. Goldwater and his supporters had misunderstood politics because they acted against the GOP's short-term interests. As a consequence, they had become easy prey to status politics. What Hofstadter misses is exactly what should form the core of cultural politics, a concept he helped pioneer: the attempt by Goldwater to break the liberal consensus and to achieve the conservative hegemony now so firmly established in the United States. What Hofstadter diagnoses as irrational can be seen instead as a far-sighted political strategy.

Hofstadter's preoccupation with the far right culminated in the volume of essays *The Paranoid Style in American Politics* (1965). Over time, the 'paranoid style' would become a catch phrase in political debate, and its equation of conspiracy theory with psychopathology dominates public discussion until today.[106] Amid a deepening crisis of postwar liberalism, psychopathology moved to the forefront of Hofstadter's writing and had its greatest cultural and intellectual impact. It will have become clear by now that paranoia is an expression of status politics: more precisely, it is a pathological symptom that articulates the status anxieties of the pseudo-conservative personality. In keeping with this symptomatic understanding of paranoia, Hofstadter attributes various surface phenomena to conspiracy theorists. The "Goldwater movement" serves as an initial example. These men and women are characterized by their suspiciousness and "conspiratorial fantasy."[107] Two features, above all, distinguish the paranoid style from the perception of actually existing conspiracies. The first is the feeling of persecution; the second is an interpretation of history as overly coherent. This leads to a tendency to connect independent phenomena in a "paranoid leap into fantasy," and the conviction that "[h]istory *is* a conspiracy."[108] To seemingly differentiate the paranoid style from clinical pathology, Hofstadter introduces three distinctions. First, its uptake by "more or less normal people" makes the phenomenon relevant politically. Second, where the clinical paranoiac finds himself personally persecuted, the representative of the paranoid style understands these persecutions to be directed against the American nation, a certain group, or persuasion. Third, the paranoid style concerns a specific mode of expression: the "way in which ideas are believed rather than [. . .] the truth or falsity of their content."[109]

These differences between culture and clinic are posited but never upheld. Even before he opposes style to content, Hofstadter states that the paranoid style has a greater affinity for bad than good causes. Shortly afterwards, he adds in a footnote that "while any system of beliefs can be espoused in the paranoid style, there are certain beliefs which seem to be espoused almost entirely in this way."[110] This conflation of political conspiracy theory and clinical psychosis has sometimes been understood as indicating a lack of coherence in Hofstadter's text—an unintended self-contradiction. However, this lack of distinction could also be said to result from the gradual transformation of paranoia into a cluster of surface symptoms. As a result, paranoia and conspiracy theory could now be attributed to texts and political actions. In the essay Hofstadter no longer refers to Freud and Adorno but takes his definition of clinical paranoia from Webster's dictionary. He quotes a psychiatric article critical of Freud's psychodynamic approach, and elsewhere regrets overemphasizing clinical motivations in describing the pseudo-conservative type. Paranoia has been transformed from a clinical structure into a style. Only two faint reminders of Freudian psychoanalysis remain, both terms in frequent use at the time. For one, Hofstadter speaks of politics as a "projective arena" in his introduction to the book.[111] Secondly, he repeatedly employs the term rationalization to describe the pseudo-conservative's expression of unconscious impulses. Blurring the distinction between culture and clinic also held political advantages. Hofstadter's goal is the denunciation of dissent perceived as a threat to liberal democracy. As he states: the term paranoid style "is pejorative, and it is meant to be."[112] Thus, Hofstadter can have no interest in separating political conspiracy theory from psychopathology. A deliberately ambiguous yet explicit demonization of political opposition, Hofstadter's paranoid style provided ideological ammunition to Cold War liberals but survives until today when its partisan origins have been forgotten.

Like status politics, the paranoid style provided Hofstadter with a link between private and public concerns. Its value, he wrote, lay in suggesting "a means by which we may better understand how political issues come to be conceived by a certain type of mind."[113] That a mind expressing itself in this style was pathological Hofstadter never doubted, yet his conception of paranoia was distinctive for a far more sweeping judgment. At times he suggested that paranoia was due to a lack of knowledge and education, without offering a cure for the illness he diagnosed. Nor did he indicate that paranoia was the psychotic's attempt at curing himself, as Freud had suggested. Hofstadter's diagnosis of paranoia was never meant to be therapeutic. There existed no cure, since for someone who applied psychology to American society this would have meant proposing large-scale political change. In contrast, Fromm's *The Sane Society* followed its diagnosis of widespread unease by exploring what curing a society would entail: "sanity and mental health can be attained only by simultaneous change in the sphere of industrial and political organization, [. . .] of character structure, and of cultural activities."[114] For Hofstadter, paranoia was exclusively negative. Where Adorno spoke of the paranoid character of enlightenment reason and identified paranoia as the "shadow of knowledge," Hofstadter only saw rationalizations that were all but rational.[115] When Leo Lowenthal and Norbert Guterman emphasized paranoia's attempt at understanding, a mistaken if necessary groping in the dark, Hofstadter remained silent.[116] For him pathology could teach nothing about normality. A final glimpse of utopian hope, as was offered in the conclusion to *The Authoritarian Personality*, which had spoken of the emancipatory powers of eros, was unimaginable in a Hofstadter text. The agency of the unconscious remained a threat, never an occasion for hope.

Hofstadter's denunciation of paranoia drew sharp criticism from some of his contemporaries. A letter written to him by a representative of The Fund for the Republic, the think tank that had commissioned his memorandum on "The Contemporary Right Wing in the United States," summarized the response of a group of highly respected academics, among them the psychologist B.F. Skinner. "[T]he group was so dubious of its own attempts, and yours to define 'right-wing extremism' that it concluded efforts to define it were simply efforts to distinguish behaviour they like from behaviour they preferred not to be identified with."[117] The letter also advanced a view that would become commonplace only later, that of an American culture of paranoia:

> We are all subject to something the group began to call 'situational paranoia'. Said one of the members of the group, 'The situation as such, the estrangement of the people, the remoteness, the mobility, the lack of being forced to consider long-run implications of momentary acts—forces on us a sense of conspiracy. [. . .] I would argue that certainly the situation is more like this now and that this is what we are reading about [. . .] We are seeing the aggravation of the experiences of social conditions that produce all kinds of paranoid behaviour in everyone.[118]

2.3 After Liberalism: Psychosis and Social Change

The Paranoid Style completes what David Brown has called Hofstadter's social-psychological trilogy, begun in 1955 with *The Age of Reform*. The final years of his life saw the war in Vietnam, the emergence of the New Left, and the rise of the counterculture. Hofstadter, in characteristic fashion, engaged with all of them and found himself on uncomfortable territory. Alexander Bloom has noted how rarely the New York Intellectuals wrote on the Vietnam War, the most hotly contested issue of the late 1960s and early '70s.[119] At first sight, this was a debate that cried out for the intellectual guidance these writers had by now offered for decades. Their relative silence stemmed from the difficult position into which they had maneuvered themselves. For those who had not completely changed sides, any war, and even more so aggression against a disproportionately smaller and poorer nation, was difficult to embrace wholeheartedly. At the same time, intellectuals like Hofstadter had moved close to power. His rare comments on the war consequently never offered a systematic critique and stalled at the level of cautious opposition.[120]

The activism of the New Left affected Hofstadter directly. The occupation of a university building by radical students divided Columbia, but Hofstadter's reaction to these events remained as evasive as his position on the war. Chosen to deliver the commencement address in place of president Grayson L. Kirk, who had been denounced as a conservative hardliner by students, he argued for institutional reform but otherwise responded to a heavily politicized situation only by urging that academics retreat from politics.[121] These years also saw a rediscovery of conflict in Hofstadter's writing. The understanding of the United States as shaped by a unifying consensus had always relied on ignoring much that defined America's past: the continent's brutal conquest, slavery, the Civil War, economic exploitation, and ethnic tensions. In one of his last essays, the afterword to a documentary history of *American Violence*, Hofstadter rehearsed old themes, criticizing the New Left, much as he had the far right, as a political style.[122] His emphasis on the role of violence in America's past was also a vehement critique, and implicitly a self-critique, of consensus history. "Shirked by our historians," Hofstadter writes in another psychologizing turn of phrase, "the subject [of violence] has been repressed in the national consciousness [. . .] We are now quite ready to see that there is far more violence in our national heritage than our proud, sometimes smug, national self-image admits of."[123] Two years after the cataclysmic events of 1968 and Richard Nixon's ascent to the presidency, Hofstadter considered the possible eclipse of a liberal politics that had taken shape with Roosevelt's election in 1932. Given the social unrest that shook the country and reached the institution at which he had taught for over two decades, it now became evident that consensus history obstructed the view as much as it provided orientation.

However, it was Hofstadter's somewhat earlier comments on what he sensed was "a new state of affairs in our cultural life" that best capture this end of an era and the beginning of a new one.[124] He described a cultural vanguard, but one whose classical attributes of rebellion, anarchism, and militancy were matched by a novel and disturbing emphasis on sensation— on fun. The basis for a modernist avant-garde had disappeared:

> We live in an age in which the avant-garde itself has been institutionalized and deprived of its old stimulus of a stubborn and insensate opposition. [. . .] American painters, seeking in abstract expressionism the outer limits of artistic liberation, find a few years later that their canvases are selling in five figures. Beatniks are in demand on university campuses, where they are received as entertainers.[125]

This new beginning could claim to reach the masses, but it had inherited a political thought that had extinguished any radicalism from itself, had destroyed the institutions and traditions of the left, exchanged collective politics for morals and religion, and found in the defense against its grand foe communism its last remaining goal. Nonetheless, this new state of affairs threatened the now old liberalism for which Hofstadter stood, even if it had incorporated much of its predecessor: its valuation of culture over economics, status over class, and ethics over politics. Once again, Hofstadter attacked an opponent with the tried and true vocabulary of illness and irrationality. Like the New Right and Left, the Beats suffered from a disorder. Their protest was not so much political, as "simply, in the current argot, further out." Echoing literary critics, he classified the Beats as another "lunatic fringe." Hofstadter himself identified with those who, "like anyone who is given to contemplating the complexities of things, [. . .] have lost the posture of militancy," and accused the new writing of "moral nihilism."[126]

Hofstadter's late engagements with contemporary issues exemplify the inability of the liberal intelligentsia to set America's agenda. As the New Deal receded into the past, Hofstadter found himself less and less able to imagine the political change the future should bring. "What most liberals now hope for," he wrote, "is not to carry on with some ambitious new program, but simply to defend as much as possible the old achievements and to try to keep traditional liberties of expression that are threatened."[127] With its repudiation of a radical heritage, from the Populist and Progressive movements to the Marxist Left of the 1930s, postwar liberalism cut itself off from the popular roots that had made the New Deal such a vibrant experiment. Instead of engaging an ever more alienated population in democratic politics, liberals betrayed a pervasive fear of the masses. In their simultaneous demonization of left and right, they conflated an elitist appeal to conservative sentiment with progressive politics. With their attack on communists and progressives, and their complicity in the destruction of unions and civil rights organizations, these thinkers exposed their own flank to the right. "When liberals came under attack they had to defend themselves from a more politically exposed position than they would otherwise have occupied," contends Ellen Schrecker.[128] The destruction of the left also weakened liberalism, today a standard term of abuse in American politics, and facilitated the ascent of neo-conservatism. Throughout his analyses of the New Right, Hofstadter exhibited an unwillingness to understand the right's sustained challenge. Against an opposition that skillfully appealed to nationalist sensibilities and religious fervor, that employed moral indignation as unscrupulously as scapegoating, Hofstadter stressed the guardianship of intellectual elites and the expert administration of the status quo. It is one of the poignant ironies of his work and historical era, and perhaps one of the few that escaped a man so tuned to the complex ironies of history, that it was not the ascendant right but a descendant liberalism whose energies were spent and that was truly non-political. Toward the end of his life, Hofstadter saw that the "unity of cultural and political tradition" he had once proclaimed had broken apart, perhaps even—as the next generation would assert—that it had been a myth all along.[129]

The end of liberal hegemony heralded a crisis of psychological accounts of US society. James Burnham has suggested that the declining influence of psychoanalysis during the 1960s was a direct consequence of liberalism's demise.[130] Wider shifts were also at play. The escalating Vietnam War sapped funding for psychiatry, and the Nixon administration proved hostile to social initiatives—a downward spiral that would accelerate under Ronald Reagan.[131] A similar disenchantment was evident in the US military and its think tanks. If the early Cold War and the War in Korea had been underpinned by psychological assumptions, Vietnam signaled the ascendancy of theories of rational choice. The same Rand experts who analyzed the unconscious motivations of the Kremlin, among them Nathan Leites, now proclaimed that the Vietcong would only retreat if sustained air bombardments proved to them the objective futility of further resistance.[132] Psychocultural approaches to national character and elite behavior seemed unable to keep their promise. Their alignment of social and psychological change appeared increasingly unrealistic as the 1960s turned ugly and hopes of the Great Society were dashed. As always, such tectonic shifts were gradual. Much public debate continued to be conducted in psychological terms. But psychological cure as social policy now seemed out of reach, or simply moved out of the picture.

These changes were also visible at the nexus of madness and female gender roles. If countercultural reevaluations of psychopathology would come to constitute the détente of Cold War madness, at times repealing the demonization of political and personal alternatives, then the diagnosis of multiple personality disorder (MPD) may be said to play a somewhat similar role at the intersection of insanity and gender. What is today known as dissociative identity would be formalized with the publication of the third edition of the Diagnostic and Statistical Manual of Mental Disorders (DSM-III) in 1980. A dramatic surge in diagnoses over the next two decades abated after serious doubts had emerged about its validity, followed by official reclassification with DSM-IV in 1994.[133] Flora Rheta Schreiber's best-selling case study *Sybil* (1973) positions itself as an explicit repudiation of Cold War domesticity. Attacking postwar America's "destructive family relationships" and "denial of self-realization" to women, Schreiber's book performs a generational and diagnostic shift.[134] Sybil's mother evokes Fromm-Reichmann's schizophrenogenic parent: a conservative and depressed housewife, whose lack of nurturing induces an early trauma in her daughter. Sybil's childhood, exposed in scurrilous detail, adds a component that will become crucial for MPD: the daughter's sexual abuse, in this case by a mother who is herself said to be psychotic. Based on her psychoanalyst's notes, as well as Sybil's diary and interviews with her, the book attempts to establish a highly literary text, told by an omniscient narrator, as indisputable fact. As Schreiber writes: ""I have also discussed Sybil's case with such notable members of the psychiatric fraternity as Dr. Karl Menninger [. . .] attesting to its reality."[135] Sensationalist detail combines with psychiatric authority to imagine an escape from the ideology of postwar femininity, but only as disorder. Sybil's alternative identities include the assertive Peggy, Vicky ("a woman of the world"), and the submissive Mary.[136] In Schreiber's account, MPD emerges as a warped attempt at liberation: a splintering of oppressive gender norms that weighs novel opportunities for American women against anxieties about their integration into a unified identity. MPD remains within the vocabulary of psychopathology but situates itself beyond established categories. In contrast to those who would classify her illness as a borderline disorder, Schreiber insists that Sybil's case should be understood as a form of hysteria. Situated between neurosis and psychosis, MPD marks a limit case, yet continues efforts to distinguish reason from unreason, acceptable from unacceptable behavior.

As early as Gunnar Myrdal's *An American Dilemma* (1944) psychoanalytical studies of group behavior turned toward black Americans. While sympathetic to their plight, Myrdal advocated individual and collective assimilation into white America as the best way to overcome racism—a recommendation based, in part, on his evaluation of black culture. "American Negro culture," he wrote, "is not something independent of general American culture. It is a distorted development, or a pathological condition, of the general American culture."[137] Civil rights leaders may have shared some of these assumptions, with Martin Luther King calling black families "psychopathic," but shone the spotlight on the prospect of cure.[138] In his sermons, King drew on psychopathology to picture racial integration as a process of healing the schizophrenic, or split, self. Bridging the racial divide appeared not simply as a political goal but an internal process that promised the unity of mental health.[139] To struggle against racism was to heal oneself from madness. The rhetoric of depth psychology, with its aura of scientific objectivity, acted as a powerful weapon in the fight against segregation and signaled black American sophistication. In stark contrast, Malcolm X's autobiography identified the desire for integration as mad, claiming that "No sane black man really wants integration" and diagnosing his fellow African Americans "mentally sick in [their] cooperative, sheep-like acceptance of the white man's culture."[140] Such self-criticism would be continued in the rhetoric of Black Power leaders Robert Williams and Stokely Carmichael, but increasingly it was the pathology of white racism that moved to the foreground. Williams's *Negroes with Guns* wildly mixed its metaphors but the message was clear, whether the racist was "a man crazed with hysteria," or racism declared "a mass psychosis." Williams still spoke of cure. Yet the treatment he advocated was not individual psychoanalysis or religious healing but mass, and if necessary violent, resistance.[141]

LeRoi Jones's *Dutchman* (1964), a foundational text in modern African-American theater, explored therapeutic violence on the model of Frantz Fanon's *The Wretched of the Earth* (1961) with far more ambivalence. In the play, the white woman Lula and a young black man named Clay meet on the New York subway. She makes sexual advances, ridicules him, and questions his masculinity until he delivers a speech that advocates murder as a solution to the black man's racial insanity.[142] Clay's firebrand rhetoric remains just that. Instead, Lula stabs him and, together with the other white passengers, throws his dead body off the train. The therapeutic value of violence also featured in Grier and Cobbs's *Black Rage*. Written by two psychiatrists who made no secret of a support for Black Power, it was unsurprising that they agreed in their diagnosis of a national sickness.[143] Their equation of such insanity with an increasing fragmentation of US society sounded a theme that would become increasingly influential in the 1970s and '80s. But what was most remarkable about their book was a positive conception of black paranoia. A term frequently associated with African Americans at the time, King had described paranoia as self-defeating. Grier and Cobbs interpreted paranoia as healthy suspiciousness necessary for survival in a hostile America—"an accurate reading of one's environment." Here, madness was traced back to the society from which it originated: "[A]fter all, who can really tell where [. . .] delusions end and reality begins in this mad, mad land?"[144] Accordingly, the authors opposed existing psychological criteria to what they called a "Black Norm." In a racist society, character traits that would otherwise be pathological were necessary adaptations. "To regard the Black Norm as pathological and attempt to remove such traits by treatment would be akin to analyzing away a hunter's cunning or a banker's prudence. This is a body of characteristics essential to life for black men in American and woe be unto that therapist who does not recognize it."[145] If *Black Rage* doubted the irrationality of madness by questioning the health of American society, the distinction was still made by a psychiatrist. In fact, expertise became all the more important, the more subtle the distinction between sanity and insanity appeared. *Black Rage* was psychiatric, not antipsychiatric protest. But in its advocacy of a necessary paranoia, the volume belonged to America's counterculture of the 1960s, which put forward similarly positive evaluations in the fiction of Thomas Pynchon or Philip K. Dick, to name just two of many authors who shared this view.

Grier and Cobbs stood in the tradition of a postwar literature that explored the freedom that madness offered black men in white society. The title of Ralph Ellison's *Invisible Man* (1952) proposes a perceptual and psycho-pathological analogy. The madness is white America's foreclosure of multi-racial reality, the inability to see black citizens as equals. The insane asylum shadowing the Southern college that the nameless protagonist attends indicates a second madness, a consequence of the first. The lack of recognition afforded black people results in social irresponsibility, an existential aloofness from the norms and values whose psychological assimilation constitutes normality. As the mad veterinarian, who resembles a medieval fool or court jester, advises when the protagonist visits the asylum: "Be your own father, young man."[146] The invisible man's attempt to create his own identity leads to his association with communism and black nationalism, both of which prove disappointments. The novel identifies a crude, mechanistic Marxism with paranoia and the nationalist leader Ras as a cold-blooded psychopath, recording Ellison's own disenchantment. Because the invisible man's sickness is social, the maddening split that defines African American existence, cure remains unavailable without credible movements for social change. In the meantime, the individual is reduced to a solitary insanity "outside the narrow borders of what men call reality."[147] Ellison's reading in existential philosophy shaped *Invisible Man* as clearly as his interest in psychiatry and psychoanalysis. The latter had already led to Ellison's support for the founding of Harlem's Lafargue Clinic in 1946. Alongside his fellow author and friend Richard Wright, he helped secure the space and contributed funds to an institution that sought to address the psychological effects of discrimination. Or as Ellison put it in an article written in support of the clinic and its director Fredric Wertham: to alleviate the "Negro's perpetual alienation in the land of his birth."[148]

Wright's *The Outsider* (1953) deepened the association between psychosis and the American Communist Party following the author's own acrimonious departure from it. In Wright's novel, communism appeared both as a potential escape from madness into meaningful community and, ultimately, insanity's identical twin. A much darker novel, *The Outsider* explored an aspect of the black experience that Ellison had only hinted at in the character of Ras. Wright's protagonist Cross Damon exhibits a cold-blooded disregard for life but his portrayal differs from a later imagination of the psychopath, which attributed a perverse pleasure in violence to this figure, particularly in the context of the Vietnam War and atrocities committed by US troops on civilians. Damon experiences violence as a radical break with existing social ties, a psychotic withdrawal from the world. "He had to break with others and, in breaking with them, he would break with himself."[149] These actions foreshadow Damon taking advantage of a freakish subway accident to leave his wife and children. Violence follows his every step. Wright, who had unsuccessfully tried to join the Navy's Psychological Warfare Unit and as a Marxist remained under lifelong surveillance by the FBI instead, emphasizes the essential madness of postwar America. His protagonist's demonic psychosis constitutes one of many varieties of insanity at a time when, suffering under political as well as racial oppression, millions are "completely cut off from humanity."[150] In a different era, Damon's separation from his society's laws and expectations might have had less violent consequences, avoiding his own death at the hands of party henchmen, and those of his victims. However, the entanglement of structural racism, individualism, and Cold War power plays, makes anything but a tragic ending unthinkable. For Wright as for

Ellison, individual therapy remains meaningless without political transformation. As Damon's opponent and fellow outsider, the hunchbacked district attorney Ely Houston, tells him: "To whom could you tell your story, Damon? A psychoanalyst? They'd be frightened of you; they'd rush out of their consulting rooms, their hair standing on end, screaming with terror."[151]

As the postwar era gave way to the Sixties, these different paths through psychopathology would be further explored by critical intellectuals, literary authors, Hollywood cinema, and the antipsychiatry movement. Madness would appear as no more than a myth, a terrible illness, and the only possible sanity, a metaphor for social fragmentation, and a superior knowledge. Even where radical activists and thinkers rejected the usefulness of mental illness to describe US society, they fell back on psychological conceptions of self and society that suffused American culture. Stokely Carmichael's famous speech at the Congress of Liberation in 1967 is an excellent example. Dismissing the importance of individual psychology for black politics, he nevertheless spoke of "the minority complex" of his community and America's "subconscious racism."[152] Like any other dismissal, reinterpretation or subversion of psychiatry, Carmichael's could be understood only against the background of its grip on America's imagination and a Cold War psychology that pathologized self and other. Here lay the basis for the contradictions that haunted left and right-wing, countercultural and mainstream, takes on madness, and this is where any understanding of them must begin.

Notes

1 Anon., "The Wise Old Man," *Time*, February 14, 1955, 62.
2 John F. Kennedy, "Special Message to the Congress on Mental Illness and Mental Retardation," accessed November 18, 2010, http://www.arcmass.org/Portals/0/-JFK%20Message%20to%20the%20Congress.pdf.
3 Ibid.
4 Joel Pfister, "On Conceptualizing the Cultural History of Emotional and Psychological Life in America," in *Inventing the Psychological: Toward a Cultural History of Emotional Life in America*, ed. Joel Pfister and Nancy Schnog (New Haven, CT: Yale University Press, 1997), 28; and Joel Pfister, "Glamorizing the Psychological: The Politics of the Performances of Modern Psychological Identities," in *Inventing the Psychological*, 167.
5 Pfister, "Glamorizing the Psychological: The Politics of the Performances of Modern Psychological Identities," in *Inventing the Psychological*, 169.
6 Ellen Herman, *The Romance of American Psychology: Political Culture in the Age of Experts* (Berkeley, CA: University of California Press, 1995), 5. In what follows, I repeatedly draw on Herman's study for my account of World War II's impact on psychiatry.
7 Sylvia Plath, *The Journals of Sylvia Plath, 1950–1962*, ed. Karen V. Kukil (London: Faber, 2000), 151 (entry dated 3.11.1952).
8 Barbara O'Brien, *Operators and Things: The Inner Life of a Schizophrenic* (Los Angeles: Silver Birch, 2011), 24.

9 Lawrence K. Frank, *Society as the Patient: Essays on Culture and Personality* (Piscataway, NJ: Rutgers University Press, 1948); and Martin Luther King, Jr., *Where Do We Go from Here: Chaos or Community?* (New York: Harper, 1967), 68.

10 Kennedy, "Special Message to Congress."

11 William H. Grier and Price M. Cobbs, *Black Rage* (New York: Basic, 1968), 158.

12 Harold D. Lasswell, *Psychopathology and Politics* (Chicago: Chicago University Press, 1930), 184. In his opening pages, Lasswell thanks a veritable role-call of leading psychoanalysts for their assistance, including Sullivan, Paul Federn, Alfred Adler, Wilhelm Stekel, Paul Ferenczi, Theodor Reik, and Franz Alexander.

13 R. E. Money-Kyrle, *Psychoanalysis and Politics: A Contribution to the Psychology of Politics and Morals* (London: Duckworth, 1951), 127.

14 Ibid., 138.

15 Ibid.

16 Harold D. Lasswell and Dorothy Blumenstock, *World Revolutionary Propaganda: A Chicago Study* (Freeport, NY: Books for Libraries, 1970).

17 Ron Robin, *The Making of the Cold War Enemy: Culture and Politics in the Military-Industrial Complex* (Princeton, NJ: Princeton University Press, 2001), 134.

18 Nathan Leites, *The Operational Code of the Politburo* (Westport, CT: Greenwood, 1972), 3–4.

19 Nathan Leites, *A Study of Bolshevism* (Glencoe, IL: Free Press, 1953), 38 and 236.

20 Richard Hofstadter, introduction to *The Paranoid Style in American Politics and Other Essays* (London: Cape, 1966), ix.

21 Lasswell, *Psychopathology and Politics*, 197.

22 Ibid. Lasswell's understanding of truth anticipated another sea change in speaking about the psychological individual. Where the 1910s and '20s had sought out the deeper knowledge that the supposedly primitive urges of the unconscious hid, most post-war American thought located truth in an ego purged of unconscious desires. See Pfister, "Glamorizing the Psychological: The Politics of the Performances of Modern Psychological Identities," in *Inventing the Psychological*, 183.

23 See Elaine May Tyler's classic study *Homeward Bound: American Families in the Cold War Era* (New York: Basic, 1988).

24 K. A. Cuordileone, *Manhood and American Political Culture in the Cold War* (New York: Routledge, 2005), xiii.

25 Alfred C. Kinsey, Wardell B. Pomeroy, and Clyde E. Martin, *Sexual Behavior in the Human Male* (Philadelphia: W. B. Saunders, 1948), 659; and see Robert J. Corber, *Homosexuality in Cold War America: Resistance and the Crisis of Masculinity* (Durham, NC: Duke University Press, 1997).

26 Betty Friedan, *The Feminine Mystique* (New York: Norton, 2013), 5.

27 Ibid., 39.

28 Ibid., 108.

29 Plath, *The Journals of Sylvia Plath*, 495.

30 Mary Jane Ward, *The Snake Pit* (New York: Signet, 1949), 20.

31 Anatole Litvak, *The Snake Pit* (1948; London: Optimum, 2004), DVD.

32 Ward, *The Snake Pit*, 173.

33 Sylvia Plath, *The Bell Jar* (London: Faber, 1966), 79.

34 Ibid., 71.

35 Plath, *The Journals of Sylvia Plath*, 429 (entry dated 12.12.1958).

36 Fromm-Reichmann, "Notes on the Development of Treatment of Schizophrenics by Psychoanalytic Psychotherapy," 263–273; and see Deborah Weinstein, *The Pathological Family: Postwar America and the Rise of Family Therapy* (Ithaca, NY: Cornell University Press, 2013).

37 Fromm-Reichmann, "Notes on the Development of Treatment of Schizophrenics by Psychoanalytic Psychotherapy," 273.
38 Ibid., 269; and Joanne Greenberg, *I Never Promised You a Rose Garden* (New York: Signet 1989), 61.
39 David S. Brown, *Richard Hofstadter: An Intellectual Biography* (Chicago: University of Chicago Press, 2006); and Daniel Joseph Singal, "Beyond Consensus: Richard Hofstadter and American Historiography," *The American Historical Review* 89 (1984): 977.
40 Brown, *Richard Hofstadter*, xiii; and Mark Fenster, *Conspiracy Theories: Secrecy and Power in American Culture* (Minneapolis: University of Minnesota Press, 1999), 10.
41 Richard Hofstadter, "History and the Social Sciences," in *The Varieties of History: From Voltaire to the Present*, ed. Fritz Stern (New York: Vintage, 1973), 363.
42 Richard Hofstadter, *The American Political Tradition: And the Men Who Made It* (New York: Vintage, 1974), xxxviii.
43 Hofstadter, "History and the Social Sciences," 361.
44 Hofstadter, *The Paranoid Style*, 185.
45 Brown, *Richard Hofstadter*, 73–75 and 89–90. I discuss the literary criticism of Howe and Trilling in chapter 6.
46 Hofstadter, "History and the Social Sciences," 367.
47 Arthur M. Schlesinger, Jr., "Richard Hofstadter," in *Pastmasters: Some Essays on American Historians*, ed. Marcus Cunliffe and Robin W. Winks (New York: Harper, 1969), 297.
48 Hofstadter, "Cuba, the Philippines, and Manifest Destiny," in *The Paranoid Style*, 53.
49 Richard Hofstadter, "A Long View: Goldwater in History," *New York Review of Books*, October 8, 1964, accessed April 15, 2010, www.nybooks.com/articles/13196; Hofstadter, *The Age of Reform*, 18.
50 Richard Hofstadter, "Goldwater & His Party: The True Believer and the Radical Right," *Encounter* XXIII-4 (1964): 3.
51 Hofstadter, "History and the Social Sciences," 362.
52 Karl Mannheim, *Ideology and Utopia: An Introduction to the Sociology of Knowledge* (London: Routledge, 1960), 139 and 140.
53 Ibid., 141.
54 Richard Hofstadter, "Democracy and Anti-Intellectualism in America," *Michigan Alumnus Quarterly Review* 59 (August 1953): 285.
55 Richard Hofstadter, *Anti-Intellectualism in American Life* (London: Cape, 1964), 27.
56 Ibid., and Hofstadter, "Democracy and Anti-Intellectualism in America," 283.
57 Hofstadter, "Pseudo-Conservatism Revisited: A Postscript," in *The Paranoid Style*, 102.
58 Ralph Ginzburg, "Goldwater: The Man and the Menace," *Fact* 1–5 (1964): 3–22.
59 Richard A. Friedman, "How a Telescopic Lens Muddles Psychiatric Insights," *New York Times*, May 23, 2011, accessed June 25, 2011, http://www.nytimes.com/2011/05-/24/health/views/24mind.html?_r=1-&ref=science.
60 Richard Hofstadter, *The Progressive Historians: Turner, Beard, Parrington* (London: Cape, 1969), 126.
61 Hofstadter, *The American Political Tradition*, 123.
62 Hofstadter, "The Pseudo-Conservative Revolt," in *The Paranoid Style*, 44. Hofstadter quotes from T. W. Adorno et al., *The Authoritarian Personality* (New York: Norton, 1969), 675.
63 For a classic statement see: Hannah Arendt, *The Origins of Totalitarianism* (Cleveland: World, 1958).

64 Arthur Schlesinger, Jr., *The Vital Center: The Politics of Freedom* (Boston: Houghton Mifflin, 1949), 64–65 and 85.
65 George Kennan, "Long Telegram," accessed April 15, 2010, http://www.truman library.org/whistlestop/study_collections/coldwar/do-cuments-/index.php?-docu mentdate=19460222&documentid=66&study-collectionid=&page-number=1.
66 Another prominent proponent of post-war psychopolitics, if as establishment critique, was the one-time editor of the modernist magazine *The Dial*, literary and architectural critic Lewis Mumford. In his essay collection *In the Name of Sanity* (1954), and more journalistic essays, such the aptly titled "Gentlemen: You are Mad!", psychosis becomes the central metaphor for the contemporary American zeitgeist and policies of nuclear armament. Lewis Mumford, *In the Name of Sanity* (Westport, CT: Greenwood, 1973); and "Gentlemen: You are Mad!" *Saturday Review of Literature*, March 2, 1946, 5–6.
67 Martin Halliwell, *Therapeutic Revolutions: Medicine, Psychiatry, and American Culture, 1945–1970* (New Brunswick, NJ: Rutgers University Press 2013), 181.
68 Although such uses necessarily simplify Freud's more complex elaboration of psychosis, they do conform roughly to Freudian conceptions. For his writings on psychosis see: Sigmund Freud, "Psycho-Analytical Notes on an Autobiographical Account of a Case of Paranoia (Dementia Paranoides)," in *The Standard Edition of the Complete Psychological Works of Sigmund Freud*, vol. 12, trans. and ed. James Strachey (London: Hogarth, 1958), 9–82; Sigmund Freud, "The Loss of Reality in Neurosis and Psychosis," in *SE* 14, trans. and ed. James Strachey (London: Hogarth, 1961), 183–187; and Sigmund Freud, "Fetishism," in *SE* 21, 155–156. Laplanche and Pontalis give an excellent overview of the development of conceptions of psychosis in: J. Laplanche and J.B. Pontalis, *The Language of Psycho-Analysis*, trans. Donald Nicholson-Smith (London: Karnac, 1988), 369–371.
69 Kennan, "Long Telegram," 15–16.
70 The essay was originally titled "The Psychological Background of Soviet Foreign Policy." For an account of its evolution see: Wilson D. Miscamble, *George F. Kennan and the Making of American Foreign Policy, 1947–1950* (Princeton, NJ: Princeton University Press, 1992), 31.
71 X [George Kennan], "The Sources of Soviet Conduct," *Foreign Affairs* 25 (1947): 567 and 573.
72 Albert Wohlstetter, "The Delicate Balance of Terror," *Foreign Affairs* 37 (1959): 211–234.
73 Sidney Hook, "Introduction: Communism's Postwar Decade," *New Leader*, December 19, 1955, 2.
74 Sidney Hook, *Heresy, Yes—Conspiracy, No* (Westport, CT: Greenwood, 1973), 26 and 35.
75 Schlesinger, *The Vital Center*, 50.
76 Hofstadter, "History and the Social Sciences," 367.
77 Max Horkheimer and Samuel H. Flowerman, foreword to *The Authoritarian Personality*, viii.
78 Martin Jay, *The Dialectical Imagination: A History of the Frankfurt School and the Institute of Social Research 1923–1950* (Berkeley, CA: University of California Press, 1996), 88.
79 Erich Fromm, "Sozialpsychologischer Teil," in *Studien über Autorität und Familie. Forschungsberichte aus dem Institut für Sozialforschung*, ed. Max Horkheimer (Paris: Alcan, 1936), 77–135. To the best of my knowledge, this central document of the early Frankfurt School has never been translated into English. All translations from the text that follow are mine.
80 Horkheimer, "Allgemeiner Teil," in *Studien über Autorität und Familie*, 8 and 21.
81 Ibid., 59.

82 Fromm, "Sozialpsychologischer Teil," 87–92.
83 Horkheimer, "Allgemeiner Teil," in *Studien über Autorität und Familie*, 43.
84 Fromm, "Sozialpsychologischer Teil," 118.
85 Ibid.
86 Ibid., 123–124.
87 Ibid., 125.
88 Adorno et al., *The Authoritarian Personality*, 618.
89 Ibid., 607–608.
90 Ibid., 481.
91 Ibid., 625, 643, 679 and 615.
92 Ibid., 675.
93 Adorno et al., *The Authoritarian Personality*, 765, 658–659, 662–663, and 483.
94 Horkheimer and Flowerman, preface to *The Authoritarian Personality*, viii.
95 Edward Shils, "Authoritarianism: 'Right' and 'Left'," in *Studies in the Scope and Method of 'The Authoritarian Personality'*, ed. Richard Christie and Marie Jahoda (Glencoe, IL: Free Press, 1954), 43 and 30.
96 Rolf Wiggershaus, *Die Frankfurter Schule: Geschichte, Theoretische Entwicklung, Politische Bedeutung* (Munich: Hanser, 1987), 458.
97 Ibid., 976. And see Herbert Marcuse, *Eros and Civilization: A Philosophical Inquiry into Freud* (Boston: Beacon, 1966).
98 Hofstadter, "The Pseudo-Conservative Revolt," in *The Paranoid Style*, 49.
99 Ibid., 43–44.
100 Richard Hofstadter, "The Contemporary Right Wing in the United States: A Memorandum," iii. Box 1, Richard Hofstadter Papers, Rare Book and Manuscript Library, Columbia University.
101 Ibid., iv–v.
102 Richard Hofstadter, "Goldwater and Pseudo-Conservative Politics," in *The Paranoid Style*, 118.
103 Hofstadter, "Pseudo-Conservatism Revisited," in *The Paranoid Style*, 69.
104 Hofstadter, "Goldwater & His Party," 3 and 8; and Hofstadter, "A Long View."
105 Hofstadter, "Goldwater and Pseudo-Conservative Politics," in *The Paranoid Style*, 114.
106 For two studies that already emulate this analogy between paranoia and conspiracy theory in their title see: Daniel Pipes, *Conspiracy: How the Paranoid Style Flourishes and Where It Comes From* (New York: Free Press, 1997); and Timothy Melley, *Empire of Conspiracy: The Culture of Paranoia in Postwar America* (Ithaca, NY: Cornell University Press, 2000). I explore Hofstadter's continuing influence on conceptions of conspiracy theory in chapter 4.
107 Hofstadter, "The Paranoid Style in American Politics," in *The Paranoid Style*, 4.
108 Ibid., 29 and 36. The emphasis is Hofstadter's.
109 Ibid., 4–5.
110 Ibid., 5.
111 Hofstadter, introduction to *The Paranoid Style*, ix.
112 Ibid., 5.
113 Richard Hofstadter, "The Paranoid Style in American Politics," 4. Box 26, Richard Hofstadter Papers, Rare Book and Manuscript Library, Columbia University. The copy of this earlier draft ends on this page.
114 Erich Fromm, *The Sane Society* (New York: Rinehart 1955), 271.
115 Max Horkheimer and Theodor W. Adorno, *Dialektik der Aufklärung: Philosophische Fragmente* (Frankfurt: Fischer, 1988), 205 [my translation]. John Cumming renders the phrase "der Schatten der Erkenntnis" as "the dark side

of cognition," a looser translation that has the effect of directly opposing paranoia and reason, rather than stressing their proximity. Edmund Ephcott translates the passage as "the shadow of cognition." Theodor W. Adorno and Max Horkheimer, *Dialectic of Enlightenment*, trans. John Cumming (London and New York: Verso, 1997), 195; and Max Horkheimer and Theodor W. Adorno, *Dialectic of Enlightenment: Philosophical Fragments*, ed. Gunzelin Schmid Noerr, trans. Edmund Ephcott (Stanford, CA: Stanford University Press, 2002), 161.

116 "As inadequate reflections of reality," Lowenthal and Guterman write about paranoid suspicions, "they might serve as starting points for analysis of the economic and political situations." Leo Lowenthal and Norbert Guterman, *Prophets of Deceit: A Study of the Techniques of the American Agitator* (Palo Alto, CA: Pacific, 1970), 24. Hofstadter refers to their study in: Hofstadter, "Pseudo-Conservatism Revisited," in *The Paranoid Style*, 67.

117 Hallock Hoffman to Hofstadter, November 12, 1958. Box 1, Richard Hofstadter Papers, Rare Book and Manuscript Library, Columbia University.

118 Ibid.

119 Alexander Bloom, *Prodigal Sons: The New York Intellectuals and Their World* (New York: Oxford University Press, 1986), 337–339.

120 Richard Hofstadter, "Uncle Sam Has Cried 'Uncle!' Before," *New York Times*, May 19, 1968, 30 and 121; and Richard Hofstadter, "The 214th Columbia University Commencement Address," *American Scholar* 37 (1968): 587.

121 Ibid., 585–587.

122 Richard Hofstadter, "Reflections on Violence in the United States," in *American Violence: A Documentary History*, ed. Richard Hofstadter and Michael Wallace (New York: Knopf, 1970), 33.

123 Ibid., 3 and 5.

124 Hofstadter, *Anti-Intellectualism*, 418.

125 Ibid., 418.

126 Ibid., 417–418 and 420.

127 Hofstadter, "The Pseudo-Conservative Revolt," in *The Paranoid Style*, 42.

128 Ellen Schrecker, *Many Are the Crimes: McCarthyism in America* (Princeton, NJ: Princeton University Press, 1998), 412.

129 Hofstadter, *The American Political Tradition*, xxxix.

130 John C. Burnham, "The Influence of Psychoanalysis upon American Culture," in *Paths into American Culture: Psychology, Medicine, and Morals* (Philadelphia: Temple University Press, 1988), 98.

131 David Mechanic and Gerald N. Grob, "Rhetoric, Realities, and the Plight of the Mentally Ill in America," in *History and Health Policy in the United States: Putting the Past Back In*, ed. Rosemary A. Stevens, Charles E. Rosenberg, and Lawton R. Burns (New Brunswick, NJ: Rutgers University Press, 2006), 236; and Gerald N. Grob, *The Mad Among Us: A History of the Care of America's Mentally Ill* (New York: Free Press, 1994), 98.

132 Robin, *The Making of the Cold War Enemy*, 201.

133 Ian Hacking, *Rewriting the Soul: Multiple Personality and the Sciences of Memory* (Princeton, NJ: Princeton University Press, 1995).

134 Flora Rheta Schreiber, *Sybil* (New York: Grand Central 2009), xviii.

135 Ibid., xix–xx.

136 Ibid., 171.

137 Gunnar Myrdal, *An American Dilemma: The Negro Problem and Modern Democracy* (New York: Harper, 1944), 928.

138 Martin Luther King, Jr., *Where Do We Go from Here*, 107.

139 Martin Luther King, "Overcoming an Inferiority Complex," in *The Papers of Martin Luther King, Jr. Vol. VI: Advocate of the Social Gospel, September 1948 –March 1963*, ed. Clayborne Carson, Susan Englander, Susan Carson, Troy Jackson, and Gerald L. Smith (Berkeley, CA: University of California Press, 2007), 305.

140 Malcolm X, *The Autobiography of Malcolm X* (New York: Grove, 1966), 246 and 312.

141 Robert F. Williams, *Negroes with Guns* (Chicago: Third World Press, 1973), 110.

142 During the Civil Rights era, associations between African American men and violence would be exploited by psychiatrists that diagnosed a tendency toward schizophrenic violence in the Black community. See Jonathan M. Metzl, *The Protest Psychosis: How Schizophrenia Became a Black Disease* (Boston: Beacon, 2009).

143 Grier and Cobbs, *Black Rage*, 31.

144 Ibid., 162 and 178.

145 Ibid., 179.

146 Ralph Ellison, *Invisible Man* (London: Penguin, 1965), 130.

147 Ibid., 464.

148 Ralph Ellison, "Harlem is Nowhere," in *Shadow and Act* (New York: Random House, 1964), 302; cited in: Shelley Eversley, "The Lunatic's Fancy and the Work of Art," *American Literary History* 13 (2001): 446.

149 Richard Wright, *The Outsider* (New York: Harper, 2008), 158.

150 Ibid., 466.

151 Ibid., 572.

152 Stokely Carmichael, "Black Power," in *The Dialectics of Liberation*, ed. David Cooper (Harmondsworth: Penguin, 1968), 162 and 169.

3 Practical Cures

From Radical Psychiatry
to Self Help

For some historians of psychiatry the book marks the beginning of the end. Albert Deutsch's exposé *The Shame of the States* castigated public asylums for failing their patients and caused a furor when it was published in 1948. An investigative journalist who had gained recognition with a history of the mentally ill and worked alongside Clifford Beers in the mental hygiene movement, Deutsch documented the conditions in almost a dozen state-run institutions across the country—from Detroit to Milledgeville, Georgia, and Philadelphia to Napa, California. Deutsch's account of overcrowded and underfunded wards infested with rats and swept by contagious diseases did not shy away from heavy-handed rhetoric. Reminding his readers of Nazi Germany's mass murder of psychiatric patients, he accused mental hospitals in his own country of "euthanasia through neglect."[1] Perhaps the most arresting aspect of Deutsch's book were the photographs that accompanied it. Male patients squatted naked in an incontinent ward in Philadelphia's Byberry Hospital, their heads turned away from the photographer's gaze, their bodies throwing contorted shadows against a dirty wall. At Napa State, Joe Rosenthal, recent winner of a Pulitzer Prize for his iconic picture of the raising of the American flag at Iwo Jima, portrayed a middle-aged woman locked into a straitjacket and then strapped to a wooden bench with a leather belt. In Cleveland, Deutsch and the photographer Herman Seid found a young woman, once declared a hopeful case, crouching naked behind rows of tables in the dining room, eating her food on the floor.

Such stark imagery could easily give the impression that Deutsch had launched a fundamental attack on public care for the insane. In his influential *History of Psychiatry*, Edward Shorter blames "Deutsch and later antipsychiatric writers" for the demise of large state hospitals, and the tragic fate of many chronically ill once they were released from them.[2] Shorter's accusation is doubly misleading. For Deutsch shared the enthusiasm and reform zeal of postwar psychiatry, professing a firm belief in medical progress. Keen to repudiate the stereotype of the crusading journalist, he situated himself as part of a wider movement aimed at institutional change. In fact, the book was itself testament to the inside perspective of its author, having become possible only by the invitation of psychiatrists keen to publicize inadequate hospital funding. In the final pages, Deutsch aligns himself with a newly formed group of liberal reformers within the American Psychiatric Association (APA), which was spearheaded by William and Karl Menninger.

Despite its air of opposition, *The Shame of the States* shares the beliefs and prejudices of the postwar medical establishment. Thus, Deutsch seems to have spoken exclusively to physicians in the course of his research. Nurses are merely counted, usually to highlight their acute shortage, and wardens are noted for their brutality toward patients. Where popular culture already saw an inhumane treatment akin to electrocution, Deutsch bemoans the lack of electro-convulsive treatment (ECT) in state hospitals and lauds the occasional exception with the scientific optimism that provided ammunition for psychiatry's critics: "Patients get a break at Brooklyn [State Hospital] [. . .] Virtually every patient who is admitted gets an early chance at shock therapy."[3] Instead of arguing for the closure of large institutions, the final chapter envisions the "ideal state mental hospital."[4] Praising federal efforts such as Harry Truman's 1947 Mental Health Act but emphasizing the ultimate responsibility of individual states, Deutsch wishes for close cooperation between different facilities. This vision of a better future in "therapeutic communities" endorses a potpourri of then fashionable treatments: from group therapy and psychoanalysis adapted to the needs of psychotics, to an increase in shock and lobotomy, the latter to be utilized with caution but endorsed on the basis of early successes.[5]

Deutsch's reform program would soon be challenged from all sides. Even before the introduction of the first antipsychotic drug, chlorpromazine, in 1954, state hospitals began to empty. They were increasingly replaced by community health centers, which lacked the close ties to remaining state facilities that Deutsch had called for. Psychoanalysis, never a realistic option for the masses of seriously ill, suffered from a loss of prestige when drug treatments proved a more effective solution that had the benefit of high profit margins for the chemical industry. Doubts about the efficacy of lobotomy and ECT were raised within the profession, to be amplified many times by patients who demanded the unthinkable—a say in their own treatment. Renegade psychiatrists and health care workers, often the nurses and wardens that Deutsch had passed over, launched stinging critiques of the medical establishment and offered their own alternatives. Journalists and filmmakers, poets and novelists, increasingly added their own voices and brought these debates to everyday Americans. For the last time, psychiatry became a matter of general concern, whether for all those who filled movie theaters to see Milos Forman's *One Flew Over the Cuckoo's Nest* (1975), or a US counterculture that welcomed a certain British psychiatrist with the bumper sticker: "I am mad about R. D. Laing."[6]

The Shame of the States presents not so much the beginning of the end, then, but the end of a beginning. Mary Ward's *The Snake Pit* (1946), which I discussed in the previous chapter, had already provided postwar culture with its first bestseller centered on mental illness, and reform writing on psychiatry would continue unabated until it peaked during the Sixties. The novel's success was equaled by its film adaptation two years later, and Deutsch addresses the millions who had read or seen it on the screen as potential allies in the quest for reform. Later critics would differ dramatically from Deutsch in their take on psychiatry but shared his reforming zeal. Liberal doctors, radical social workers, angry ex-patients, and neo-conservative politicians all made it their mission to fundamentally change the mental health system. In the process, they politicized psychiatry in a way it had never been before, and has not been since. Arguably, this is the meaning of Shorter's curious designation of Deutsch as an antipsychiatric writer. For authors like Laing, the conservative libertarian Thomas S. Szasz, not to speak of countercultural fictions like *One Flew Over the Cuckoo's Nest*, and the grassroots movement for mental patients' liberation, share little apart from their insistence that madness concerns everyone and is therefore a political issue.[7]

In the hands of many psychiatrists and historians, the term antipsychiatry has come to mean an absolute opposition to their medical specialization, ignorant of its advances and lost to an unscientific romanticism. Applied widely and loosely—Shorter also counts the sociologists Erving Goffman and Thomas Scheff, as well as the philosopher Michel Foucault as antipsychiatrists—the term makes little sense. Neither does it serve a critical analysis of arguments and positions or allow for a differentiation between individual authors and movements. Unfortunately, this use of antipsychiatry, in effect serving as a term of denunciation, has become widespread. Andrew Scull's *Madness in Civilization*, sub-titled *A Cultural History of Insanity*, is quick to dismiss writers he agrees were "lumped together as 'anti-psychiatrists'" and never engages in any depth with critiques that formed a dominant perspective on his topic for two decades.[8] Clinical psychologist Richard Bentall, author of *Madness Explained*, spends 600 pages arguing for an integration of biological and psychological perspectives on mental illness, but is quick to distance himself from a concept he clearly views as toxic.[9]

Antipsychiatry retains a value as an umbrella term for mid-century critiques, but in this chapter I prefer to speak of such separate if overlapping movements as radical psychiatry, alternative therapy, and mental patients' liberation. From the late 1950s to the early '80s, these movements shook to the core an institution of immense power, and of immediate concern to millions of people. On an average day in 1946, writes Deutsch, 635,769 Americans found themselves patients of mental institutions, filling more than half of all hospital beds in the country. Estimates of the number of mentally ill in America ran to a staggering 8 million, then 6 percent of the total population.[10] Despite these figures, critical mental health workers, ex-patients, and authors were fundamentally optimistic about the possibility of change, a hope that drove them to protest in front of hospital gates, write essays and poems, cobble together a newsletter on the cheap, or open drop-in centers for the homeless mentally ill. For reasons this chapter will discuss in detail, their protest came at an opportune moment. If it ultimately ended in defeat, their criticism and activism left traces and produced legacies that continue even after a narrowly biological understanding of madness was canonized with the third edition of the Diagnostic and Statistical Manual of Mental Disorders (DSM) in 1980. At the outer reaches of this movement, the question that animated liberal reformers like Deutsch and the influential Menninger brothers, how to better care for the mentally ill, was transformed into something fundamentally different: a conception of madness that sought healing in a liberation *from* psychiatry. One of the stories to be told here is that of an increasing divergence in understanding insanity. To the detriment of both, this split has often left medical psychiatry and the arts and humanities unable to find a shared language.

The first section of this chapter considers a number of highly controversial thinkers of the Sixties: Szasz, Goffman, Foucault, Laing, and Phyllis Chesler all made madness and mental illness the central concern of their writing during those years. Their research and polemics not only criticized institutional psychiatry but sought to regain an understanding of madness that was not limited to a medical perspective. At the same time, their reflections were concerned with more than psychopathology. By way of its imagery they grappled with one of the most pressing issues of Cold War America: the question of power, and the possibility of freedom from an ever-expanding state apparatus. Goffman and Foucault came from disciplines outside of the mental health system and would turn to other topics as their careers progressed. The oppositional prefix assigned to them misses the mark because their primary interest was never psychiatry, and because they sought a perspective on madness that preceded its capture by medicine. Others, such as Szasz and Laing, are better described as radical psychiatrists: authors who developed a critique from *within* the profession, and did so from a pronounced left- or right-wing political stance.[11]

This overview of representative thinkers is followed by a discussion of what may be termed alternative therapy. Initiated by disgruntled physicians and nurses, this movement rejected the existing mental health system for community care and constituted a small but influential element within the wider counterculture of the 1970s. Alternative therapy sought social transformation and at times advocated outright revolution, but it also contributed to a popular self-help psychology that spelled a retreat from the political goals it espoused. In this and the final section on mental patients' liberation, my analysis concentrates on movement magazines, specifically *The Radical Therapist* (later titled *Rough Times*), *Issues in Radical Therapy*, and *Madness Network News*. These publications rarely feature in scholarship on the Sixties or histories of mental illness but provide much more than a frequently neglected source of information.[12] Edited by mental health workers or former patients, sent out to thousands of subscribers, and sold in counterculture bookstores, they constituted their movements' main forum for spreading ideas and stimulating debates between professionals and non-professionals. *The Radical Therapist*, *Issues in Radical Therapy*, and *Madness Network News* were the media through which protests were organized and where readers looked for like-minded people to start community centers or shared their experiences as hospital patients. Spreading far beyond metropolitan centers, professional associations, or single hospitals, these magazines established regional, national, and increasingly international networks and drew in new participants. In many ways, they *were* the movement. As one health-care worker recalled years later: "Once I got to (social work) school [. . .] I began to [. . .] follow old issues of the journal *The Radical Therapist*. I was intrigued and discovered I could do therapy."[13]

Sections two and three share an interest in alternative publications and grassroots movements. Yet alternative therapy and the ex-patients' movement, despite occasional collaboration and overlaps, also eyed each other with suspicion. Radical therapists accused mental patients' liberation of focusing too narrowly on psychiatry, forgetting about the larger goals of the left. In turn, the ex-patient movement came to bar professionals from participating in its conferences, newsletters, and self-help centers. Envy played its part. Middle-class radicals yearned for recognition by working-class patients who sometimes resented their privilege and viewed them as the friendly face of an institution they were trying to escape. At the center of the ex-patients movement until it ceased publication in 1986 stood *Madness Network News*, which plays a central role in my analysis. In addition, this final section looks at two women who perhaps best represent its literary and social legacy. Judi Chamberlin's *On Our Own* (1978), a founding document of mental patients' liberation, functions as a theoretical justification and a practical handbook for the establishment of alternative care centers. Finally, Marge Piercy's *Woman on the Edge of Time* (1976) is usually read as a classic of both feminist and science fiction. But Piercy was also associated with Boston's Mental Patients Liberation Front and contributed several poems to *The Radical Therapist* over the years. Her utopian novel represents a lasting attempt to translate the aspirations of the movement into fiction.

3.1 Madness at the Crossroads: Cold War Psychiatry and Its Radical Critics

In the introduction to *The Myth of Mental Illness*, Szasz recalls starting work on his best-selling book in 1954, the same year, in which antipsychotic medication was first used in US hospitals. Biomedical psychiatry and the doyen of American 'antipsychiatry' are usually seen as polar opposites, and to most of his colleagues Szasz remained a red flag until his death in 2012. In a series of articles and books that came to dominate critiques of institutional psychiatry in the United States, Szasz kept repeating a small number of forceful arguments. The term mental illness was merely a metaphor, since most of these diseases could not be proven to have an organic cause. Psychiatry constituted an institutionalized form of violence akin to the Catholic Inquisition. Many mental patients were in fact malingerers, Szasz wrote: "lazy or lethargic, sick or stupid" poor people and women intent on exploiting physicians.[14]

Born in Budapest in 1920, Szasz fled to America at the age of 18 and took an intense hatred of state authority with him. Thus, communism was a "political and moral evil" that should be resisted with violence, if necessary.[15] Liberal intervention was no better: arguing for a strict separation of state and medicine, he opposed not only involuntary hospitalization but any form of public health insurance. In Szasz's Cold War libertarianism, the subject was simultaneously imagined as completely autonomous and its autonomy threatened by state power. To the horrors of institutional medicine, he opposed a utopia of "the freely contracting individual." The care of those unable to afford private therapy was to be left to charities.[16] Here as elsewhere, Szasz evinced a staggering disregard for the patients he ostensibly sought to defend, a majority of which were women, came from ethnic minorities, or were working class. Szasz's writings, first formulated in the late 1950s and popularized in the following decade, positioned him squarely on the right. His explicit conservatism did nothing to stem his embrace by the counterculture—witness an enthusiastic letter sent to him by Timothy Leary, who declared *The Myth of Mental Illness* to be the "most important book published in the twentieth century"—or Szasz's uptake by the ex-patients' movement.[17]

In retrospect, Szasz's critique prefigures the transformation of US psychiatry since the 1950s. The vitriolic exchanges with mainstream psychiatrists obscure fundamental similarities. Szasz took aim less at psychiatry per se but at its extension beyond a biomedical paradigm, exploiting very real weaknesses. The postwar emphasis on psychological causes had allowed for a dramatic extension of psychiatry's reach but threatened its medical status.[18] The etiology of many supposedly somatic diseases remained in the dark, and the 'talking cure' could just as well be delivered by health care workers without a medical degree. The further psychiatry moved beyond medical terrain, offering sociodynamic explanations and only custodial care for the chronically ill, the more it exposed itself to laymen and dissenters within its own ranks. To mention only the most infamous example: homosexuality was removed from the DSM's classification of mental diseases only in 1973, after vocal protests by gay activists and liberal psychiatrists.[19] As Robert Castel has argued, psychiatry's functionality for state authorities lies in providing administrative solutions for social conflicts, specifically the antagonism between public order and individual freedom.[20] The way in which both the warehousing of the chronically insane and the pathologization of homosexuality came to be seen as indefensible provides two examples of postwar psychiatry's failure at conflict resolution.

Clearly, a readjustment was needed. Szasz led the way in his insistence on an essentially libertarian conception of personal autonomy. Alongside the attacks on his own profession, Szasz also insisted that psychiatry could become a science if it restricted itself to somatic medicine. His understanding of biomedical psychiatry may have been outdated, but Szasz's accordance of an unquestioned objectivity to physiological medicine, his conviction that "the phenomenology of bodily illness is indeed independent of the socio-economic and political character of [. . .] society" accorded with the views of its more orthodox representatives.[21] This is not to claim that Szasz's suggestions had a direct influence on the eventual resurgence of biological psychiatry. On the contrary, some historians of psychiatry have claimed that the move toward a strictly medical psychiatry was motivated, in part, by the desire to counter antipsychiatry. In any case, biochemic and genetic research reestablished the link between medicine and psychiatry, which had been threatened by psychoanalysis.

Szasz's importance for understanding Cold War madness lies in his function as an essential link between postwar psychiatry, alternative or countercultural therapies, and the neoliberal mental health system that emerged out of the cauldron of the Sixties. All three constitute themselves around a libertarian conception of the self, and a corresponding conception of treatment. As a consequence, mental health care as it has emerged since the 1980s in the United States shows remarkable parallels with Szasz's prescriptions: from contemporary psychiatry's self-understanding as a politically neutral bastion of medical science, to the shift from hospitalization to out-patient services that seemingly uphold the patient's individual freedom. Szasz's polemics did not provide these solutions. Yet his frequently simplistic arguments played their part in provoking answers that were equally simple, at least rhetorically. If Szasz and his followers accused psychiatry of being a pseudo-medical enterprise, its scientific credentials (now phrased in the jargon of genetics and neuroscience) had to become indisputable. Another, more ambitious, option seemed possible. This would have involved renewed efforts at a scientific integration of social and physiological perspectives, paying heed to the fundamental insight that body and mind cannot be understood without taking their social environment into consideration. Under the leadership of Robert Spitzer and the return to Kraepelian classification in DSM-III this was a road emphatically not taken.[22]

Szasz's distrust of state institutions found a more sophisticated counterpart in a study published the same year as *The Myth of Mental Illness*. Sociologist Erving Goffman's seminal *Asylums* (1961) turned the mental hospital into the cipher of a bureaucratic society that mortifies its subjects and denies them the "self-determination, autonomy, and freedom of action" that defined the self for him.[23] As a "total institution"—the term invoking German and Soviet totalitarianism on home turf—America's mental asylums stood in for advanced bureaucracy, and Cold War society as whole. "I have argued the [. . .] case in regard to total institutions," Goffman wrote. "May this not be the situation, however, in free society, too?"[24] Szasz had concentrated on graphic examples of abuse, understanding psychiatry as a regime of physical violence. For Goffman, psychiatric power lay less in the destruction of individual lives than in producing the social role of the patient. Somewhat hyperbolically, *Asylums* claimed that psychotics suffered not from mental illness but from the bad luck of becoming institutionalized. Goffman may have relished the provocation, but his argument also aligned him with his French contemporary Foucault. Psychiatry, Goffman contended, bore responsibility for symptoms it merely claimed to discover. It masqueraded as objective science by situating a social dynamic in the patient's psyche. To an extent, Goffman remained caught in the dynamic he sought to deconstruct. His study aimed at developing a sociological theory of the self as a "stance-taking entity" that moved between identification and opposition to larger structures. But ultimately, *Asylums* left its readers, and perhaps its author, without a viable conception of the self. Total institutions, defined as making resistance to them impossible, dismantled even the minimal self-determination of stance-taking, and denied Goffman's initial assumptions about personal autonomy. Goffman's politics fell in line with this pessimism. Despite his damning assessment, he confessed that he could not imagine any meaningful change to mental hospitals.[25] Szasz and Goffman share far more than their conservatism. Unlike the former, Goffman did not deny the existence of mental illness, yet neither distinguished between mental illness and madness. Insanity may be physiological in cause or socially determined but an illness it certainly was—and nothing more. Not only did this understanding concur with psychiatry's own conception, it also marked the limits of their challenge to it. As I show in chapter 4, the countercultures of the 1950s and '60s pursued a line of inquiry similar to Szasz and Goffman's imagination of the state as authoritarian instance of control. There, the table was turned by consistently declaring society itself insane or madness the only true sanity.

A similar logic guides the writings of the European thinkers who had the greatest impact on America's Cold War culture of madness: Laing and Foucault. The latter's star turn in the United States arrived only in the 1980s, when he became an academic celebrity in the wake of his writings on sexuality and biopower, a trajectory I return to in the final chapter. Laing's fame preceded Foucault's and went far beyond academia. Starting with *The Divided Self* (1960), his books sold several million copies throughout the Sixties. In 1971, *Life* magazine reported that the paperback edition of *The Politics of Experience* had reached a run of 400,000 within five years. Laing's contemporary Peter Sedgwick recalls two young women describing themselves as "chicks who dig Coltrane, *The Dead* and R.D. Laing" in the *Village Voice* and media reports accorded the Glaswegian psychiatrist the status of a veritable rock star. *Life*'s five-page photo spread began with a close-up of Laing's middle-aged face, his brow furrowed, his head held between

Figure 3.1 The Scottish psychiatrist R.D. Laing, whose books inspired the US counter-culture, as portrayed by John Haynes for a photo series in *Life*. Courtesy of Lebrecht Music & Arts Photo Library

his hands, his dramatic expression suggesting deep anguish that could be read as verging on madness. The short text accompanying the photographs both made and rejected this implication, and the remaining shots showed Laing in carefully choreographed existential poses: sitting barefoot in front of the window of his study, his silhouette almost black against the winter light; meditating, sometimes dressed only in his underwear, in yoga positions; and walking through the London park of Hampstead Heath, where he eventually climbed a tree and looked, still barefoot, into the distance.[26]

Laing's countercultural self-stylization appears comic today and has led to ridicule by unsympathetic critics. His writing resists easy dismissal. Existential psychiatry and French phenomenology left a lasting impression on him, as it did on Foucault. Laing also referenced American authors such as Goffman and Gregory Bateson's influential theory of the "double bind," according to which contradictory communication within families caused schizophrenia.[27] On the page, this heady mixture often combined into inspired prose. Laing distinguished himself from many of his peers by his ability to write empathetically about the experience of the mad, and to retain their perspective when examining a supposedly sane society. His meteoric rise to fame and later distancing from countercultural views has led commentators to propose a sharp divide between the early and later Laing. But as early as 1960, he accords madness a certain epistemological privilege: "the cracked mind of the schizophrenic may *let in* light which does not enter the intact minds of many sane people."[28] Statements such as these have led to accusations of irresponsible naivety. However, Laing also emphasizes a "genetically determined inborn tendency toward schizophrenia," and the loneliness and despair of those affected.[29] Rather than identifying all psychosis as illness, Laing describes some instances of madness as a partial insight. Hallucinations and delusions express a limited awareness of the oppressive phantasy systems that define dysfunctional families, which Laing sees as the root cause of schizophrenia. Such madness is distinct from true sanity, which overcomes social alienation and leads to a newly integrated ego. Laing's emphasis on "schizophrenogenic families," which adapted Fromm-Reichman's similar and highly dubious description of mothers, was not entirely unproblematic either.[30] It remained unclear what functional families looked like, and the promise of a comparative study was never fulfilled.

As the Sixties progressed, Laing widened the scope of his analysis. It was a measure of his increasing alienation that Western society now took on the qualities that had earlier distinguished the family unit. Laing expresses this sentiment most clearly in *The Politics of Experience* and his talk at the Congress on the Dialectics of Liberation, organized by the American psychotherapist Joseph Berke, and held in London in July 1967. Describing a world he experienced as having gone mad, Laing writes: "Only by the most outrageous violation of ourselves have we achieved our capacity to live in relative adjustment to a civilization apparently driven to its own destruction."[31] Madness consisted in humankind's adaptation to the everyday reality of the Cold War, its constant threat of nuclear annihilation, and anti-communism's construction of a mortal enemy. Recalling the case of a 17-year-old girl in a mental hospital who believed she carried the atom bomb inside her, Laing contrasted her with the "perfectly adjusted bomber pilot" and the "statesmen of the world who boast and threaten that they have Doomsday weapons."[32] Which of them, he asked, were more dangerous and more estranged from reality? The reference to Stanley Kubrick's black comedy *Dr. Strangelove* and its deranged military men provided the answer. It was in this political context that Laing famously perceived madness as a healing process, a utopian attempt at rebirth. Based on work undertaken with Berke and Cooper at the alternative community Kingsley Hall in London, he saw psychosis as taking a course that led to a non-alienated state and true sanity. If the minds of most people had been forced shut, this journey through madness might help them to perceive the light again when they passed out of it. Even here Laing was careful to qualify his more fanciful remarks: madness was as much breakdown as breakthrough, could lead to renewal but also threatened disintegration. It was unavoidable that such caveats were lost in the heady romanticism that pervaded the late Sixties, not least Laing's own work.

A similar fate befell Foucault when he first came to the attention of American readers. Based on an abridged French paperback version that cut 300 pages and 800 footnotes from the original text, *Folie et Déraison* arrived in English translation as *Madness and Civilization* (1964)—and with ringing endorsements by Laing and Cooper. In the years that followed, Foucault's history of madness was fitted into a narrative of psychiatric abuse and the continued incarceration of the mad, seemingly cited far more often by critics than read. Cooper's enthusiastic introduction provided a blueprint for its later uptake in the writings of Szasz, Chesler, and many others. "Madness has in our age become some sort of lost truth," Cooper began, and continued with a recap of asylum atrocities and a pseudo-medical psychiatry, all the while attributing these statements to Foucault.[33] Scrutiny of the actual text paints a different picture. Marking a shift from his early phenomenological work to structuralism, *Madness and Civilization* moved between the historical experience of madness and a "structural study of [. . .] notions, institutions, judicial and police measures, scientific concepts."[34] Foucault's main concern was neither the abuse of mental patients nor the history of psychiatry. Rather his study aimed at disrupting such a historiography in style and method. For Foucault the reduction of madness to mental illness silenced other ways of understanding its experience: whether as an existential encounter with the unknown in the Middle Ages, or as speaking the truth of man's folly in the works of Renaissance writers like Shakespeare and Cervantes. A medical understanding of madness could arise only after this gradual act of silencing, Foucault argued. Thus psychiatry's founding act already constituted a decidedly political act, which would continue to characterize its "monologue by reason *about* madness."[35] Foucault's contention was therefore not the simplistic accusation that psychiatry was a pseudo-science, but that all scientific method bore the ideological imprint of its historical circumstances.

Where *Madness and Civilization* did engage directly with institutional medicine, it sometimes made for uncomfortable reading for the likes of Laing and Cooper, who had been so eager to co-opt its author. In particular, Foucault criticized the obsession with the family unit, arguing that psychiatry's prestige was based in part on parental authority, so that even critical psychiatrists remained entangled in its power structures. When Laing and Foucault appeared together at the "Schizo-Culture" conference in New York in 1975, this criticism was renewed by philosopher Gilles Deleuze and psychiatrist Félix Guattari, who had recently co-authored *The Anti-Oedipus* (1977).[36] Nonetheless, Foucault could be swept up by romantic notions of madness as much as any other Sixties writer. At one point in *Madness and Civilization* he suggested that "[m]admen then led an easy wandering existence" in the Middle Ages.[37] Such is perhaps the risk that inheres in writing that makes history the occasion for philosophical reflection. Even in his rhapsodic conclusion, however, Foucault held back from identifying psychosis with artistic genius. If the link between them existed, then only insofar as art was frequently built by the sane against the tide of madness, and in a creative defense—Foucault mentioned Antonin Artaud and Friedrich Hölderlin—against its onset.

Laing and Foucault arrived on American shores at the tail end of a fascination with phenomenology and existential philosophy. Inspired by earlier psychiatrists such as Ludwig Binswanger, the two European thinkers explored the experience of madness with novel complexity. Their writings, often as lyrical as they were analytical, added a decisive inflection to homegrown attacks on psychiatry, which critiqued its methods but often accepted the designation of insanity as illness. Laing and Foucault's insistence on the subjective reality of the mad chimed with a counterculture for whom intensity of experience became the single most important virtue. Their impact can be seen throughout the radical therapy and ex-patients' movements, which the remainder of this chapter discusses. It is equally visible in Phyllis Chesler's *Women and Madness* which sold a million copies in the 1970s and represents a uniquely feminist contribution to radical psychiatry. Chesler set out to systematically relate madness to female gender roles, and her definition of the former staked out a position that defied both Szasz and Laing. Madness should not be romanticized, she wrote, nor should it be confused with political or cultural revolution. It also wouldn't do to deny the existence of madness, describing its "divinely menacing behaviour from whose eloquence and exhausting demands society protects itself through 'reason' and force."[38] These comments seemed applicable to both genders, but Chesler was quick to point out the specificity of female experience. The book's first chapter looked at the lives of four American women, including Zelda Fitzgerald, the wife of the novelist and short story writer F. Scott, and poet Sylvia Plath. Short sympathetic portraits, they highlighted the mistreatment of women in mental asylums since the late nineteenth century and formed the basis for understanding women's flight into psychosis as "an expression of powerlessness and an unsuccessful attempt to reject and overcome this state."[39] These tragic lives also showed, Chesler argued, that many women who found themselves in the clutches of psychiatry were not mad, or suffering from physiological illness, but were simply unhappy and driven to self-destructive behavior.

These observations and Chesler's interviews with sixty American women set the stage for the conceptual thesis of the book. What appeared as female madness was the complete submission to a society that demanded passivity from women, a reaction Chesler identified with clinical depression, anxiety, and paranoia. In contrast, the rebellion against this conservative gender identity led to diagnoses of schizophrenia. Chesler's sociodynamic theory posed as many questions as it answered: could madness be understood simultaneously as lack and excess of gender conformity? Did such a view reproduce outdated stereotypes of Cold War femininity at a time, the early 1970s, when the feminist movement was on the upswing? How could diagnoses of paranoia and schizophrenia be understood in men if they seemed so tightly bound to female identity? In retrospect, Chesler's theoretical abstractions seem the weakest link in a book that reprinted many of the interviews she had conducted. There, in heartbreaking detail, Chesler unearthed proof of women's oppression by their families, their partners, and a collusive mental health establishment. As she documented, during the 1960s more women than men were patients in psychiatric wards, private hospitals, community centers, and private therapy—and their numbers were rising. Looking back at *Women and Madness* nearly twenty years later, Chesler described the lack of adequate care for the women she had interviewed, and the need for feminist and radical therapy. The next section analyzes this movement, and its development from the late 1960s onward.

3.2 Revolutionary Healing: The Radical Therapy Movement

Radical therapy stood at the intersection of so many postwar developments that it can only be seen as a quintessentially Sixties phenomenon. Founded by disillusioned mental health workers, it resulted from an explosion in psychological services and contributed to their further diversification. Emerging in the final years of the 1960s and blossoming in the following decade, radical therapy bore the imprint of a US society that was splintering into numerous subcultures and causes, from feminism to more esoteric quests for happiness, and the further radicalization of a left fringe. In an early issue, the editors of *The Radical Therapist* (*RT*) laid out a pluralistic understanding of what such therapy could amount to: organizing a community against war, racism, and environmental damage; awareness of the social rather than individual causes of psychic trouble; opening a therapy center for the young. The list concluded on a note that brought all of them together under the roof of countercultural experience: "Life-style is crucial."[40] For the activist-journalists that published this and other dissident magazines, radical therapy was grounded in political engagement and sought fulfillment in everyday conduct.

Still, a marked tension existed between politics and life-style. The movement's radical wing, which sought to unify Marxism and psychology, frequently berated the new therapy collectives and drop-in centers for their "'do-your-own-thing' ideology" and accused them of an abdication of duty.[41] For Marxist psychologists, political liberation trumped a liberated lifestyle—a priority that wasn't at all self-evident to those who sought healing in self-help. New Haven, Connecticut's, Number Nine, an alternative or counter-institution, as it called itself, was fairly typical. Named after the Beatles song "Revolution 9" and founded in late 1969, it employed fifteen full-time staff and provided ten spaces for young people going through personal crises. In addition, the center also came with its own psychedelic bus and rock band. Number Nine offered the usual mix of individual and group therapy, a drop-in center and an emergency phone line. What brought all of these activities and the people involved in them together was a somewhat fuzzy sense of mission. As one staff member wrote: "Our activities are unified through our growing [. . .] conception of ourselves as a community within a larger alternative culture, which is working for broad changes in the fabric of our society."[42] The house prided itself on its acceptance of difficult behavior, former patients often became members of staff, and everyone lived together in a commune. Concrete goals were harder to come by: beyond the rejection of the status quo, Number Nine limited its vision of an alternative society to the phrase "growth through counseling."[43] Such vague conceptions of political change laid bare another contradiction. Radical therapist defined their movement in fundamental opposition to the mental health care system but usually provided alternative services instead of direct contestation. Rather than seeking alliances with sympathetic psychiatrists, nurses, and ex-patients, they opened community centers and offered group therapy to other members of the counterculture. Often, these patients turned out to be as white and middle class as the therapists who helped them. As one essay in *Issues in Radical Therapy* (IRT) cautioned, the movement was limited to major cities and liberal university towns "and as of yet has had no impact on any third world community."[44]

Another crucial oversight emerges from the study of these journals. With very few exceptions, the gathering storm of a genetic and biochemical psychiatry emits no response in them. We may attribute this curious absence to the movement's conviction in the social causes of mental illness, and the necessity of political change to combat it. In other words: why engage with what you already know to be false? As important was the increasing distance of countercultural therapists from mainstream institutions and psychiatric research. Radical therapy therefore also presents a case study of the gap that opened up between the self-consciously political understanding of madness in the counterculture and the turn toward medical models in psychiatry. To an extent, this split persists today: between medical practitioners and many of their colleagues in social work, nursing and psychology; as well as between humanities and social science scholars and researchers in the biological sciences. Radical therapy journals were central to this development. Psychiatrists Michael Glenn and Michael Galen had taken part in the APA's annual meeting in Miami in 1969, during which its liberal caucus adopted the moniker radical for the first time. Frustrated with the APA's resistance to progressive demands, Glenn and Galen returned to the Air Force base at Minot, North Dakota, where they were stationed, to start *RT* in the following spring. Claude Steiner, the movement's chief theorist and another member of the radical caucus, began publishing *IRT* three years later after opening his own alternative center in Berkeley.[45]

For these psychiatrists, the break with the APA also led to a gradual distancing from their own professional identity—not always a smooth process. *RT* characterized itself as a 'professional' journal in the founding issue, yet Glenn's opening manifesto also called for the demystification and deprofessionalization of psychotherapy.[46] What exactly this process entailed constituted a central debate of early issues. Some contributors advocated a process of sharing skills to democratize therapy. Others extended Szasz's famous argument to declare skills a myth. Much of the frustration stemmed from what radical therapists felt to be the irrelevance of a medical education to their daily work. In Steiner's center, twelve months of collective learning that rejected psychiatric terminology and individual sessions for "soul healing" in a group setting replaced medical training.[47] This alternative institution was titled the Radical Psychiatry Center, but as Steiner acknowledged the reference to psychiatry was somewhat of a misnomer and meant primarily as a provocation. Despite rhetorical similarities, the early debates about professionalism distinguished themselves from the writings of critics like Szasz, Goffman, Foucault, and Laing. Neither Szasz and Laing, the two psychiatrists among them, showed much interest in making therapeutic techniques available beyond their own profession. In contrast, radical therapy's emphasis on skill-sharing and non-professional healing allowed it to become a movement that was anchored around two journals but extended to community teaching, drop-in centers, and regular conferences.

As the movement's primary means of communication, *RT* and *IRT* show many parallels with the Sixties dissident press.[48] Made possible by the accessibility of cheap photo-offset printing, the era saw a boom in underground publications that made up for amateurish layout and design with unabashed idealism. Like their colleagues across the nation, the editors of *RT* and *IRT* saw themselves as activists first, journalists second—priorities reflected in the uneven quality of writing and inconsistent spelling to be found in their journals. Radical therapy publications also shared a chronic lack of money and establishment hostility with their more distant forerunners in antebellum abolitionism and the nineteenth-century labor movement. All these publications linked and shored up communities, supported and in many cases initiated grassroots action, and opened their pages to the community they served. *RT* and *IRT* counted prominent reformers, scholars, and novelists as their authors, among them Barbara Ehrenreich, Deirdre English, Todd Gitlin, and Marge Piercy. Yet their most notable characteristic was a fundamentally democratic ethic: produced by a collective of activists, subscriptions were offered free to prisoners, mental patients, and anyone who suffered from a "real lack of money."[49] Articles, letters, and poems by current and former psychiatric inmates filled their pages. Others contacted the journals when they wanted to start their own therapy center. As reader C. A. Fairfield, describing himself as a former psychiatric aide in Los Angeles, wrote:

> I want to establish a commune in Northern California whose 'thing' it will be to provide the setting for schizophrenics to ride out their trips sans shock sans drugs sans shrinks (except a hip shrink or whathaveyou) and sans silly ass psychiatrisms—do you know of anyone already doing the Laing-like community in a rustic setting?[50]

This countercultural outlook continued in the visual makeup of the magazines. In keeping with other publications, *RT* and *IRT* freely reprinted articles and illustrations that were shared via the Underground Press Syndicate and Liberation News Service. Cartoons that expounded Mao quotes alternated with photographs taken at political rallies, woodcuts by Frans Masereel, and comic strips by Robert Crumb. Drawings of the raised and clenched fist—made popular by Black Power—could be found next to ads for Atlanta's "Liberation Records" and the "Gay Liberation" magazine.

Radical therapy publications also distinguished themselves from the wider underground press. Serving a tight-knit community on the edges of a huge movement, its publications reached a far smaller audience, which probably never exceeded the *RT*'s print run of 5,000 copies and a roughly equal number for *IRT*.[51] In contrast to magazines like the Los Angeles *Free Press* or the *Chicago Reader*, which could count on a large urban readership, theirs was a national and sometimes international audience. Although they could be described as social movement media, the two journals also resembled special interest publications and academic journals in their thematic focus and specialized vocabulary. Confronting this hybrid identity, *RT*'s founding editorial asked in its title, "How Revolutionary is a Journal?".[52]

It admitted that such publications, aimed at a highly literate audience, ran the danger of being elitist and ineffective. Yet, the editors argued in self-defense that a journal could serve to clarify issues and rally support, bringing its readers together for social action. This rhetorical commitment to community politics was soon followed by the call to go *beyond* journalism, and the founding of a grassroots initiative called Open in Minot. Despite the local community health center withdrawing its offer to provide space in an unused building after town pressure, Open soon offered a training group for aspiring therapists, housed a women's liberation and GI group, and provided drop-in services for college and high school students.[53]

Despite or because of such grassroots work, an ideological and personal struggle erupted in *RT*'s second year. Following publication of an issue dedicated to writings by members of Berkeley's Radical Psychiatry center, an editorial questioned the Californians' involvement in wider struggles and accused them of a "middle-class emphasis on groovy fun and individual solutions."[54] Coinciding with a move from North Dakota to Somerville, Massachusetts, a suburb of Boston, these debates led to editor Glenn leaving the journal, a name change, and the birth of *IRT*. After the final issue of 1971 critiqued the journal's title *Radical Therapist* (radical for its trendy overuse, therapy for its professional connotation), it began appearing as *Rough Times*. The motivations for this switch became abundantly clear in June 1972: "We participate in the world-wide revolutionary force, not within the confines of 'radicals in the professions.' We want [. . .] total revolution, not just reforms."[55] The shift in editorial policy showed in a special section on "Vietnam & Psychology," articles on mental patients' liberation, and the German Socialist Patient Collective, located in Heidelberg and equally committed to revolution. Increasingly, *Rough Times* looked beyond US borders to guide the movement's efforts. Wilhelm Reich mixed with Frantz Fanon, the ever-present Szasz was discussed next to the Italian reformer Franco Basaglia. Reich, in particular, highlighted the contradictions between this eclectic blend of writers, and their uptake by alternative therapists. His combination of Marxist and psychoanalytic credentials endeared Reich to radical psychologists but the emphasis on sexual liberation played into the hands of a narcissistic retreat into private life, whether that took the shape of a commune or more traditional arrangements. As the feminist writers Ehrenreich and English warned in an astute analysis a couple of years later, the supposed radicalism of sexual liberation fed a commercial pop psychology that sapped the flame of left-wing politics.[56]

In the meantime, *IRT* provided a new forum for the Radical Psychiatry group around Steiner. Emerging after their fallout with *RT*'s editors, the West Coast journal featured higher production values, as well as longer and more academic articles, but understood itself as part of the same movement. The founding editorial referred to *IRT* as a practical journal, emphasized community organizing and vowed to resist cooptation by liberal psychiatrists and a hip, depoliticized counterculture. In 1976, the editorial collective and local organizers launched the "Radical Psychiatry Summer Institute," and soon thereafter the "Midwest Radical Therapy Conference," which attracted 250 participants to a campsite near Iowa City when it first took place in May. Workshops during the four-day event included "feminism for men," "visual techniques in therapy," and "herbal and psychic healing."[57] Regional initiatives coexisted with growing internationalization: British psychoanalyst Susi Orbach joined as a contributing editor, the summer institutes brought the US movement in touch with German, Canadian, and Swedish colleagues, and articles focused on Basaglia's work in Northern Italy, *The Anti-Oedipus*, and a post-revolutionary psychiatry in Nicaragua.

Therapeutically, these examples remained in the shadow of Steiner's own approach, which he distilled from the work of Eric Berne. Berne, the founder of transactional analysis, rejected diagnostic concepts for a therapeutic encounter that focused on social interaction. Despite acknowledging his apolitical liberalism, Steiner based his therapy on Berne's work and made alienation the key term. Two basic premises guided Steiner: the first was a chimerical belief in absolute harmony; the second saw alienation at the root of all psychiatric conditions. At this point, the psychoanalytic spotlight on family dynamics combined uneasily with an understanding of alienation as political oppression. As a consequence, Steiner declared that healing could not be based on individual insight but had to evolve out of a group fighting for its liberation. Precisely how this journey from awareness to action should be accomplished remained a bone of contention throughout *IRT* and radical therapy's existence. The Szaszian elements in Steiner's worldview proved less controversial, and the rejection of medical terminology perhaps owed as much to the former as to Berne. These debts were thrown into stark relief in an interview Steiner conducted with Laing in the latter's home in London in 1975. By then, Laing had repudiated his left-wing rhetoric of the late 1960s and was living contentedly, as he claimed, in a nuclear family of his own. After Laing's curt dismissal of communes—"they don't seem to be particularly better," he observed—the conversation turned to madness. Laing met Steiner's insistence that madness, like mental illness, was merely a form of emotional upset with equal derision: "Well, some people are pretty crazy," Laing replied.[58]

The contradiction between healing and change became only more acute as the counterculture's drive evaporated in the late 1970s. After swinging back from an extreme left position to self-help, *RT* reported financial problems and, after a final name change to *State and Mind*, folded in 1976. Now the sole publication of the movement, *IRT* showed more longevity and was published in the Bay Area until 1983, when editorial responsibility shifted to the Illinois Radical Therapy Collective in Springfield for another three-year period. The journal became more streamlined, its briskly written editorials approximating the mainstream press. With Reagan's election to the presidency, the ascendancy of the right began to worry contributors but the changing times also showed within the movement. Rhetorically, *IRT* remained steadfast in its commitment to socialism and collective healing. Yet some articles and movement activities struck a different note. Reporting from a "Radical Therapy Theory Conference," held in February 1984 in San Francisco, the author complained about the time wasted by the democratic process of agenda setting and advocated individual accountability to replace the "'tyranny of structurelessness.'"[59] Like a decade earlier, the meeting had been organized by an alliance of ex-patients, therapists, and academics but the article's managerial perspective was a far cry from the spirit of the Sixties, as was the focus on theory and limiting participation to invited speakers.

The gradual absorption of radical therapy into the mainstream was unmistakable. Similar in some ways to the fate of ex-patients' liberation, this outcome recalled one of the most piercing assessments of the movement. Written by Mona Field, of the Radical Therapy Training Collective in Los Angeles, the article confronted movement members with a narrower but even more painful failure.[60] By 1977, when Field's short essay was published, revolutionary change in the United States had receded even for die-hard believers. At a time when the dissident press was fading, dealt a final blow by the end of the Vietnam War, radical therapists continued to publish their own journal, organize conferences, and run community centers. This alone counted as a remarkable success. But Field's community activism in a traditionally left-wing neighborhood had taught her that far from reaching the masses of ordinary Americans, or mounting an effective challenge to institutional psychiatry, radical therapists hadn't even convinced fellow leftists. Yes, activists saw conventional psychotherapy as oppressive, an argument that writers like Steiner, Glenn, and Galen had made from the start. Neither, however, did they recognize radical versions of it as a political tool. To them, mental illness remained a personal, not a political, problem. Even those of Field's acquaintances who saw therapists preferred the apolitical approaches that the movement had been criticizing all along—or, perhaps, had simply helped gain in popularity.

3.3 Ex-Patients between Liberty and Neoliberalism

Despite considerable overlap, radical therapy and ex-patient activism constituted two separate movements at their inception, and drifted apart further as they unfolded. This division appears by no means inevitable. *Madness Network News* (*MNN*), the voice of mental patients' liberation from 1972 to 1986, was the brainchild of left-wing mental health workers and former patients in the Bay Area of California. It remained a collaborative project until the latter excluded all professionals from the editorial board. Boston's Mental Patients' Liberation Front, one of the most vociferous advocacy groups to emerge in the United States, held its first meetings in the offices of

RT, which had only recently moved from North Dakota to Massachusetts. Patient activists such as Chamberlin or Leonard Roy Frank, *MNN*'s long-time editor, repeatedly contributed to *RT* and *IRT*. Regular conferences, launched in Detroit in 1973, provided a shared platform until separatism took hold.

Ultimately, class and ideological divisions proved too powerful. Both movements came into being as a consequence of psychiatry's explosive expansion and diversification in the postwar era, but they constituted different elements within it and their proponents took their place on opposite sides. Radical therapy evolved out of the political activism of progressive psychiatrists and remained, despite calls to deprofessionalize, a mainly middle-class phenomenon within the countercultural bohemia of the Sixties. Mental patients' liberation took root in a very different milieu. Patient publications had existed before, but *MNN* spoke for a movement because a majority of psychiatric patients came to live outside of large hospital complexes, where they had once been housed. Released more quickly and at an earlier age, many found that an existence outside of psychiatric institutions was fundamentally different but not necessarily easier as they often struggled with meager benefits, homelessness, unemployment, or menial jobs, social stigma, and fragile health. In this situation, patients depended on peer-support like never before. For those who were still in hospital care, were too ill, or lived far from alternative centers, *MNN* provided a decentralized therapeutic space, in which the community could share past and current experiences and discuss solutions in a sympathetic environment. One recurrent problem addressed in the magazine was the reactions of new acquaintances or potential employers to a history of institutionalization. *MNN*'s editors encouraged its reader to come out, often with success. A reader who gave her name as Virginia Davis wrote to *MNN* thanking the magazine for helping her to make this step: "It's becoming easier and easier to say, 'I've been crazy'."[61]

From a high point of more than half a million patients in mental institutions after World War II, numbers had dropped to less than a third two decades later. As the 1960s drew to a close, self-help groups spread rapidly across the country, starting with Portland's Insane Liberation Front in 1970, the Mental Patients' Liberation Project in New York City a year later, and the Network Against Psychiatric Assault (NAPA) in San Francisco in 1972, to name just a few. These activists often came from working-class backgrounds and found collective living to be an economic necessity rather than an aspirational lifestyle. Their foremost goals were the establishment of support networks and patient rights: the freedom to choose and—above all—to refuse treatment. Upon reading *MNN*, it quickly becomes evident how low revolution and countercultural experience rank among the priorities of its contributors. It would be misguided, however, to dismiss the movement's political nature. The insistence on freedom from treatment added direct contestation to the construction of alternative institutions—from demonstrations to boycotts and lawsuits. Radical therapy might have had loftier ambitions, built on a sophisticated understanding of psychiatry's place within US capitalism. But for more than a decade, mental patients' liberation was built around a core of fundamental opposition.

The last section of this chapter focuses on the dominant strand of ex-patient activism during the 1970s and early '80s. The era coincides with the meetings that brought activists and sympathizers together at the yearly "Conferences on Human Rights and Against Psychiatric Oppression," and the existence of its major public platform. Sold for 50, later 75 cents, *MNN* boasted a print run of 4000 copies, roughly the same as *RT* and *IRT*. Under the title, alongside a sun and moon, the header riffed on no less than the *New York Times* to proclaim itself mad America's newsletter of record: "All the Fits That's News to Print." Where radical therapy publications leaned toward professional journals in their outlook and terminology, *MNN* shows many historical parallels with black, gay, and women's liberation magazines like *Black Panther* and *Come Out!*, which was first published in late 1969.[62] Advertisements for *MNN* printed in other countercultural newspapers referred knowingly to the kinship between these movements in an illustration that showed a wild-haired man, dressed in flowing garments, mouth opened wide as if shouting, his right fist raised high. These publications sprang up as the civil rights and student movements split into identity-based creeds, and countercultural publications began to address smaller and more closely knit communities. The ex-patients' movement does not stop with *MNN*. However, as the Cold War came to an end, so did mental patients liberation as it had existed for more than a decade: its challenge to institutional psychiatry waned, and militant opposition gave way to a form of advocacy that defined mental patients as consumers.[63] Over the next few pages, I trace this shift from liberty to neoliberalism but close on what is perhaps the most lasting achievement of mental patients' liberation beyond the pages of *MNN*, Marge Piercy's novel *Woman on the Edge of Time* (1976).

Begun as a community newsletter for the Bay Area of California, *MNN* soon attracted a national and international readership and contributors. Some of these were disillusioned psychiatrists, but from the beginning the main emphasis lay on the self-assertion of current and former patients. Aiming to protect the "rights and dignity of those people labeled crazy," the editors also called for patients sending in letters, poems, illustrations, and essays to give their real names in order to "break the myth of mental illness."[64] An early contribution of this kind was "Shock," a short article written by Cyril Kolotronis, who gave his address as Western State Hospital in Lakewood, Washington. The author detailed his ECT treatment, mourning the memory loss that left him unable to do math and made him much worse, he added, at playing Bridge and Pinochle. Kolotronis wasn't content merely to describe his experiences in a neutral manner, drawing on popular Cold War imagery to denounce psychiatry. Electroshock constituted a war crime, in his case committed by a "foreign doctor, who went to the same school as Fidel Castro," and recalled the medical experiments conducted in

Auschwitz.⁶⁵ "Can this be America?" Kolotronis asked in closing. The essay may have wildly mixed its references to communism and national socialism, but the understanding of psychiatry as a totalitarian institution engaging in torture was fairly standard in the pages of *MNN*, as were comparisons between McCarthyism and the oppression of the mentally ill. Like the radical therapy press, *MNN*'s contributors occasionally dabbled in Reich and Fanon, but its ideological outlook was dominated by Szasz. His denial of madness and mental illness, rephrased as problems in living, led to *MNN*'s insistence that treatment should only ever happen on a voluntary out-patient basis, even if the alternatives were the "mental patient ghettos" that several contributors reported on, or the private care homes and welfare hostels that were springing up in city centers and suburbs.⁶⁶ Rarely was this libertarian worldview questioned. In one such debate, a member of the self-consciously Marxist Mental Patients Liberation Front questioned calls for individual responsibility that had arisen in the context of violence attributed to released mental patients. Instead, he called for a revolutionary overthrow of oppressive institutions. The reaction by *MNN*'s editorial board was swift: "As far as responsibility goes. What's wrong with that? You quote Karl Marx, then reach a conclusion that just doesn't follow."⁶⁷ Szasz himself was fully aware of his prominent position in the movement and expressed his admiration for *MNN*, sending a check for a two-year subscription alongside his letter.

The insistence on individual responsibility formed a central plank of mental patients' liberation. Not only did this sit rather uneasily with Szasz's occasional remarks about lazy and stupid patients, it also begged the question what, if anything, distinguished the mad from other downtrodden people. Such reflections could have opened the way for working-class alliances but their pursuit was cut off by identity politics and a purely negative conception of liberty as freedom from treatment. Self-assertion could also pose other problems. Celebrations of insanity, from a "Festival of Creative Psychosis" to Laingian workshops on madness as breakthrough, foreshadowed the later Mad Pride movement but contradicted the reduction of mental illness to social difficulties.⁶⁸ These strategic deficits notwithstanding, the yearly conferences and *MNN* became a rallying ground for legal and public activism. In 1975, a lawsuit filed by seven inmates of Boston State Hospital, who had been members of the local liberation group, established a limited right to refuse drug treatment in Massachusetts, with similar reforms following in New York and California.⁶⁹ In 1976, a month-long sit-in at the office of governor Jerry Brown led to the establishment of patient rights and advocacy groups in California counties. Celebrating this success, *MNN*'s October issue printed a photograph of two women sitting on a couch in the governor's office and holding up placards that read: "Mad Women Fight Back" and "Bet Your Ass We're Paranoid."⁷⁰ In a later campaign, movement activists succeeded in adding a question on banning electro-convulsive treatment to the city election ballot in Los Angeles in 1982. Soon after it was passed with more than 60 percent of votes, the ban was lifted again due to a lawsuit filed by psychiatrists.⁷¹

Figure 3.2 Two female protesters pictured during a month-long sit-in in the office of California governor Jerry Brown in 1976. Photo by Richard Cohen, courtesy of *Madness Network News* (www.MadnessNetworkNews.com)

These partial successes might have contributed to a more sustained legacy had it not been for another far-reaching error. After complaining about the elitism of their professional allies at the 1975 conference, patients started holding closed meetings. Chamberlin fondly recalled: "for the rest of the Conference, most of the ex-patients could be found behind a door with a very clear 'Keep Out' sign for anyone who hadn't done time in a mental institution."[72] Soon, activist groups in Boston and New York became limited to former patients, and in 1976 *MNN* followed suit after what Chamberlin described unceremoniously as a coup. Taking inspiration from Black Power and radical feminists, separatism was a reaction to very real differences in class and power. It was also rooted in fundamental political disputes: radical psychiatrists, even where they defended patients against physical and drug treatment advocated therapy as an emancipatory tool and lobbied for its expansion. Liberation activists, in contrast, viewed any attempt to cure them skeptically and often called for the complete abolition of therapeutic intervention. Given these conflicts, a lasting alliance between the two groups would have been difficult to sustain. Yet separatism, pursued by such a small and powerless group with few natural allies, further weakened the movement.

The decision to go it alone also showed in the community centers established by activists. In *On Our Own*, an influential handbook of mental patients' liberation, Chamberlin began by recounting a fairly typical story of growing up as a woman in the Cold War. Born to working-class parents in Brooklyn, Chamberlin finished high school only for her life to follow a course that she summarized with the words: "a secretarial job, boredom, and marriage."[73] Suffering from severe depression, she was institutionalized in 1966 and continued to see a therapist thereafter. "That my depression might be telling me something about my own life was a possibility no one considered, including me," she wrote.[74] After leaving her husband with the support of a women's liberation circle and joining an ex-patient group, Chamberlin underwent another crisis in 1973, which she spent in an alternative center in Vancouver. This experience, described in glowing terms as a Laingian tale of breakdown and rebirth, formed the basis for Chamberlin's unmitigated rejection of psychiatry and advocacy of patient-organized alternatives. Incapable of imagining that professional psychiatrists could be of help to anyone, Chamberlin foresaw the complete replacement of mental hospitals by community facilities run by their clients.

In the overview of alternative treatment centers that followed the account of her own institutionalization, Chamberlin distinguished between three models. First came partnerships between professionals and patients, in which their roles remained separate, as in most halfway houses or Laing's alternative community Kingsley Hall. The second kind saw patients and non-patients as equals and allowed professionals only in external roles, as supporters and advisors. The third, separatist, model excluded everyone who wasn't a former or current patient. Chamberlin rejected the first option and remained suspicious of the second. Yet, her main example of a completely non-professional institution, the Elizabeth Stone House in Boston, also highlighted serious drawbacks to even the most successful alternatives. Started with the help of a 1974 conference on "Women and Madness," the house provided a refuge center downstairs, where women could stay for up to two weeks, and an upstairs therapeutic community. In addition to its restriction to women, the house did not accept violent or suicidal patients, or those with drug or alcohol problems. It also limited the amount of time any individual could stay. These restrictions excluded the most serious cases in advance. Financial difficulties and the reliance on local volunteers were another chronic source of insecurity. In her introduction, Chamberlin had already rejected criticism of exclusively non-professional care with the usual Szaszian truisms: "It will be objected that this will leave untreated many people who require 'treatment.' But two hundred years of institutional psychiatry have shown that mental hospitals cannot help the unwilling."[75] The facile demeanor with which Chamberlin sidestepped the need for custodial and geriatric care, revealed another limitation of mental patients' liberation: drawing their ranks from comparatively young and able-bodied former inmates, who had recovered to live independently or had never been seriously ill in the first place, activists claimed to speak for all patients, and disregarded those unable to take responsibility for their lives anymore.

These weaknesses took their toll once the political climate turned against radical movements. In the course of 1975, a new self-definition crept into *MNN*: the patient turned consumer. The term would become more frequent over the following years, but for the time being this tendency co-existed with more radical self-assertions. At the seventh annual conference in 1979, a Dutch activist became the first non-American speaker following a visit from European ex-patients. *MNN* increasingly found a wider echo. As early as 1972, the author Ken Kesey had written to the magazine to thank it for updating him on recent developments while he was working on the screenplay for *One Flew Over the Cuckoo's Nest*. In 1977, Guattari visited liberation groups in New York, sharing his address in Paris with *MNN*. Around the same time, a French reader of *MNN* reported that she had passed a few issues to Foucault at a conference.[76] Special sections on the European antipsychiatry movement were followed by articles on Germany's Socialist Patient Collective and an essay by Basaglia. Ever skeptical of professional meddling, Chamberlin remarked that activists on the other side of the Atlantic were rarely former patients. Yet given the dearth of financial resources in the movement, these grassroots exchanges were quite remarkable.

In the meantime, mental patients' liberation faced growing competition at home. Founded in 1979, the National Alliance for the Mentally Ill (NAMI) would eventually develop into the largest advocacy group for psychiatric patients in the country. The name was telling in itself: where ex-patients had asserted their right to speak in their own voice, the new group consisted of parents and relatives who spoke *for* them. These families, often more middle-class and respectable, as *MNN* noted, began to build the alliances with existing institutions and sympathetic professionals that liberation activists had often shunned. Hand in hand went their enthusiastic adoption of biological models of mental illness: support for genetic and biochemical explanations aligned NAMI with the new psychiatric orthodoxy, but also absolved parents from accusations that they were responsible for their children's illness. Arguably, the libertarian underpinnings of mental patients' liberation laid the groundwork for NAMI's later emphasis on consumer choice. What allowed it grow in influence so rapidly, however, were neoliberal reforms. During Reagan's tenure as governor, California's health care system became a testing ground for the marketization he would unleash nationwide during his presidency. Under the cover of strengthening individual rights, the so-called Lanterman-Petris-Short, coming into full effect in 1972, led to a further drop in patient numbers. *MNN* explicitly defended the law from criticism, but the reforms played into the hands of organizations like NAMI.[77] When the mainstream media blamed a number of sensational murders on released patients, who now found themselves crammed into hostels or sleeping on the streets, moderate self-help groups were at hand to alleviate the effects of understaffed and underfunded psychiatric wards, or simply to provide a fig leaf for politicians eager to deflect from the consequences of their actions. The founding of their own National Alliance of Mental Patients by liberation activists in 1985 came too late—at least for their long-standing movement organ. *MNN*'s final issue announced the dissolution of the editorial collective, ending with a bleak outlook into the future:

> A real lack of communication and trust in recent years among people has been another major cause [. . .] [of] co-opting the movement [. . .] Very few anti-psychiatry projects remain. Those that do tend to be isolated. It remains to be seen whether or not a visible, organized anti-psychiatry movement will continue to exist.[78]

Things did not turn out quite as bleak, but the collapse of *MNN* initiated a dry spell for radical patient activism that lasted until after the Cold War. Many of its founding figures remained active, however, and a younger generation would come to the forefront in the 1990s and 2000s. The government funding that became available for patient initiatives in the 1980s flowed elsewhere, and in another symbolic defeat the yearly movement conferences underwent a name change that signaled the end of a principled opposition. The earlier focus on human rights and oppression was soft-pedaled in meetings that were newly titled "Mental Health Alternatives."

In Piercy's *Woman on the Edge of Time* liberation from psychiatry equally presents an on-going battle. A prolific poet and novelist, Piercy was involved in Students for a Democratic Society (SDS) in the 1960s and contributed several poems to radical therapy journals and *MNN* before *Woman on the Edge of Time* appeared. Her acknowledgments refer to many of the movement's leaders and organizations, including *RT* editor Michael Galen, Phyllis Chesler, Boston's Mental Patients' Liberation Front, and Paul Lowinger, of the APA's radical caucus. Piercy also made a point to thank past and present inmates and staff who had helped her gain access to psychiatric institutions and shared their experiences.[79] Like other feminist utopias of the Sixties, Piercy's future society was not perfect but in continuous flux. On the upside, women were freed from childbirth, children from growing up in nuclear families, gender identity had become fluid, and humanity embraced grassroots socialism. At the same time, this imaginary world was still at war with capitalist strongholds. Opposed to this hopeful outlook, stood a bleak present and the 37-year-old Chicana woman, Connie. The novel begins with Piercy's protagonist seeing a person who isn't present in her time. What ordinarily might be taken as a sign of madness turns out to be Connie's ability to establish contact across time and space.

This romantic vision of madness is offset by Piercy's portrayal of institutional psychiatry. Described as an underworld of the economically and socially oppressed, the novel offers detailed descriptions of the hospitals in which Connie is held: her slow shuffle across day rooms and bleak hallways that she recognizes as a side effect of chlorpromazine, the nurses' habit of viewing complaints about their care as signs of deep-seated illness. Several episodes reveal Piercy to be a close reader of movement magazines and liberation activism. Electroshock experiments conducted on homosexual patients in the novel pick up on a paper that reported a similar "aversion therapy" at the 1970 APA conference and led to vocal protests.[80] The theme of mind control through psychosurgery and psychotropic drugs plays an equally important role in *Woman* as it does in *MNN*. This focus on psychiatric abuse demonstrates the proximity between Piercy's novel and mental patients' liberation. The same can be said for Connie's portrayal as a persecuted but otherwise sane person. Here as in *MNN*, mental illness appears a myth. Yet the novel's future also affords a different perspective, introducing a distinction between madness and disease. Here, people go mad to "see visions, hear voices of prophecy, bang on the wall, relive infancy, [. . .] to disintegrate, to reintegrate."[81] Toward the end, Connie escapes the hospital and psychosurgery. When she is caught and returned, she poisons the staff but *Woman* breaks off before the consequences of her action are revealed. Piercy's science-fictional time-travel narrative imagines psychiatric activism as part of a wider struggle between a humane future and a totalitarian modernity—and thus opposes a mad rationality to a sane madness. American antipsychiatry relegated such a positive conception of madness to its edges, to brief acknowledgments and references to Laing's imported writings. Far more dominant was the denial of its existence, a pragmatic but also a defensive tactic. It is only in the imaginary space opened up by American literature and culture that madness flourishes as true freedom and utter horror, as sheer intensity of experience and ultimate truth. The next chapter turns to these countercultural fictions of insanity and critiques of a psychotic Cold War reality.

Notes

1 Albert Deutsch, *The Shame of the States* (New York: Harcourt Brace, 1948), 96.
2 Edward Shorter, *A History of Psychiatry: From the Era of the Asylum to the Age of Prozac* (New York: Wiley, 1997), 278.
3 Deutsch, *Shame of the States*, 161.
4 Ibid., 182.
5 Ibid., 184. The term "therapeutic community," later popularized by Maxwell Jones, here refers to a paper by the British psychiatrist Thomas Main, "The Hospital as a Therapeutic Institution," *Bulletin of the Menninger Clinic* 10 (1946): 66–70.
6 Peter Sedgwick, *Psycho Politics: Laing, Foucault, Goffman, Szasz, and the Future of Mass Psychiatry* (New York: Harper, 1982), 67.

7 The term "anti-psychiatry" was coined by the South African psychiatrist David Cooper, a close collaborator of Laing. Cooper defined it as the development of concepts and practices antithetical to institutional psychiatry. David Cooper, *Psychiatry and Anti-Psychiatry* (London: Tavistock, 1967), ix.
8 Andrew Scull, *Madness in Civilization: A Cultural History of Insanity from the Bible to Freud, from the Madhouse to Modern Medicine* (London: Thames & Hudson, 2015), 318.
9 Richard Bentall, *Madness Explained: Psychosis and Human Nature* (London: Penguin, 2004), xv.
10 Deutsch, *Shame of the States*, 30–1.
11 My understanding of the term "radical psychiatry" differs from its use by historians such as Lucas Richert, whose focus lies on the radical caucus within the APA. See Richert, "'Therapy Means Change, not Peanut Butter': American Radical Psychiatry, 1968–1975," *Social History of Medicine* 27 (2013): 104–21.
12 But see Richert for a brief discussion of the first two. Richert, "Therapy Means Change," 115–118. Michael Staub's recent study of social psychiatry from World War II to the 1980s considers an anthology put out by the editors of *The Radical Therapist*. Michael E. Staub, *Madness is Civilization: When the Diagnosis was Social, 1948–1980* (Chicago: University of Chicago Press, 2011), 123.
13 Cited in: David Wagner, "Radical Movements in the Social Services: A Theoretical Framework," *Social Service Review* 63, no. 2 (1989): 273.
14 Thomas S. Szasz, *The Myth of Mental Illness: Foundations of a Theory of Personal Conduct*, rev. ed. (New York: Harper & Row, 1974), 164 and 175.
15 Thomas S. Szasz, *The Manufacture of Madness: A Comparative Study of the Inquisition and the Mental Health Movement* (New York: Harper & Row, 1977), 223.
16 Ibid., 37.
17 Timothy Leary, "Letter to Thomas Szasz," accessed October 12, 2015, http://www.szasz.com/leary.html.
18 Norman Dain, "Critics and Dissenters: Reflections on 'Anti-Psychiatry' in the United States," *Journal of the History of the Behavioral Sciences* 25, no. 1 (Jan 1989): 3–25.
19 Staub, *Madness is Civilization*, 126–7.
20 Robert Castel, *Die psychiatrische Ordnung: Das goldene Zeitalter des Irrenwesens*, trans. Ulrich Raulf (Frankfurt: Suhrkamp, 1983), 20–1.
21 Szasz, *Myth of Mental Illness*, 48.
22 Hannah S. Decker, *The Making of DSM-III: A Diagnostic Manual's Conquest of American Psychiatry* (New York: Oxford University Press, 2013).
23 Erving Goffman, *Asylums: Essays on the Social Situation of Mental Patients and Other Inmates* (Garden City, NY: Anchor, 1961), 43.
24 Ibid., 320.
25 Ibid., 384.
26 John Haynes, "Philosopher of Madness: A Striking Look at R.D. Laing, Controversial Psychiatrist and Author," *Life*, October 8, 1971, 86–90.
27 Gregory Bateson, "Toward a Theory of Schizophrenia," in *Steps to an Ecology of Mind: Collected Essays in Anthropology, Psychiatry, Evolution, and Epistemology* (London: Intertext, 1972), 201–227. Bateson's theory, which referenced Frieda Fromm-Reichmann's concept of the 'schizophrenogenic mother,' understood schizophrenia as the result of a traumatic breakdown in family communication that left the patient unable to understand the world around him, or express himself within it.
28 R.D. Laing, *The Divided Self: An Existential Study in Sanity and Madness* (London: Tavistock, 1969), 76. Italics in the original.

29 Ibid., 204–5. As Laing emphasized in an interview in 1975: "I never had that sort of split in my mind between the chemicals and the social thing. [. . .] I was also very interested in genetics—still am." Claude Steiner and Spence Meighan, "R.D. Laing: An Interview," *Issues in Radical Therapy* 3, no. 4 (Fall 1975): 9.

30 Frieda Fromm-Reichmann, "Notes on the Development of Treatment of Schizophrenics by Psychoanalytic Psychotherapy," *Psychiatry* 11 (1948): 263–273.

31 R.D. Laing, *The Politics of Experience* and *The Bird of Paradise* (London: Penguin, 1970), 64.

32 Ibid., 99; and R.D. Laing, "Preface to the Pelican Edition," in *The Divided Self* (London: Penguin, 1990), 12.

33 David Cooper, "Introduction," in Michel Foucault, *Madness and Civilization: A History of Insanity in the Age of Reason*, trans. Richard Howard (London: Routledge, 1989), vii-ix.

34 Michel Foucault, "Preface to the 1961 Edition," in *History of Madness*, ed. Jean Khalfa, trans. Jonathan Murphy and Jean Khalfa (London: Routledge, 2010), xxxiii.

35 Ibid., xxviii. The emphasis is Foucault's.

36 See my discussion of this event in chapter 6.

37 Foucault, *Madness and Civilization*, 6.

38 Phyllis Chesler, *Women and Madness* (Garden City, NY: Doubleday, 1972), xx.

39 Ibid., 15–6.

40 Anon., "On Practice," *The Radical Therapist* 1, no. 5 (Jan–Feb 1971): n. p.

41 Phil Brown, "Political Psychology," *Issues in Radical Therapy* 20 (Fall 1977): 24.

42 Denis Jaffe, "Number Nine: Creating a Counter-Institution," *The Radical Therapist* 1, no. 5 (Jan–Feb 1971): 10.

43 Ibid., 11.

44 Joy Aronson and Enid Klauber, "Counter-Hegemony and Radical Psychiatry," *Issues in Radical Therapy* 17 (Spring 1977): 3.

45 Richert, "Therapy Means Change," 112–3.

46 Michael Glenn, "Manifesto," *The Radical Therapist* 1, no. 1 (Apr–May 1970): 2.

47 Claude Steiner, "Radical Psychiatry—Manifesto," *The Radical Therapist* 1, no. 2 (June–July 1970): 12.

48 For an overview of underground publications see: Rodger Streitmatter, *Voices of Revolution: The Dissident Press in America* (New York: Columbia University Press, 2001); and for a more detailed study of the 1960s: John McMillian, *Smoking Typewriters: The Sixties Underground Press and the Rise of Alternative Media in American* (New York: Oxford University Press, 2011).

49 *The Radical Therapist* 1, no. 6 (Feb–Mar 1971): 1.

50 C.A. Fairfield, "Letter," *The Radical Therapist* 1, no. 4 (Oct–Nov 1970): 2.

51 The relative obscurity of the two magazines also meant that they escaped concerted efforts by local police and the FBI to harass, infiltrate, and undermine the underground press. See Streitmatter and McMillian for documentation of the FBI's frequently illegal activities.

52 The Editors, "How Revolutionary Is A Journal?," *The Radical Therapist* 1, no. 1 (April–May 1970): n. p.

53 Anon., "RT in Practice," *The Radical Therapist* 1, no. 1 (Jan–Feb 1971): 17.

54 The Editors, "Critique," *The Radical Therapist* 2, no. 3 (Oct 1972): 31.

55 Anon., "Editorial," *Rough Times* 2, no. 7 (June 1972): 1.

56 Deirdre English and Barbara Ehrenreich, "Politics of Sexual Freedom," *Issues in Radical Therapy* 2, no. 3 (Summer 1974): 15–17.

57 Anon., "Movement News," *Issues in Radical Therapy* 4, no. 3 (Summer 1976): 29.

58 Steiner and Meighan, "R.D. Laing: An Interview," 6 and 8.

59 Patricia Parsons, "Radical Therapy Theory Conference," *Issues in Radical Therapy* XI, no. 2 (Spring 1984): 30.

60 Mona Field, "Left Turn at Echo Park," *Issues in Radical Therapy* 19 (Summer 1977): 7.

61 Virginia Davis, "Letter to the Editor," *Madness Network News* 2, no. 3 (June 1974): 23.

62 Streitmatter, *Voices of Revolution*, 223–225 and 243.

63 For an excellent overview of the ex-patients movement since the 1970s, including its radical and liberal strands, see: Linda J. Morrison, *Talking Back to Psychiatry: The Psychiatric Consumer/Survivor/Ex-Patient Movement* (New York: Routledge, 2005).

64 *Madness Network News* 1, no. 5 (1973): 2.

65 Cyril Kolotronis, "Shock," *Madness Network News* 1, no. 5 (1973): 9.

66 Bob Harris, "Testimony by Ex-Inmate Activists," *Madness Network News* 4, no. 4 (Fall 1977): 32.

67 Stephen Soldz, "Letter to the Editor," *Madness Network News* 2, no. 2 (Feb 1974): 21; and Sherry Hirsch, "Dialogue," Ibid., 22.

68 Nick Crossley gives a brief overview of the British Mad Pride movement in: Nick Crossley, *Contesting Psychiatry: Social Movements in Mental Health* (New York: Routledge, 2006), 205-207.

69 Judi Chamberlin. "The Ex-Patients' Movement: Where We've Been and Where We're Going," in *Challenging the Therapeutic State: Critical Perspectives on Psychiatry and the Mental Health System*, special issue of *The Journal of Mind and Behavior* 11, no. 3–4 (Summer/Autumn 1990): 333.

70 See back cover of *Madness Network News* 4, no. 1 (Oct 1976): n. p.

71 Judi Chamberlin, "The Ex-Inmates' Movement Today," *Issues in Radical Therapy* XI, no. 4 (1985): 15.

72 Judi Chamberlin, "Organizing? or Disorganizing?" *Madness Network News* 3, no. 3 (Oct 1976): 4.

73 Judi Chamberlin, *On Our Own: Patient-Controlled Alternative to the Mental Health System* (N. p.: Mind, 1988), 22.

74 Ibid., 23.

75 Ibid., 18–19.

76 Linda Morrison, *Talking Back to Psychiatry: The Psychiatric Consumer/Survivor/Ex-Patient Movement* (New York: Routledge, 2005), 72.

77 Anon., "Notes from LAMP . . . about Psychiatry and the Law," *Madness Network News* 2, no. 1 (Dec 1973): 8–10.

78 *Madness Network News* 8, no. 3 (1986): 2; cited in Morrison, *Talking Back to Psychiatry*, 82.

79 Marge Piercy, *Woman on the Edge of Time* (London: Women's Press, 2001), 7.

80 Richert, "Therapy Means Political Change," 114–5.

81 Piercy, *Woman on the Edge of Time*, 66.

4   A Sane Madness?

Psychosis and Cold War Countercultures

In November 1975, a largely unknown science fiction writer by the name of Philip K. Dick shared the cover of *Rolling Stone* with the Grateful Dead, the Weather Underground, and Rod Stewart posing with the Swedish actress Britt Ekland. Five years had passed since the end of the 1960s, but those assembled on the cover all hailed from the previous decade, its student revolts, the hippy communes of Haight-Ashbury, and London's Mod culture. Paul Williams's feature on what the magazine proclaimed to be "The Most Brilliant Sci-Fi Mind on Any Planet" has been understood as the beginning of Dick's critical recognition as the most influential science fiction author of the later twentieth century.[1] Williams's essay portrayed a personable if highly paranoid loner lost in plots possibly of his own imagination, and this snapshot of his late years dominates Dick's reputation to this day. A full-page illustration by the artist Kent Bellows, painted in acrylic in a sort of psychedelic realism, accompanied the article. Bellows visualized his subject reading in an armchair during a thunderstorm, a smoldering joint and spilled tablets of speed on display on a coffee table. Dick's paranoid delusions took the shape of a tentacled monster, its fangs exposed, reaching in through the window as it was about to engulf the author.

As I will argue throughout this chapter, such metaphors of psychosis dramatize a perceived loss of agency: a threat to the individual subject dramatized with the help of a literary tropology of madness. These countercultural fictions may be understood as symbolic solutions whose inadequacy calls forth ever new attempts at regaining in full what seems forever partial and fleeting. Dick and Bellows share this recourse to psychopathology with a dominant strand of the postwar United States and America's counterculture. Therefore, this chapter reads Dick's fiction alongside a number of his peers, from Jack Kerouac to Allen Ginsberg, and from William Burroughs to Ken Kesey and Thomas Pynchon, and considers central documents of the Sixties imagination: the "Port Huron Statement" (1962), written by members of Students for a Democratic Society (SDS), and Theodore Roszak's *The Making of A Counter Culture* (1969), the study that coined the term. Some of these authors will also feature in my discussion of paranoid narrative, a major element of countercultural psychopathology,

Figure 4.1 The author Philip K. Dick, portrayed in a painting by Kent Bellows as featured in the November 5, 1975, issue of *Rolling Stone*. Courtesy of Phyllis Bellows

in chapter 5. As part of their aesthetic and political revolt, these texts reverse dominant valuations of madness and emphasize the freedom and purported wisdom of the schizophrenic. Yet their attempts remain ambivalent and partial, hampered as much by madness's long-standing pathologization as irrational as by Cold War associations of psychosis with a demonized left.

Almost all of Dick's novels over a thirty-year period concern themselves with madness, a dialogue sustained by a lifelong reading in psychology. In fact, it is difficult to think of another major US writer of the late twentieth century in whose work madness plays such a dominant role. As Fredric Jameson has argued in a number of influential assessments, Dick "was the epic poet of [. . .] schizophrenia of a 1960s counterculture," of "an end to individualism so absolute as to call into question the last glimmers of the ego."[2] As a consequence, his work allows for unparalleled insight into cultural appropriations of psychoanalysis in the United States after World War II: its rise as a major science of human behavior and the gradual subsumption under brain research—what Nathan Hale has called the rise and crisis of psychoanalysis.[3] Dick's oeuvre takes us from early Cold War satires of Freudianism and the antipsychiatric novels of the mid-1960s, to the shift to neurology late in life. While partaking in countercultural reevaluations of madness, Dick also stands out for his rejection of facile romanticism. Where other Sixties authors at times celebrate the freedom and supposed authenticity of the schizophrenic, Dick's fiction pays equal attention to the loneliness and fear that madness often brings.

The final section argues that there is another reason to single out Dick's oeuvre. After experiencing a series of hallucinations in February and March 1974, Dick spent much of his remaining years writing about their possible significance, ceaselessly ruminating and self-diagnosing. A 900-page excerpt was published as *The Exegesis of Philip K. Dick* in 2011. As tediously repetitive as they are often poignant and exhilarating, his diary entries see him leave behind conventional conceptions of personal agency. Dick's alternative vision of madness escapes medical diagnosis and conceptualizes an "individual [that] is not an individual."[4] Replacing the imagery of fragmentation and individual loss for the integration into wider networks of meaning, Dick's emergent subjectivity retrospectively evokes the rise of the World Wide Web and mobile communication. These passages also form the final twist in Dick's engagement with psychiatry, coming as they do on the cusp of its biological revolution and during the last years of his life. With the publication of the third edition of the Diagnostic and Statistical Manual of Mental Disorders (DSM-III), new syndromes join the serious mental illnesses and add to the postwar erasure of the boundary between neurosis and psychosis. In closing, I compare Dick's post-psychiatric imagination to Leslie Marmon Silko's novel *Ceremony* (1977), which follows a World War II veteran suffering from post-traumatic stress disorder (PTSD). Silko's protagonist seeks an escape from pathology in the reengagement with his

Native American community and returns us to the very beginnings of the Cold War.

Born in 1928, shortly before the onset of the Great Depression, Dick was too young to really be a Beat and too old to grow up a Hippie, even if a life spent in California meant he came in close contact with both. Just out of high school, in 1947 he moved into a rooming house in Berkeley and made friends with Jack Spicer and Robert Duncan, two central proponents of the San Francisco Renaissance. If Dick missed New York's Beat scene and Haight-Ashbury in the mid-1960s, he was briefly part of what Duncan described as the birth of the rejuvenated poetry scene in San Francisco, "the group of writers who met around him [Duncan] in Berkeley during the 1940s."[5] His acquaintance with Spicer and Duncan encouraged Dick to pursue a career as a mainstream literary writer, which would remain a lifelong and unfulfilled dream for him, and for a while led to a loss of interest in the science fiction that had been his obsession since childhood.[6] The politics of the Berkeley scene also left its mark on the young author. What Davidson identifies as the anarchist or anarcho-pacifist politics of the Duncan circle coincides much more closely with Dick's early work than common characterizations as either Marxist or liberal. No one who savors the anti-militaristic satire and revolutionary coups of Dick's novels of the 1950s and early '60s can doubt what he retrospectively called his fireball radicalism "back in my youth in politically active Berkeley."[7]

This is a distinctively Cold War politics, however, anxiously asserting the freedom of the individual at the same time that it yearns for collective change. Dick's individualism found one of its expressions in a similarly individualist ethics of literary production: a private mythology of spontaneous creation, fuelled by an addiction to amphetamines, and exemplified by Dick's pride in his furious typing speed. The parallels with the creation of Jack Kerouac's *On the Road* (1957), a novel Dick admired, are striking. Kerouac and Dick's forceful assertion of spontaneity and authorship betrayed a deep cultural anxiety about the individual subject, an anxiety that was accompanied by an ideology of hyper-masculinity and frequent sexism. Not only did Dick share elements of a common history and creative self-understanding with the San Francisco Renaissance and the Beats. He also casually identified himself with them and was proud to be called a "Berkeley Beatnik" by his soon-to-be third wife Anne Rubenstein. At the time, she was married to the poet William Rubenstein, one of the editors of the little magazine *Neurotica*, which published early works by Kerouac and Ginsberg. Dick stressed his literary affinity to the Beats but distanced himself from its social scene—an ambiguity he shared with Duncan and Spicer who publicly criticized some of Ginsberg's more provocative actions.[8]

The perceived threat to individual autonomy found its most pervasive metaphor in a literature of madness. In Kerouac's *On the Road*, the protagonist, and the essence of Beat, Dean Moriarty, is repeatedly diagnosed by himself and others as psychotic. As Old Bull Lee, a character based on William Burroughs, says: " 'He seems to me to be headed for his ideal fate, which is compulsive psychosis dashed with a jigger of psychopathic irresponsibility and violence.' "[9] In the novel, Kerouac understands madness, exemplified by the psychotic Dean, as the ultimate severance of all ties with a society that stifles freedom. Only the absolute outside of madness promises liberation. Kerouac writes of rebellion as psychological escape rather than political action. Thus he provides an understanding of madness not as the dissolution of subjective agency but exactly its opposite: the singular authenticity and spontaneity of a fully autonomous subject. Kerouac's novel ends, however, on the flipside of such autonomy—absolute isolation. "The last time I saw him was under sad and strange circumstances," recounts the narrator, Sal Paradise. "Dean couldn't talk any more and said nothing."[10] It is this madness, the psychological devastation of institutionalized mental illness induced by an alienating postwar society, which Allen Ginsberg famously refers to when he begins his poem "Howl": "I saw the best minds of my generation destroyed by/madness."[11] As Ginsberg knew only too well, this fate had befallen earlier generations as well. Whereas his own time in a psychiatric hospital was relatively short-lived, his mother Naomi spent most of her later life in various institutions. Ginsberg questions his own mental health in "Kaddish," the famous elegy to his mother and classifies sanity as a mere "trick of agreement."[12] Yet the poem draws its tragic force from Naomi's lobotomy, to which her son consented following the advice of her doctors. Rather than alleviating symptoms, her persecution complex only intensified—imagining a Cold War fantasy of espionage and mind control at a time when her son could only concur that apocalypse was never more than "a flash away."[13] Where "Kaddish" eulogizes a mother, it also mourns the lost utopia of her radical youth. In Ginsberg's mother, as in Cold War America, communism becomes madness and dreams of revolution founder alongside youthful sanity.

In response, what Ginsberg imagines as a "natural ecstasy" seeks shelter from Moloch, the sacrificial god of American capitalism, exemplified by its "madtowns of the/East" and "invincible mad/houses," and finds it in the promise of community, the return to a simpler life.[14] Both understandings of madness, flipsides of a sought-after unity of the subject that promises authenticity and threatens isolation, seek to escape the anonymity and reification of an urban late modernity. This is clearest perhaps in Ken Kesey's *One Flew Over the Cuckoo's Nest* (1962), told from the perspective of Chief Bromden, a Native American mental patient. Torn from the community of his tribe, Kesey imagines the novel's psychiatric hospital as the machinic production of robots for the conspiratorial "Combine." It is only by way of the body, pitting the organic against the technological, that its power can be challenged. Against the hospital's emasculation of its patients—"Moloch in whom/I am a consciousness without a body!" Ginsberg had written—Kesey positions the sheer physical force and hyper-masculinity of Randle

McMurphy, his tragic-comic hero.[15] McMurphy's resistance to the oppression of the tyrannical Nurse Ratched reconnects the patients with their bodies in the physical exertion of a fishing trip and the visit by two prostitutes and exposes the machinic as bodily when McMurphy rips apart the nurse's uniform, laying her flesh bare to his fellow patients. After McMurphy's enforced lobotomy, likened to castration in the novel, Chief Bromden escapes to his native village.

Kesey's depiction of psychiatry was based on his own, maybe somewhat skewed, observations. Living in an artist community in Northern California after completing a creative writing program at Stanford University, Kesey was introduced to Freudianism by a graduate student in psychology, who also told him about experiments with psychomimetic chemicals at a near-by mental hospital.[16] Kesey volunteered, and found himself a test subject in experiments the CIA conducted as part of its secret MK-Ultra program to ascertain the suitability of LSD for interrogation.[17] Wolfe claims that Kesey conceived of Chief Bromden while high on LSD. More importantly, Kesey would go on to popularize the drug as a recreational activity. Synthesized by a Swiss biochemist in 1938, psychiatrists in the 1950s were drawn to LSD for two reasons: firstly, its use led to intense self-reflection, an experience that allowed some patients to break free from depression or addiction. Secondly, the hallucinations induced by the substance were said to mimic psychosis. Using LSD could therefore provide psychiatrists and nurses with insight into the condition, but these effects also gave rise to speculation about the origins of mental illness, including the first biochemical theory of schizophrenia, published by the psychiatrist Humphrey Osmond. Kesey's happenings with the Merry Pranksters—the road trips described by Wolfe and the first acid raves—swapped the slightly more solemn promotion of psychedelics led by Harvard psychologist Timothy Leary for an emphasis on otherworldly fun. Picking up on the Beat fascination with drugs—Neil Cassady became a core member of the Merry Pranksters, as he had been for the clique around Burroughs and Ginsberg—Kesey turned the experience of madness into entertainment. The exploration of these states constituted the core of the psychedelic movement and offered an essentially apolitical alternative to the activism of radical students and civil rights campaigners. That the heavy use of LSD might actually result in psychosis apparently did not cross Kesey's mind, at least initially. As Wolfe writes, recounting the fate of a woman who had to be institutionalized during one of their road trips: "She roared off into the void and was picked up by the cops by and by, and the doors closed in the Country psychiatric ward, that was that, for the Pranksters were long gone."[18]

In ways similar to *One Flew Over the Cuckoo's Nest*, William Burroughs's *Naked Lunch* (1959) depends on the graphic presence of the body to stem the fragmentation of human subjectivity, its transformation into ghost and machine, the insect and the schizophrenic. "The Vigilante," Burroughs writes early on, "copped out as a schizo possession case: 'I was stand-ing outside myself [. . .] I am a ghost wanting what every ghost wants—a body.'"[19] Burroughs attempts to hold onto his textual bodies, and the body of the text, with the help of a deathly painful pleasure of sexuality and addiction: a brutal amplification of destruction, decay, and gratification. It is to Dick's credit that he came to resist most of these symbolic solutions, organic community as much as the self-presence of the body. Where Dick's mainstream novel *Confessions of a Crap Artist* already portrayed the 1950s as a suffocating hell of dysfunctional families, his science fiction allowed him to go a step further. *Time Out of Joint* (1959) seems to be set in the same decade, a way for Dick to build on his mainstream writings, and uses science fiction devices only to frame the narrative. The novel's protagonist seemingly lives a somewhat stagnant existence in a small-town shadowed by the threat of nuclear annihilation. Even this existence represents an illusion, however: to be more precise, it is a delusion, for he has withdrawn from the year 1997 to a fantasy of his postwar childhood. Step by step, Ragle Gumm's imaginary world disintegrates. In a famous scene, a soft-drink stand disap-pears before his eyes, one episode of many that confronts the psychotic pro-tagonist with reality. Ragle's sanity returns him to an insane world. Earth is waging a pointless war against its own kin, human settlers on the moon decried by the government as lunatics. The retrospective small-town idyll, the childhood past as refuge from the anxiety of the early Cold War, does not exist, Dick insists. *Time Out of Joint*, in its satire of the nuclear family, strikes at the integrity of the community that underlies postwar ideology and will be partially superseded in the Sixties by the countercultural group.

In building a sham 1950s for Gumm, who has the ability to predict the impact point of rockets fired from the moon, the US government has torn apart families and rearranged them to fit with larger political concerns.[20] Dick unmasks the social construction of intimacy, a critical energy that would soon extend to the physical body. *The Simulacra*, published five years after *Time Out of Joint*, features concert pianist Richard Kongrosian, whose increasing mental disturbances lead to the breakdown of any boundaries between body and world, self and other. In a memorable passage, Kongro-sian uses his psychokinetic powers to literally absorb a vase of roses. In its place appear, quivering and blood red, his inner organs. Like the community of the nuclear family, Dick understands the individual body as a social and psychological fantasy. Neither Kesey's physical and sexual prowess nor the bodily force of Ginsberg's "natural ecstasy" are available to a writer who continually denied both assurances to his characters and readers. As in Bur-roughs, Dick's bodies are constantly in the process of organic breakdown and inorganic fusion, countering fragmentation not with individuality and unity but with an assemblage of the human and machinic. Whereas Bur-roughs relies on the fleeting ecstasy of the body, the frantic incantation of its presence by sexual and psycho-chemical orgasms, sexuality and drug use offer not union but only further isolation in Dick's novels. The body and community, the machine and the authentic individual, were major themes of postwar culture that found themselves refracted in discourses of madness. This recourse to psychopathology testified to a wider integration of its vocabulary into US society, a development not welcomed by everyone. In her report on a Ginsberg reading for *Partisan Review*, Diana Trilling, the wife of Lionel, Ginsberg's former teacher at Columbia University, compared the Beats to the literary bohemians of the 1920s and '30s. Trilling noted that "[o]ne didn't use pathology in those days to explain or excuse or exhibit oneself."[21] What arouses Trilling's indignation is not the spread of psychopathological terms per se. After all, the literary establishment, of which the Trillings were such a formidable part, showed little hesitation in pathologizing political opponents. Trilling objects to the appropriation of madness for popular self-diagnosis: the production of a cultural imagination of the mad subject.

Establishment voices notwithstanding, few countercultural texts escaped the pervasive psychologization of literature and politics. "The Port Huron Statement," a central text of the 1960s political imagination, had spoken of "the schizophrenic public-military, private-civilian economy of our epoch" and the "characteristic of paranoia" taken on by American anti-communism.[22] Roszak's *The Making of A Counter Culture* repeatedly draws on the vocabulary of pathology as well. Roszak defined his subject by its disaffiliation from mainstream society, so much at a remove from the postwar consensus that for some, Diana Trilling among them, it took on "the alarming appearance of a barbaric intrusion."[23] Roszak, himself a sympathetic observer, sanctioned the popular assumption of an end of ideology and rejected black militancy and conventional political analysis for a communitarian and aesthetic revolt. Perhaps of necessity, then, America's counterculture was not so much a radical rejection of the status quo but a meeting point between youthful dissent and the hope for a better future within the bounds of advanced capitalism. It had only been four years, for instance, since President Lyndon B. Johnson built on Kennedy's rhetoric of the "New Frontier" to promise the "Great Society." As Johnson said in a speech at the University of Michigan's graduation ceremony in 1964: "We have the opportunity to move [. . .] upward to the Great Society [. . .] where the city of man serves not only the needs of the body and the demands of commerce but the desire for beauty and the hunger for community."[24]

Where Roszak differed radically from Johnson was in his skepticism regarding the power of government and technological progress. Adopting a criticism that enjoyed wide currency with centrist and liberal circles as much as on the left, Roszak denounced the consequences of a de-humanizing modernity: a narrow conception of reason, reality, and progress would force humanity to understand its frustration with such limited goals as madness—a madness for which a booming psychiatry provided therapies based on a similarly instrumental view of mental health.[25] Reminiscent of Kesey's attack on institutional psychiatry in *One Flew Over the Cuckoo's*

Nest, Roszak criticizes an "adjustive psychotherapy" for its collusion with a technocratic dystopia. At the same time, Roszak understands the potentialities of man, and of the rebellious youth in particular, as psychological. Technocratic government does not create the wish for political change. It drives people crazy. "[B]uilding the good society is not primarily a social but a psychic task," Roszak writes. Against a "mad rationality," a term he borrows from Lewis Mumford, the goal can only be a sane madness:[26]

> To deny that the true self is this small, hard atom of intense objectivity we pilot about each day as we build bridges and careers is surely to play fast and loose with psychopathology. [. . .] And yet this is what the counter culture undertakes [. . .] by way of its mystical tendencies or the drug experience [. . .] In doing so, it once again transcends the consciousness of the dominant culture and runs the risk of appearing to be a brazen exercise in perverse nonsense.[27]

The shift from politics to psychology effects a switch from the collective to the individual. The future begins "not at the level of class, party or institution but rather at the non-intellectual level of the personality."[28] Like the literature of the Beats, cultural and political change is driven by personal commitment and the examination of the self and has to pass through the individual psyche: a dynamic that calls forth an ethics of unique individuality, personal authenticity, and the spontaneous experience that is assumed to spring from it. Such absolute freedom comes at a price. "Dean couldn't talk any more and said nothing," Kerouac had written of Dean Moriarty.[29] This inability to reach out beyond the community of intimates or even engage with them threatens both Roszak's counterculture and Dick's lonely schizophrenics. More broadly, it amounted to the decisive failure of the Sixties in the United States—the lack of cooperation between a largely middle-class student movement and working-class struggles. Existing class differences presented serious hurdles aggravated by the destruction of much of the Old Left of the 1920s and '30s, but the ideology of authenticity played its part in this failure. Intimately tied to youth and subcultures, the expression of authentic individuality frequently allowed for a politics of the small group, but seldom for mass action. Distancing himself from his depiction of revolutionary change in earlier texts, Dick professed similar attitudes in the 1970s. He upheld his belief in America's rebellious youth but distinguished the counterculture from direct political engagement. "I do not necessarily mean politically active youth, those who organize into distinct societies with banners and slogans—to me that is a reduction into the past, however revolutionary these slogans may be." Such organization was merely "one group using force against another."[30] What distinguished the counterculture was precisely its escape from psychological predictability, and thus, for a writer who associated predictability with the schizoid personality, its authentic humanity. The youth Dick imagined to fulfill this role was not part of a mass organization but an individual who would act as a member of cliques and subcultures. Recounting an episode that later found its way into the novel *A Scanner Darkly* (1977), Dick tells how a friend had stolen cases of Coca-Cola from a truck and, after she and her friends had drunk all of it, returned the bottles for deposit.[31]

Such small group action points to two deeply interrelated concerns of the counterculture. A longing for community, in this case for the understanding and security of the clique, already underlay Duncan and Spicer's San Francisco circle and the Beats. A deep alienation from contemporary society combined with a Utopian persuasion that had already informed America's beginnings.[32] This alienation could find expression in the symbolic restoration of rural, ethnic, and working class communities, as in Kesey's *One Flew Over the Cuckoo's Nest,* or in the countercultural artistic or political group. Simultaneously, such communitarian formations acted as a critique of mass organization and the state. Community bound by the confines of individual authenticity retained an ethics of the small group, rather than being a politics of the mass. Here lay perhaps the widest rupture between New and Old Left. Writers like Burroughs or Pynchon no longer sought control as a necessary instrument for the domestication of a rapacious capitalism but feared and ridiculed it as the madness of an irrational reason. Increasingly allied with the state as bureaucratic unions or the Stalinist party, a left politics that sought to organize under the banner of class was identified with disciplinary state apparatuses. Countercultural writers supplemented existing theories of the hubris of state control with biting satire and an aesthetics of rejection and rebellion. The next section looks more closely at how Dick's novels came to phrase such a cultural politics in the vocabulary of madness.

4.1 "We Need a Quack": Philip K. Dick and Psychoanalysis in America

Dick's science fiction must be understood against the rise of the social sciences, and psychology in particular, in Cold War America. It would be wrong to say that his novels replace the natural with the social sciences, rather Dick applies the speculative questioning that science fiction developed in its appropriation of hard science to psychoanalysis and psychiatry. As Brian Attebery has noted for the magazine science fiction of the 1940s, with which Dick grew up, its major innovation was the "application of experimental method and technological innovation not to physical problems but to fundamental questions about society and the mind."[33] Dick's protagonists still travel in space ships and through time, they continue to colonize far-away planets. Yet most of Dick's creative energy is taken up by the psychological portrayal of his characters and the consequences of social change upon them. Chapter 2 of this book traced the application of psychology to Cold War historiography and politics. Even more so than was the case for the social sciences, Dick's oeuvre moves from an eager appropriation of depth psychology to an increasing skepticism that follows the trajectory of the rise of psychoanalysis and its gradual loss of prestige. In Dick's case, this development is complicated by a fundamental ambivalence.

Dick first came into contact with psychoanalysis as a high school student when his mother sent him to a Jungian therapist in San Francisco, then one of only three American cities with followers of the Swiss psychiatrist.[34] This encounter seems to have induced a mixture of intellectual fascination and emotional dread in the young Dick and would decisively shape his work. Indeed, Jung remained an important reference for him until his death. Dick's ambivalence toward Jung, however personal its motivations might have been originally, soon grew into a subtle awareness of the Janus-faced status of psychoanalysis as disciplinary apparatus and emancipatory self-examination. Dick's is a Jungian world, a world in which police officers boast of their reading of him and his theories are common knowledge. In what follows, I analyze Dick's appropriation of Jung to trace the transfer of psychoanalysis to mid-century America and to highlight an intellectual tradition that has received far less critical attention than that which followed in the footsteps of Freud.[35] Thus, rather than restricting Dick's references to psychiatry in a reading that repeats postwar psychologizations of politics, this section reverses this movement and aims to historicize the psychological.

When discussing Dick's reading of Jung, most critics mention only the most popular aspects of his depth psychology, the concept of archetypes and theory of artistic creation.[36] Yet Jungian thought pervades Dick's fiction at a much more fundamental level. Dick takes from Jung his understanding of schizophrenia and ontology, two dominant concerns of his work. But why was Dick so committed to Jung rather than to a Freudian orthodoxy far more prevalent in the United States? We have seen already how Dick first received psychoanalysis by a Jungian therapist. The answer to this question goes far beyond biographical details, however, and presents us with a fascinating portrait of the American reception of psychoanalysis. Widely popular among artists and writers in the late 1910s and '20s, Jungian psychoanalysis failed to gain an institutional basis comparable to a Freudianism whose ranks were swelled by Jewish emigration. By the late 1940s, besides New York, only San Francisco and Los Angeles had established Jungian centers. The San Francisco Jung Institute, across the bay from Berkeley where Dick grew up, was unique for its strong links to psychiatry and the establishment of a Jungian presence at the University of California's Langley Porter Clinic and at Stanford University.[37] It was at Langley Porter that Dick first received psychotherapy in 1946–47, and later he would also be treated at Stanford's Hoover Pavilion.[38] More than merely a psychological theory, Jungianism became medical practice in California. The San Francisco Institute also contributed to a second wave of popularity for Jung's work in the 1960s, when it organized lectures and workshops for a lay audience.[39] Jung's exclusion from a psychiatric mainstream dominated by Freudian ego psychology and his rediscovery by the counterculture might have added to his appeal for Dick. But the two authors also share a variety of interests. In contrast to Freud, who moved into psychiatry via the study of the neuroses, Jung's point of entry had been schizophrenia, and this remained a personal and professional focus throughout. At its most simple, schizophrenia represents an inversion of libido for Jung, a withdrawal of psychic energy from reality, and investment in an interior world of fantasy and myth.[40] Overwhelmed by unconscious forces, the person's ego splits or fragments: an understanding that shows the influence of Pierre Janet's "dissociation" and Eugen Bleuler's neologism "schizophrenia," literally the splitting of the mind.[41]

These aspects of Jungian schizophrenia—fragmentation and withdrawal— are central to Dick's portrayals of madness. As Jack Bohlen says of the android school teachers in *Martian Time-Slip*: "[Y]ou teaching machines are going to rear another generation of schizophrenics [. . .] You're going to split the psyches of these children."[42] However, it is Jung's understanding of schizophrenic withdrawal that dominates *Martian Time-Slip* (1964). The novel follows Manfred Steiner, age ten, a boy so withdrawn from his surroundings that he has never spoken a word. Manfred's condition is described as autism, "a childhood form of schizophrenia."[43] In his understanding of autism as infantile schizophrenia, Dick follows contemporary understandings of the condition, but Jung also uses the term in *Psychology of the Unconscious*. Once again, Jung takes on a concept coined by Bleuler, from whose writings it found its way to its current usage as autism. The schizophrenic shuns reality and replaces it with his own psychological equivalent, argues Jung. "Therefore, I must grant to Bleuler the right to reject the conception of autoerotism, taken from the study of hysterical neuroses, [. . .] and to replace it by the conception of autismus."[44] The passage is key for an understanding of Jung's thought. As his reference to autoeroticism indicates, he rejects Freud's theory of libido and by implication also his understanding of psychosis.[45] Jung's early work with Bleuler had revealed to him, he thought, evidence of a deeper level of the unconscious, an unconscious that was collective because it had access to an underlying ground of being, or unus mundus.[46] For Jung, Freud's assumption of a sexual libido collapsed when confronted with the psychotic's access to this primordial reality and the construction of dreams and myths arising from it. Here was a form of libidinal investment that went beyond sexuality. As a consequence, autoeroticism, or its later form of narcissism, could not be seen as underlying the psychoses, as Freud had claimed in his essay on Schreber five years earlier.[47] However convincing one may judge the evidence for Jung's collective unconscious to be, it opened up a rich space for Dick's imagination, space that would have remained closed to a Freudian.[48] *In We Can Build You* (1972) this inner world takes its most Jungian form and explanation. Louis Rosen, a small entrepreneur whose company produces androids, falls in love with the beautiful but schizoid Pris and suffers a psychotic breakdown.

First in a hotel room, where he is confronted by his family, and then in a psychiatric clinic, he withdraws into a fantasy of a happier life with Pris. Rosen's illness is consistently explained in Jungian terms. Louis is diagnosed by his psychiatrist with "the Magna Mater type of schizophrenia." He is under control of the archetype of the great mother, who is represented by Pris. As Louis explains to his business partner before checking into the mental hospital: "That's what an attack of schizophrenia is, a weakening of attention so that unconscious processes gain mastery and take over the field. They capture awareness, very archaic processes, archetypal."[49]

Dick also follows Jung in his description of the stages of psychotic breakdown and the general course of mental illness. At one point Pris is described as having been schizoid by the age of ten, obsessive compulsive by thirteen, a full-blown schizophrenic by seventeen. All three mental states are closely connected for Jung. Obsessional neurosis is the closest relative to schizophrenia within the neuroses. Schizoid states, which Jung likens to dissociation, are in their most severe form a symptom of psychosis.[50] Many more examples of Dick's appropriation of Jungian thought could be given, but Jung's decisive contribution to his oeuvre remains his theory of schizophrenia. Jung's belief in the schizophrenic's access to a deeper reality opens up psychosis to the literary imagination in a way Freud's rival conception never did. His epistemological privileging of the schizophrenic, credited with an ability to experience what remains hidden from the sane, exerted a strong fascination on the 1960s counterculture. For Dick, the primordial being of Jung's *unus mundus* came to constitute the core of the ontological questioning that characterizes his later novels, and thus the most famous aspect of his fiction.

Before moving on to a discussion of Dick's Jungian ontology, I first want to consider Dick's satirical critiques of psychoanalysis. The novels in which Dick felt that these disciplines were a worthy target of his wit stem mostly from the late 1950s and early '60s. During these years psychoanalysis enjoyed its greatest reputation in the United States and became part of mainstream society. As part of this institutional rise of psychoanalysis, Freud's sexual emphasis was muted at the same time that the person Sigmund Freud came to stand in for a whole discipline and cultural field. So successful were practitioners in establishing themselves in the postwar years that the terms psychiatrist and psychoanalyst became interchangeable. Dick's early novels reflect this rapid rise but remain ambivalent in their evaluation. In *Confessions of a Crap Artist*, Jack Isidore reflects on his sister's regular trips to a psychoanalyst in San Francisco and notes her husband's reaction to them: "Charley [. . .] took as holy writ whatever she reported. Any man who charged twenty dollars an hour had to be good."[51] This critical distance becomes even clearer in *Time Out of Joint*. After being diagnosed with a reversion to infancy by a neighbor who doubles as an amateur analyst in his spare time, Vic Nielson is unequivocal in his response: "'What rubbish,' Vic said."[52] Such ambivalence easily turns into satire.

In *Eye in the Sky* (1957), Dick ridicules the conservative psychoanalysis of the postwar years. Caught in the private world of a religious fanatic, Jack is confronted with strange insights. One scientist in particular takes critiques of Freud's libido theory to a new level. The founder of psychoanalysis, he remarks to Jack, developed the concept of libido as a sublimation of artistic creativity. Only when this drive fails to find an outlet does it morph into its surrogate form: sexual desire.[53]

These reflections on psychoanalysis moved toward the center of Dick's fiction in the early 1960s. Two novels stand out: *The Simulacra* and *Clans of the Alphane Moon* (both 1964). Always acutely aware of social developments, Dick's ambivalence intensifies to the point where he depicts the fall from grace of psychoanalysis in the rather accurately imagined twenty-first century society of *The Simulacra*: Working in collusion with a sort of celebrity authoritarianism, a German pharmaceutical company has convinced the world of the sole effectiveness of drug therapy for mental illnesses. Psychoanalysis has been declared illegal. As an artificial journalist, a "reporting machine," proclaims: "'Like the practice of bloodletting, psychoanalysis has thrived and then waned and now a new therapy has taken its place."[54] Despite its continued expansion and popularity, psychoanalysis had come under intensified attack in the mid- and late-1950s. Condemning it as unscientific, behaviorists and neurologists began to develop new drug treatments, and many psychoanalysts noticed a decline in the prestige of their profession soon after.[55] It would be too simple to describe Dick as a staunch critic of psychoanalysis, however. *The Simulacra* clearly depicts a dystopian society, and psychoanalysis' loss of prestige could be seen as the result of political oppression. Yet in line with criticism by skeptical psychiatrists, the novel extends its satirical treatment to the point of questioning the efficacy of psychoanalysis. When the last remaining analyst, Dr. Superb, is allowed to see one more patient, he hopes for a change of heart on the part of the powerful. Instead, he is kept in business not to cure a patient, but rather the opposite: "You won't be able to help him; that's exactly why we want you there. If he obtains chemical therapy he'll recover his mental balance. [. . .] we need [. . .] a quack."[56] By the mid-1960s, Dick increasingly directed his critical energy at institutional psychiatry. In *The Three Stigmata of Palmer Eldritch* (1965), Dick's so-called drug novel, it is not a human psychoanalyst who finds himself under attack but a suitcase psychiatrist connected to a central computer, whose purpose it is to make one of the characters mentally ill.[57] This shift may be seen as reflecting the subordination of psychoanalysis to psychiatry, part of a trend in which long-term analysis was replaced by shorter and cheaper interventions, group and drug therapy.[58] Perhaps Dick's replacement of a human therapist by a machine reacts to such atrophy of individual attention, in any case Dick's attacks on psychiatry became increasingly intense.

Clans of the Alphane Moon confronts a group of mental patients living in outer space with a psychiatrist eager to return them to their wards on earth. The novel satirizes Cold War pathologizations of political opponents, which branded competitors within the United States and communist regimes around the world psychotic. Asked, this time by a human reporter, why she doesn't leave the inhabitants of the moon to themselves and respect their culture, psychiatrist Mary Rittersdorf replies: "'What values could mentally ill people develop?'"[59] Quickly, a public relations officer turns the situation around by portraying the mad settlers as dangerous. The colonization of the moon becomes an act of self-defense. Throughout the novel, Dick exposes the self-righteousness of the American invaders, while the threat of confinement transforms the different castes on the Alphane Moon, made up of diagnosed schizophrenics, paranoiacs, maniacs, and hebephrenics, into a functioning society. Reflecting on the moon's successful self-governance, one of Rittersdorf's companions asks her: "How would it differ from our own society on Terra?"[60] The psychiatrist's reply takes the form of a distinction between sanity and madness: the Alphanes are mad, the psychiatrists charged with treating their illness sane. Dick's answer to this dichotomy is to erase it. It is at this point that we enter his antipsychiatric novels.

4.2 From Antipsychiatry to Neuropsychiatry

At first sight, a definition of Dick's writings as antipsychiatric might seem questionable. The major writers associated with antipsychiatry in Europe and the United States do not feature in his work, an absence all the more striking given his intense reading in psychiatry. R. D. Laing seems to have had no impact on Dick, nor did David Cooper, Franco Basaglia, or Thomas S. Szasz, although important and popular books by Laing and Szasz would have been available to him. Neither can Dick be said to follow a looser understanding of madness, sometimes associated with antipsychiatric writings and influential upon a number of its thinkers, that views the schizophrenic as a visionary spirit in a mad society. Such a romantic understanding of madness was adopted by parts of the counterculture and informs Kerouac's portrayal of Dean Moriarty in *On the Road* and Ken Kesey's portrayal of Chief Bromden. Further afield, related conceptions of madness guide Foucault's early work and Deleuze and Guattari's *Anti-Oedipus*.[61] Dick's schizophrenics may possess a certain epistemological privilege that at times allows them to see the future. Yet their ability is rarely of any value to themselves or society. What they see does not confer knowledge, nor do they discover beauty. Instead, they are confronted with decay and horror. Rather than being free, Dick's schizophrenics are caught in desperate isolation. Dick's fiction can then be seen as antipsychiatric in a sense that is at once broader and more precise. This definition forms the core of Foucault's conception of antipsychiatry in his lectures titled *Psychiatric Power*. Foucault's reading of psychiatry as part of larger shifts in practices of power usefully supplements my account of

Dick. As Foucault writes, antipsychiatry can be understood as the denial of and freedom from the absolute right of non-madness over madness.[62]

Having failed in her mission and full of newly found respect for the Alphane Moon's inhabitants, Mary Rittersdorf decides to settle with the clans. When she and her husband Chuck, who has accompanied her, take a psychological test, she is diagnosed with clinical depression. Admitting her own illness breaks down earlier distinctions between her own sanity and the *in*sanity of Alphane's inhabitants. In a final twist, Chuck Rittersdorf, who is classified as sane, founds a new caste community to supplement those already existing on the moon, "the Norm settlement."[63] Sanity takes its place among the mental illnesses. Except that on a world inhabited by the mad, individual normality is the only true madness. "'Nobody'll ever show up and live with you in your settlement,'" says one character to Chuck. "'You'll spend the rest of your life in isolation—six weeks from now you'll be out of your mind; you'll be ready for every other settlement on this moon.'"[64] The false neatness of this solution, the refusal to recognize psychiatry's continuing power, that arguably makes *Clans of the Alphane Moon* a weaker novel than *Martian Time-Slip*. Only one short episode indicates a more forceful alternative. During the confrontation between the invaders and the settlers, Mary Rittersdorf witnesses a hallucination imagined in Jungian terms: "The shape was that of a master lizard and she realized at once what she was witnessing; this was a schizophrenic projection, part of the primordial world experienced by the advanced psychotic [. . .]—except why was *she* seeing it?"[65] Rather than merely denying psychiatry's power over madness in a breakdown of binary distinctions, Dick depicts madness's alternative power. What was once deemed subjective, denied value by objective reason, disables rational explanation.

Such overt erasures of the boundary between sanity and madness are paralleled by the narrative structure and voice of Dick's novels in the early 1960s. Eschewing the single authorial narrator of his early science fiction, *Clans of the Alphane Moon* and *Martian Time-Slip* shift narrative perspective between chapters and six to eight characters of almost equal importance.[66] In a fascinating interview passage, Dick identifies this use of shifting perspectives with the radical heterogeneity of subjective viewpoints, an insight further dramatized, he insists, by the use of schizophrenia.[67] Characters who claim access to an indisputable reality are contradicted by continuous shifts of narrative voice, which expose contradictory perception without offering a privileged viewpoint. Even such an intersubjective reality disintegrates in *Martian Time-Slip*. Dick's novel follows two psychotics, the young boy Manfred and Jack Bohlen. Jack, who suffered from schizophrenia in the past, is hired to help exploit the child's supposed cognitive abilities and remembers his earlier breakdown: "And then the hallucination, if it was that [. . .]. He saw the personnel manager in a new light. The man was dead. He saw, through the man's skin, his skeleton."[68] What torments Bohlen is not so much the vision per se but its ontological status. Was it a hallucination? Or did it reveal something else? Perhaps, he conjectures, the personnel manager was an android. In that case, "[i]nstead of a psychosis, he had thought again and again, it was more on the order of a vision, a glimpse of absolute reality."[69] The novel repeatedly affirms the truthfulness of Jack's perception, which exposes the radically dehumanizing being of Jung's *unus mundus*. Yet *Martian Time-Slip* arguably goes beyond the admission of the psychotic's subjective truth in its remarkable central chapters. Here, narrative voice shifts to Manfred Steiner, whose schizophrenia Dick understands as the consistent exclusion from the symbolic and the continuous corporeal experience of the real. Dick's popular fiction can maintain such an extreme perspective only for brief periods of time, but for its duration it results in the breakdown of narrative time, the disintegration of intersubjective speech, and finally perception itself:

Stop, he said to it.
Gubble, gubble, gubble, gubble, it answered.
Dust fell on him from the walls. The room creaked with age and dust, rotting around him. Gubble, gubble, gubble, the room said. The Gubbler is here to gubble gubble you and make you into gubbish.[70]

These passages exercise madness's power over social reality. More than simply withstanding or disabling rational explanations as in *Clans of the Alphane Moon*, madness dismantles social reality. Arguably, Dick's novel acts as what Foucault describes as a counter-conduct in *Security, Territory, Population*, enacting opposition to psychiatric power. For Foucault, such counter-conducts are signs of broader contradictions in governmentality, in concrete terms the crisis of institutional psychiatry, of which antipsychiatry can be taken as an expression.[71] This does not mean that madness becomes true sanity in these novels. The social isolation of Dick's schizophrenics results in their inability to influence reality, as when the Alphane Moon's self-appointed spiritual guides fail to stem the invasion of their home despite their advance knowledge of the event. Manfred Steiner's access to absolute reality reveals only decay and horror and leads to an existence of unbearable solitude. For all of Dick's insistence on schizophrenia's truth, its terrible visions are opposed to the empathy of human relationships, on which *Martian Time-Slip* ends and from which schizophrenics remain excluded. Dick thus clearly rejects idealizations of madness as liberation.

What Kim Stanley Robinson called Dick's "reality breakdowns" do not appear for the first time in *Martian Time-Slip*.[72] The earliest scene of this kind takes place in *Time Out of Joint*, when a soft-drink stand disappears in front of Ragle Gumm. One afternoon in the park, Ragle walks up to a drink stand and asks for a beer. What happens next must count as one of the most memorable scenes in Dick's fiction. Reality freezes, and the soft-drink stand disintegrates into its constituent molecules until it vanishes, to leave behind nothing more than its signifier printed on a piece of paper.[73]

Unless we assume that Ragle's world suddenly falls apart because he asks for alcohol at a *soft-drink* stand, we need to look for a more comprehensive interpretation. Step by step the novel reveals that Ragle is slowly returning to sanity. That Ragle's delusions would need slips of paper—of which he discovers quite a few early in the novel—as prompts, or that these hallucinations could be maintained by them, seems far-fetched. But what marks an important contrast to later episodes of this kind is that it enacts a progression from psychosis to mental health, not from supposed sanity to madness. The socially accepted grounds of an intersubjective reality hold fast, and the novel's characters accept rationality's power to explain the drink stand's disappearance. The drink stand fades away, but unlike in *Martian Time-Slip*, we are not exposed to the horrors of decay, nor to the transformation of the human into a machine.

The gradual disintegration of intersubjective reality and its replacement by madness in Dick's fiction has been identified as his ontological turn.[74] However, it has escaped critics that this shift can be explained by Dick's conception of madness. As Jack Bohlen's descriptions of his visions as 'absolute reality' show, the later scenes expose Jung's unus mundus, the ultimate ground of being, from which the archetypes and the psychotic's hallucinations derive. The Jungian emphasis upon the privileged experience of the schizophrenic provides the intellectual basis of Dick's ontological questioning. The concrete imagination of this absolute reality in *Martian Time-Slip* also owes to the existential psychologists, the most famous of whom, Ludwig Binswanger, worked with Bleuler and Jung at the Burghölzli clinic in Zurich. In particular, Dick's description of doom and decay stems from the essay collection *Existence: A New Dimension in Psychiatry and Psychology*.[75] Dick's account of Manfred's private universe, his "Tomb World," closely parallels the experience of the schizophrenic patient Ellen West in Binswanger's case study in *Existence*. Binswanger describes this world as dull, dark, and without any signs of life.[76] Dick's characters are first and foremost social beings. Sanity therefore means the integration into the symbolic, the social and linguistic fabric of society. Mental illness, by logical extension, follows from the exclusion from symbolic reality. As Dick writes of Manfred: "The reality which the schizophrenic fell away from—or never incorporated in the first place—was the reality of interpersonal living."[77]

The critic Darko Suvin influentially divided Dick's then still incomplete oeuvre into three distinctive stages: his apprentice work from 1952 to 1962, the increasingly complex "character systems" of his novels of the mid-1960s, and the ontological shift fully implemented with *Ubik* (1969).[78] Suvin traces what he sees as a decline from politics to ontology—and from an earlier multi-vocal narrative to the "solitary anxieties" of the later work—to a breakdown in Dick's humanist ethics.[79] It seems more fruitful to return to the distinction made here between Dick's earlier and later reality breakdowns. What changes from *Time Out of Joint* to *Martian*

Time-Slip is that the narrative in the latter work depicts a progression from mental health to schizophrenia rather than moving from madness to sanity. Dick's increasingly frantic efforts to provide an explanation for the reality breakdowns that became an increasing feature of his fiction and private life are taken to their highest pitch in *Palmer Eldritch*. Its eponymous villain conjures the novel's irruptions of a drug-induced real into terrifying images, but cannot banish their power. The attempts at providing a narrative solution for what erupts but cannot be narrativized finally fail in the face of *Ubik*: the abstract logic of capital, which constantly tears apart and reconfigures human reality, cannot not be deciphered, cannot be integrated, into conspiracy thinking.

As I wrote at the beginning of this chapter, a perceived loss of personal agency and the attempt to slow or even reverse the subject's fragmentation should be seen as central to Dick's fiction. It is with regard to such a disintegrating subjectivity that Dick, so often understood as a highly idiosyncratic science fiction writer, brings something *within* the genre to its logical conclusion. Dick shares this anxiety, one could argue, with science fiction as such. A popular genre whose classical form had its heyday in the 1930s to '50s during the establishment of Fordism and the hegemony of large monopolies, science fiction is characterized by a certain disbelief in the necessity of individual subjectivity. The logical conclusion that science fiction could do without the individual, without the protagonist, haunts Dick's oeuvre. Why should this trouble Dick? The first reason is Dick's complex libertarianism, but his personal convictions intersect interestingly with the politics of the genre. A novel without a protagonist to advance the narrative and reflect on it, if it were a novel at all, would likely fail as science fiction—a genre from which most readers expect identifiable heroes and plots. With the exception of *VALIS*, perhaps, Dick's novels deliver both. But his protagonists are usually as powerless as they are passive and depressed, white collar workers who feel past their prime and lament their domination by stronger women.

This contradiction between the individual's troubled agency and its generic and political desirability finds various expressions in Dick's work and greatly influences its overall development. One indicator of the protagonist's diminished ability to advance Dick's narratives is their combination of breakneck-speed plots and literary landscapes jammed with science fiction tropes—his novels are not robot, telepathy, or post-Holocaust fictions but all of these wrapped in one, with a few spaceships thrown in for good measure. Understood as a generic device rather than an individual idiosyncrasy, these agglomerations of robots and spaceships function as fillers in the sense that they add weight and time to the narrative. The convoluted, high-speed plots draw on another popular genre frequently raided by science fiction, namely detective novels, to produce their narrative momentum. In the first instance, however, this diminished individuality is propped up by the paranoid logic of Dick's conspiracy theories, which dominate his novels of the 1950s. How central this structure is for Dick's fiction can be seen from the fact that despite the many revolutions that take place in his novels, state power—with the exception of *Dr. Bloodmoney*—remains in place.[80] What promised a different future turns out to have been merely a change of faces because Dick's protagonists depend on the productive power of the state for their agency. Its all-perceiving eye sustains the protagonists that seek to destroy it.

Following a tradition I traced in chapter 2, Dick maintains no clear distinction between conspiracy theory and paranoia.[81] When Charles McFeyffe, the security officer in *Eye in the Sky*, accuses the character Marsha Hamilton of being a socialist, her husband Jack responds with a psychiatric diagnosis: " 'You're sick,' he said to McFeyffe, [. . .] 'You're destroying innocent people. Paranoiac delusions.' "[82] In *Time Out of Joint*, Ragle instantly identifies his own attempts to understand the conspiracy that envelops him as pathological: "I'm a retarded—psychotic. Hallucinations. [. . .] Daydreams, at best. Fantasies about rocket ships shooting by overhead, armies and conspiracies. Paranoia. A paranoiac psychosis."[83] Dick's acceptance of a Cold War psychology that built on elements of Freudian psychoanalysis to equate conspiracy narratives with mental derangement is illustrated in his rare discussions of the term paranoia. "For us there can be no system," he writes in "The Android and the Human": "maybe all systems [. . .] are manifestations of paranoia."[84] Paranoiacs, as Dick says in an earlier text, are " 'rational' psychotics"—and Dick's perspective on paranoia varies with his valuation of a rationality characteristically placed here in inverted commas.[85] Where this rationality is understood as totalizing, Dick will view paranoia as dangerous, in line with postwar denunciations of social planning. In the *Clans of the Alphane Moon*, Mary Rittersdorf's quest to diagnose the inhabitants of the moon has her visit its caste of paranoiacs, or "paranoiac schizophrenics":[86]

> [W]ith the acute paranoid a systemized and permanent hostility could be anticipated [. . .] The paranoid possessed an analytical, calculating quality; he had a good reason for his actions, [. . .], cure or even temporary insight was virtually impossible. Like the hebephrenic, the paranoid had found a stable and permanent maladaptation. [. . .] the paranoid seemed rational. The formal pattern of logical reasoning appeared undisturbed. Underneath, however, the paranoid suffered from the greatest mental disfigurement possible for a human being. He was incapable of empathy, unable to imagine himself in another person's role.[87]

All elements of Dick's earlier definition of the conspiracy theorist as paranoid are present, corresponding to dominant Cold War sentiment: his or her pseudo-rationality, the totalizing, rigid quality of the conspiracy theorist's thought, and finally, the unique threat emanating from his rationalizing pathology. But, of course, *Clans of the Alphane Moon* is an antipsychiatric satire, and Rittersdorf will soon be exposed as no more sane than the former mental patients she wants to lock up.[88] The inhabitants of the Alphane Moon, mistrustful of their visitor's motives, only escape their renewed incarceration thanks to their paranoia.

Dick's conception of conspiracy theory suffers from a certain irresolution that follows suit from its equation with paranoia. Unless all conspiratorial narratives, political or other, are seen as spurious, their outright pathologization is out of the question. In turn, identifying conspiracy theory with an understanding of paranoia that foregrounds its rigidity and boundless systematizing, makes a wholesale endorsement equally impossible. "We are faced with the clear and evident possibility," Dick notes, "that at least in the case of paranoids—or, anyhow, some paranoids—the 'delusions' are not delusions at all, but [. . .] accurate perceptions of an area of reality that the rest of us cannot [. . .] reach."[89] As an author, Dick is not alone in his uncertainty. Thomas Pynchon's *Gravity's Rainbow* (1973) similarly moves between contradictory positions. Pynchon's continuous classification of different forms of paranoia, from operational to drug-induced, from proverbs for paranoids to creative paranoia, for all its variation equally falls into seeing paranoia as either true, or the expression of a mad rationality. What is revealing is how rarely Dick or Pynchon feel the need to define or discuss what is after all a psychiatric term. Dick, in the few instances where he reflects on paranoia, never refers to psychiatric or psychoanalytic sources, a constant feature of his writings on schizophrenia. Much more so than schizophrenia, the term paranoia and its identification with conspiracy had become common sense by the time Dick and Pynchon wrote their fiction. Although these authors appropriate the term for their self-understanding, the countercultural embrace of conspiracy as a political and epistemological tool never sheds its threatening pathology.

In his left-wing appreciation of Dick's early novels, Suvin famously lauded the political quality of their conspiracy theories.[90] Instead, Dick's conspiracy narratives should be read as deeply ambivalent, or as what Foucault describes as the liberal "fantasy of the paranoiac and devouring state."[91] While this pervasive distrust of the state spread far beyond liberals in postwar America, Foucault is surely right to emphasize its results. In its manifestation as liberal ideology, the fantasy of the devouring state participates in the radical extension of market logic that we know as American neoliberalism. Here we can detect the source of the final major development of Dick's fiction. This phase of Dick's final novels, from *A Scanner Darkly* to *The Transmigration of Timothy Archer* (1982), coincides with a last attempt to counteract the perceived fragmentation of the subject. In the earlier novels, the diminished status of the individual protagonist had been deflected by generic borrowing, or the experience of his disintegrating agency halted in conspiracy narratives. The decisive step is taken when Dick transforms the logic of this disintegration into the dynamic of his fiction.

The most pertinent change for our purposes concerns Dick's growing interest in neurology. The 1970s were a period of retrenchment for psychoanalysis in the United States.[92] The ties between Freudianism and psychiatry were severed, and drug therapies based on new neurological insights became standard treatment, an ascent that continues with genetic research until today. *A Scanner Darkly* contains all the ingredients of a typical Dick novel: conspiracy theories and political oppression, drugs and madness, a hapless protagonist, and his miserable love-life. It is how these ingredients are reinterpreted and combined that makes it so informative. From early on in the text, psychosis is understood as brain damage. "Receptor-sites" and "speech-center damage," the "occipital lobe," and "Neural-Aphasia Clinics" have replaced the hallucinating madmen of the 1960s.[93] Gone are the days when psychosis was madness, a state of mind rather than a deterioration of the brain. "Sometimes I wish I knew how to go crazy. I forget how," says Bob Arctor, the novel's protagonist. "It's a lost art," replies his boss.[94] Instead, *A Scanner Darkly* quotes psychiatric literature on brain damage, and the novel's psychiatrists perform numerous tests on Arctor.[95] *A Scanner Darkly* features the most sustained discussion of neurology in Dick's fiction, but a similar picture emerges in other late novels. Three years earlier, *Flow, My Tears, the Policeman Said* had explained the creation of two parallel realities with reference to brain toxicity affecting one of its characters. This novel, which shares with *A Scanner Darkly* the setting in a dystopian California, also suggests the source of Dick's departure from countercultural understandings of madness. Where *Flow, My Tears* directs its critique at Nixon's repressive politics and features a subplot of radical students hiding beneath burnt-out campuses, *A Scanner Darkly* represents Dick's turn against the Sixties. Political radicalism and alternative lifestyles have deteriorated into mortal drug addiction. This change of perspective was epitomized by a letter written to the Department of Justice in February 1973, in which Dick proposed to dedicate the novel to Richard Kleindienst, attorney general under Nixon.[96]

Dick's appropriations of psychopathology had given form to a perceived dismantling of individual subjectivity. With conspiracy theories receding into the background, the new reliance on neurology comes to shape the structure of *A Scanner Darkly*. Reinforcing earlier conceptions of schizophrenia as splitting, the novel literalizes research on brain dissociation in the disintegration of Arctor's consciousness, his breakdown into the two personae of Bob and Fred. This process is all the more remarkable given the novel's premise. *A Scanner Darkly* tells the story of Bob Arctor, alias Fred, a drug-addicted Californian hippie hired by the police to spy on his friends. What marks the novel as science fiction is the so-called "scramble suit," consisting of a thin membrane that visualizes the features of random persons and protects Fred's identity from his police superiors. In the course of the novel, Bob becomes the main suspect and Fred, Arctor's police persona, begins non-stop surveillance of himself. At first sight, this hyperbolic instance of surveillance would seem to replicate earlier themes of power in Dick, in which the identity of the protagonist is upheld by the state. Yet Arctor, the hippie drop-out, is given a second identity as a collaborator spying on his friends and his own alter ego for a morally questionable state apparatus.

This rarely mentioned dilemma forms the ethical core of *A Scanner Darkly*. The novel dramatizes the conflict faced by Dick in his rejection of the counterculture and support for what Nixon in 1969 termed a 'war on drugs.' Arctor's final descent into irreversible brain damage commemorates the inevitable failure of an autonomous countercultural subject and interrogates Dick's short-lived allegiance to a repressive state. That the novel ends on a decidedly less ambivalent note adds another political dimension. In the final scene, Arctor finds the organic source of the novel's fictitious drug—the so-called war on drugs, Dick implies, can be won. If Dick's antipsychiatric fiction had indicated a larger crisis in governmentality, then the neurological paradigm of his late novels participates in its renewal: the language and practice of brain research, of pharmaceuticals, and genetics, comes to the rescue of establishment psychiatry in the 1970s and beyond. Foucault famously termed this new form of governmentality bio-power, and it is remarkable how *A Scanner Darkly* not only performs the failure of surveillance and discipline on their own terms but introduces a new language of profits, of distribution costs, and calculation into Dick's work.[97] Rather than standing at the center of disciplinary controls, we learn toward the end of the book that Arctor and his circle of friends merely functioned as expendable instruments in wider considerations aimed at a heavily drug-using American population. Here is a form of power that no longer concentrates solely on disciplining the individual subject, as Foucault writes, but that excels in the management of populations. In this, his darkest novel, Dick's original anxiety finds its confirmation.

4.3 A Healing Light: Madness beyond Pathology

Dick's last major novel, published as *VALIS* a year before his death in 1982, seemed to confirm his turn against the counterculture. Early in the book, its protagonist Horselover Fat is admitted to an Orange County mental hospital and the scenes that ensue constitute the most detailed description of a psychiatric institution in Dick's fiction. Yet, where Dick had earlier excelled at antipsychiatric satire, such impetus is conspicuously absent from *VALIS*. Instead, the novel is at pains to distance itself from countercultural critiques of psychiatry. In an implicit reference to Kesey's *One Flew Over the Cuckoo's Nest*, Dick disputes the portrait of neglect and abuse painted by "mythic novels" and commends the hospital for its excellent care. A similar picture emerges in relation to drugs, continuing the reevaluation begun in *A Scanner Darkly*. "By now the epoch of drug-taking had ended," the narrator opines.[98]

By the mid-1970s, the circumstances of Dick's life had changed drastically. Settling in suburban Southern California he stepped back from a Sixties communal lifestyle edging ever closer to mental and physical breakdown. Only in his mid-forties, Dick was beset by chronic health problems and led a life that was reclusive but seemingly stable, sharing a household with his fifth wife Tessa and his young son Christopher. Then, in February and March of 1974, Dick underwent a series of visions or hallucinations: a sudden flash of pink light transmitting information, night-long series of psychedelic images, suburban California fading to expose ancient Rome underneath, cryptic messages from a voice Dick described as artificial intelligence.

VALIS, a narrative quest for metaphysical certainty, presented a clear break, if not with Dick's fiction, then at least with its reputation. In the novel's thinly veiled account of Dick's mystical experiences, theology supplanted countercultural politics, a narratological hall of mirrors skewed genre fiction beyond recognition. Dismissed or simply ignored by a first generation of Dick scholars, more recently critics have taken *VALIS* as a basis to hail him as a Christian author.[99] The novel provides grounds for neither, and the posthumous publication of *The Exegesis of Philip K. Dick*—a constant reference in *VALIS* and the source of its philosophical reflections—complicates matters further. At 900 pages, the excerpts collected in the volume are disproportionately longer than anything Dick published in his lifetime; yet the complete diary entries, typed and handwritten between 1974 and 1982, run to over 8,000 pages.[100] Previously, only a much shorter edition without any claim to represent Dick's thought over such a sustained period, was available to his readers.

Dick's theological references are highly pluralistic in the *Exegesis*, adding apocryphic and New Age Christianity to Biblical sources and the Gnostic tradition, dabbling in Buddhism, Taoism, and Hinduism, and taking in Greek and German philosophy to construct an idiosyncratic metaphysical system. Nevertheless, Dick's spirituality is very much of his time: as Erik Davis argues, Dick is representative of the countercultural seekers that were so numerous in the American, and particularly Californian, 1960s and '70s.[101] Thus, Dick's onto-theology might be described as post-Christian: a counterculture shading ever more into New Age spirituality, a religious self-discovery that circles around but never remains tied to Christianity. Something similar can be said about Dick's relation to psychiatry across these pages: Jungian psychoanalysis remains a mainstay, the existential psychiatrists make an appearance, and Dick picks up on neuropsychiatry and Abraham Maslow's human potential movement. Jung, above all, forms the basis of repeated attempts at self-diagnosis—the lifelong habit of an author who was as versed in medical jargon as his therapists. In the course of the *Exegesis*, Dick explains his visions as a total collapse of his ego and a return to the collective unconscious, then describes himself as suffering from "[s]chizophrenia with religious and paranoid coloring—of the ecstatic type," or as completely cured.[102] So far, so familiar. What emerges most forcefully from the *Exegesis*, however, is what I am tempted to describe by the same prefix as Dick's religiosity. If his theology is post-Christian, then the medical terminology is post-psychoanalytic. No one therapeutic ideology dominates the *Exegesis*. As for the authority figure of the healer or analyst, he is increasingly replaced by the ideology of self-help that flourished in the 1970s. Dick's movement toward alternative religion and self-help highlight a steady mutation of the wider counterculture, its increasing de-politicization and gradual integration into a society whose liberal pluralism it helped create.

The term exegesis commonly refers to the clarification of a holy text. Dick's starting point, however, is his own mystical experiences. It is in seeking to understand them that his fiction (particularly the novels *Ubik*, *The Three Stigmata*, *A Scanner Darkly*, and *VALIS*), as well as dreams, messages from the AI voice, and his continuing hallucinations are accorded the status of scripture. The *Exegesis* thus becomes a sustained exercise in interpretation. Yet an overdue emphasis on this aspect runs the risk of seriously misrepresenting the importance of the *Exegesis* to its author and to an understanding of Cold War madness. Faced with the heavily repetitive nature of the *Exegesis*, in constant orbit around the experiences Dick referred to by the shorthand "2–3–74," one cannot help but notice that its primary function is pragmatic. "[I]t is a way of preserving the memory of it all, this endless rehashing; that is the real point, to keep the memory—which is so cherished—alive."[103] Dick's entries, often several of them a day covering multiple pages, reinvoke and tame the unfathomable, integrate the inexplicable into symbolic frameworks to hold off further psychotic breakdowns. Graphomania undoubtedly plays a role in all of this, but the enjoyment its author gains in the writing of the *Exegesis* seems equally palpable.

Dick's madness is everything but unrelated to the pragmatic aspect of the *Exegesis*. In a letter to his editor at Harcourt Brace, Eleanor Dimoff, Dick wrote as early as 1960: "I believe that my weakness is that I am too much in the hands of my material. It is too real to me. Too convincing. Not 'fictitious' enough."[104] Dick's life and writing had long veered toward the edges of what could be rationally understood and represented. At times his fiction brilliantly captured, at times it visibly struggled with, what was "too real"—the disappearance of the soft-drink stand in *Time Out of Joint* comes to mind. Neither was Dick's perception of a pink information beam in February 1974 his first hallucination. What Dick seems to have experienced is the signifier as *real*, information whose existence he cannot doubt but whose meaning appears ineffable. Given the elusiveness of meaning, Dick focuses much of his energy on what information *does*, and the *Exegesis* becomes a practical exercise in what writing *can do*. The relative success of this undertaking also marks the distance between Dick's earlier and later hallucinations. As he writes: "My 3–74 experiences are an outgrowth of my Palmer Eldritch experience [. . .] I knew him to be real [. . .] but only in *Ubik* does he begin to appear as benign."[105] At times, Dick gives voice to his terror and anguish in the face of his extraordinary experiences, but the overall picture is one of joy and scholarly absorption in his task.

The *Exegesis* constitutes Dick's final wrestle with the fate of the autonomous subject—what he terms "the prison [. . .] of the atomized individual."[106] Liberation means the integration into larger networks, an imagination for which Dick variously appropriates technological, biological, and theological language to assert that the "individual is not an individual."[107] This is neither a smooth process, nor does it lead to an identifiable body of theory but the practice of writing provides Dick with an escape route from disintegration. The particular achievement of the *Exegesis* may be gauged best by returning to the vocabulary of madness, which he made his own like no other American writer of his time. The remarkable parallels with one of psychiatry's most famous patients can serve as a reference: like Daniel Paul Schreber, the Prussian judge whose account of his illness inspired Freud's theory of schizophrenia, Dick pictures himself as "a womb for the divine," a penetration with sacred information that brings forth a new savior.[108] Like Schreber, Dick cannot question the reality of his visions but doubts everyday reality as ancient Rome replaces Orange County. In contrast to Schreber, Dick experiences his reproductive role as a form of enlightenment. Nor does he seem to be disturbed by his strange femininity. These textbook examples of schizophrenic withdrawal and megalomania give way to something less defined and more contemporary—a subject that does not depend on conventional morality and social authority.

Writing at the historical juncture of the late 1970s, as the political force of the Sixties is blunted but its cultural transformations take hold, Dick imagines the rise of a novel humanity. This "new historical type" is defined by an "inner truth," a rejection of law for what he calls a "godly anarchy." That these thoughts of an egalitarian network, "a positive decentralization of power and authority," never stabilize may reflect the fragility of Dick's psyche as much as it indicates a gradual transition in dominant forms of subjectivity, which I discuss as a shift toward ordinary psychosis in the next chapter.[109] In the absence of a safe harbor, Dick navigates the time and space of his final years day by day. In the labor and joy of writing, the *Exegesis* itself becomes a healing practice, an always temporary cure. Dick's final journey leads him beyond a self forever on the edge of fragmentation. Despite his interest in neuropsychiatry late in life, the *Exegesis* pushes him toward imagining madness without pathology. His vision of an post-individualist subject rejects autonomy for community, hierarchy for egalitarianism, and a violent masculinity for a generous passivity.

These reflections occur at a time of rapid change for psychiatry. The radical alternatives that characterized the Sixties fade but influence a new generation of popular self-help, while depth psychology is replaced by a resurgent biological science within medical institutions but lives on in urban enclaves and as intellectual endeavor. These years also witness fundamental changes in diagnosis, in part formalized with DMS-III. New diagnoses allow for new narratives of the self, and in turn react to emerging conceptions of madness and mental illness. One particular addition to psychiatric nosology seems crucial in this context, offering a variation on Dick's new age perspective on psychosis. Post-traumatic stress disorder (PTSD) reformulated earlier diagnoses such as shell shock and battle fatigue, and entered the spotlight with the return of US soldiers from Indochina.

Marmon Silko's *Ceremony* follows a former World War II soldier of mixed Pueblo and Mexican heritage but was read, not without reason, as engaging with the plight of Vietnam veterans upon its publication in 1977. Released from a psychiatric hospital in Los Angeles, Tayo returns to his village in New Mexico. Recurring hallucinations of his dead cousin and the horrors of combat continue to plague him. Tayo's illness is physical, psychological, and metaphysical all at once—never separate from but in aching relation with the fate of Native Americans on the reservation. His nausea reacts to the self-destruction of his fellow veterans, and Tayo remains as torn with guilt as the Laguna Pueblo are riven with poverty, racism, and generational conflict. What holds true for his illness, Tayo realizes, also extends to any attempt at healing. "His sickness was only part [126] of something larger, and his cure would be found only in something great and inclusive of everything."[110] The ceremony Tayo undergoes with the help of the medicine man Betonie imagines his own reconciliation with Pueblo culture, and his people's with their fate under Western civilization. All of them come together at the uranium mine situated on the reservation: the source of nuclear testing observed by his grandmother, the nuclear bombs dropped on the Japanese men and women whose screams echo in Tayo's memory, and the military threat establishing a fragile Cold War equilibrium. What brings about their convergence and returns the protagonist to sanity appears indistinguishable from madness: the meaning-making of a paranoia that has no end and "knew no boundaries."[111] Such reasoning may upturn cause and effect, past and present. Yet what others call delusion assures a meaningful existence for a protagonist for whom "the world had come undone."[112] *Ceremony*, in particular, and America's counterculture in general, derive their strength from the conviction that the latter may trump the former. As Silko writes of her protagonist as he returns, a second time and now truly, to his community and the land of his ancestors: "He was not crazy; he had never been crazy. He had only seen and heard the world as it always was: no boundaries, only transitions through all distances and time."[113] The next chapter explores in detail the delusions and truth of such a paranoid reason.

Notes

1　Paul Williams, "The True Stories of Philip K. Dick," *Rolling Stone*, November 6, 1975, 44–50 and 88–94.
2　Fredric Jameson, "Philip K. Dick, In Memoriam," in *Archaeologies of the Future: The Desire Called Utopia and Other Science Fictions* (London: Verso, 2005), 347.
3　Nathan G. Hale, Jr., *The Rise and Crisis of Psychoanalysis in the United States: Freud and the Americans, 1917–1985* (New York: Oxford University Press, 1995).

4 Philip K. Dick, *The Exegesis of Philip K. Dick*, ed. Pamela Jackson and Jonathan Lethem (Boston: Houghton Mifflin Harcourt 2011), 835.

5 Michael Davidson, *The San Francisco Renaissance: Poetics and Community at Mid-Century* (Cambridge: Cambridge University Press, 1989), 125. While Davidson does not mention Dick, Ekbert Faas's biography of the young Duncan wrongly identifies him as a poet: "With such young poet celebrities as Jack Spicer, Philip K. Dick and George Haimsohn living at 2208 McKinley Street, the rooming house had become a focus of literary activity even before Duncan's arrival." Faas also mentions an improvised poetry session, recorded at the house with Dick's help. Ekbert Faas, *Young Robert Duncan: Portrait of the Poet as Homosexual in Society* (Santa Barbara, CA: Black Sparrow Press, 1983), 252–253. Rickman's *To the High Castle* devotes most space to Dick's relation to the San Francisco Renaissance. Gregg Rickman, *To the High Castle: Philip K. Dick: A Life, 1928–1962* (Long Beach, CA: Fragments West/Valentine, 1989), 169–185.

6 Lawrence Sutin, *Divine Invasions: A Life of Philip K. Dick* (London: Harper Collins, 1994), 57, 62, and 92–93. Rickman also quotes Kleo Mini, Dick's second wife, as saying of his acquaintance with Duncan and Spicer "that it helped to validate an artistic vocation for Philip." Rickman, *To the High Castle*, 177.

7 Philip K. Dick, " 'Headnote' for 'Beyond Lies the Wub,' " in *The Shifting Realities of Philip K. Dick: Selected Literary and Philosophical Writings*, ed. Lawrence Sutin (New York: Pantheon, 1995), 106.

8 Sutin, *Divine Invasions*, 98, 101, and 200; and Davidson, *The San Francisco Renaissance*, 60.

9 Jack Kerouac, *On the Road* (London: Penguin, 2000), 133.

10 Ibid., 280.

11 Allen Ginsberg, "Howl," in *Howl and other Poems* (San Francisco: City Lights, 1956), 9.

12 Allen Ginsberg, "Kaddish," in *Collected Poems, 1947–1997* (New York: Harper, 2006), 220.

13 Ibid., 217.

14 Ginsberg, "Howl," 21–22.

15 Ibid., 22.

16 Tom Wolfe gives an account of Kesey's introduction to LSD in: Tom Wolfe, *The Electric Kool-Aid Acid Test* (New York: Picador, 1968).

17 Erika Dyck, *Psychedelic Psychiatry: LSD from Clinic to Campus* (Baltimore: Johns Hopkins University Press, 2008), 5.

18 Wolfe, *The Electric Kool-Aid Acid Test*, 87.

19 William Burroughs, *Naked Lunch: The Restored Text*, ed. James Grauerholz and Barry Miles (London: Harper, 2005), 8.

20 Dick's scenario shows interesting parallels with Norbert Wiener's work on the guidance and control of anti-aircraft fire during World War II. As Lily Kay has argued, this work established the foundation for Wiener's later development of cybernetics and, in its definition of weapon systems as assemblages of human and machine parts, also of the cyborg. Lily E. Kay, "Cybernetics, Information, Life: The Emergence of Scriptural Representations of Heredity," *Configurations* 5, no. 1 (1997): 23–91.

21 Diana Trilling, "The Other Night at Columbia: A Report from the Academy," *Partisan Review* XXVI (1959): 220.

22 Tom Hayden, *The Port Huron Statement: The Visionary Call of the 1960s Revolution* (New York: Thunder's Mouth, 2005), 79.

23 Theodore Roszak, *The Making of a Counter Culture: Reflections on the Technocratic Society and its Youthful Opposition* (London: Faber, 1970), 42

24 Cited in James T. Patterson, *Grand Expectations: The United States, 1945–1974* (New York: Oxford University Press, 1996), 562.

25 Roszak, *The Making of a Counter Culture*, xiii.
26 Ibid., xiv, and 49; and Lewis Mumford, *The Transformations of Man* (New York: Collier, 1978), 122.
27 Roszak, *The Making of a Counter Culture*, 99.
28 Ibid., 49.
29 Kerouac, *On the Road*, 280.
30 Philip K. Dick, "The Android and the Human," in *Shifting Realities*, 191.
31 Philip K. Dick, *A Scanner Darkly* (London: Gollancz, 1999), 209.
32 Davidson, *The San Francisco Renaissance*, xi–xii.
33 Brian Attebery, "The Magazine Era: 1926–1960," in *The Cambridge Companion to Science Fiction*, ed. Edward James and Farah Mendelsohn (Cambridge: Cambridge University Press, 2003), 39.
34 Sutin, *Divine Invasions*, 49–50; and Thomas B. Kirsch, *The Jungians: A Comparative and Historical Perspective* (London: Routledge, 2000), 58.
35 If I begin my discussion of psychopathology in Dick with Jung, I nonetheless steer clear of a strategy that has hampered existing studies on the topic. Dick's fiction is filled to the brim with literally hundreds of implicit and explicit references to psychiatric authors and texts, the sheer number of which makes it almost impossible to follow up. This means it's all the less desirable to identify a limited number of texts read by Dick and interpret his work through them.
36 See, for instance: Christian Strowa, *Things Don't Like Me: Paranoia, McCarthyism and Colonialism in the Novels of Philip K. Dick* (Trier: Wissenschaftlicher Verlag Trier, 2008), 10; Patricia S. Warrick, *Mind in Motion: The Fiction of Philip K. Dick* (Carbondale, IL: Southern Illinois University Press, 1987), 34 and 99; Anthony Wolk, "The Swiss Connection: Psychological Systems in the Novels of Philip K. Dick," in *Philip K. Dick: Contemporary Critical Interpretations*, ed. Samuel J. Umland (Westport, CT: Greenwood, 1995), 120.
37 Hale, *The Rise and Crisis of Psychoanalysis in the United States*, 62; and Kirsch, *The Jungians*, 58, 62–64, and 122.
38 Sutin, *Divine Invasions*, 49; and Williams, "The True Stories of Philip K. Dick," 46.
39 Kirsch, *The Jungians*, 82.
40 Anthony Stevens, *Jung: A Very Short Introduction* (Oxford: Oxford University Press, 2001), 18.
41 Anthony Storr, introduction to *The Essential Jung*, by Carl Jung, ed. Anthony Storr (London: Fontana, 1986), 14; and C. G. Jung, "Recent Thoughts on Schizophrenia," in *Collected Works*, vol. 3, trans. F. C. Hull (London: Routledge, 1960), 251.
42 Philip K. Dick, *Martian Time-Slip* (London: Gollancz, 2007), 89. Not surprisingly given this view of education, the novel speaks of a dramatic rise in cases of schizophrenia, an epidemic affecting one in six people—literally a malady of its time. Ibid., 88–89.
43 Ibid., 76.
44 C. G. Jung, *Psychology of the Unconscious: A Study of the Transformations and Symbolisms of the Libido. A Contribution to the History of the Evolution of Thought*, trans. Beatrice M. Hinkle (London: Kegan Paul, 1922), 84. The German term "Autismus" is left untranslated in Hinkle's English version.
45 Ibid.
46 For a definition see Stevens, *Jung: A Very Short Introduction*, 57.
47 Jung, *Psychology of the Unconscious*, 84; and Sigmund Freud, "Psycho-Analytical Notes on an Autobiographical Account of a Case of Paranoia (Dementia Paranoides)," in *The Standard Edition of the Complete*

Psychological Works of Sigmund Freud, vol. 12, trans. James Strachey (London: Hogarth, 1958), 62.

48 In an interview, Dick explained his preference for Jung over Freud: "Freud would say the unconscious is just a repository of nasty thoughts we don't want to face; and Jung says no, the unconscious is extremely positive and powerful and very often correct, and compensatory to the conscious." Rickman, *To the High Castle*, 203.

49 Philip K. Dick, *We Can Build You* (London: Harper Collins, 1997), 231.

50 Jung, *The Essential Jung*, 43; and C.G. Jung, "The Meaning of Psychology for Modern Man," in *Collected Works*, vol. 10, 139.

51 Philip K. Dick, *Confessions of a Crap Artist* (London: Gollancz, 2005), 77.

52 Philip K. Dick, *Time Out of Joint* (London: Gollancz, 2003), 23.

53 Philip K. Dick, *Eye in the Sky* (London: Gollancz, 2003), 125.

54 Philip K. Dick, *The Simulacra* (New York: Vintage, 2002), 6–7.

55 Hale, *The Rise and Crisis of Psychoanalysis in the United States*, 301 and 331.

56 Dick, *The Simulacra*, 12.

57 Philip K. Dick, *The Three Stigmata of Palmer Eldritch* (London: Gollancz, 2003), 3–6

58 Hale, *The Rise and Crisis of Psychoanalysis in the United States*, 339.

59 Philip K. Dick, *Clans of the Alphane Moon* (London: Harper, 2008), 33.

60 Ibid., 79.

61 See chapter 6 for a discussion of their respective positions.

62 Michel Foucault, *Psychiatric Power: Lectures at the Collège de France, 1973–1974*, ed. Jacques Lagrange, trans. Graham Burchell (New York: Picador, 2008), 345.

63 Dick, *Clans of the Alphane Moon*, 199.

64 Ibid., 199–200.

65 Ibid., 166. Italics in the original.

66 What Fredric Jameson called Dick's "character systems": Fredric Jameson, "After Armageddon: Character Systems in *Dr Bloodmoney*," in *On Philip K. Dick: 40 Articles from Science-Fiction Studies*, ed. R.D. Mullen, Arthur B. Evans, Veronica Hollinger, and Istvan Csicsery-Ronay, Jr. (Terre Haute, IN: SF-TH, 1992), 26–36.

67 Rickman, *To the High Castle*, 205–207.

68 Dick, *Martian Time-Slip*, 83.

69 Ibid., 84.

70 Ibid., 171–172.

71 Michel Foucault, *Security, Territory, Population: Lectures at the Collège de France, 1977–1978*, ed. Michel Senellart, trans. Graham Burchell (New York: Picador, 2009), 356 and 389. One reaction to this crisis in the United States was Kennedy's 1963 Community Mental Health Act, supported by fiscal conservatives eager to save money, which led to a drastic drop in hospitalized psychiatric patients. It is interesting to observe that in *Martian Time-Slip*, published in 1964 but written two years earlier, Manfred Steiner stays in a psychiatric institution, while *Clans of the Alphane Moon*, written in the year the Mental Health Act was passed, revolves around psychiatric patients freed from confinement. For a short account of the consequences of Kennedy's bill, see: Hale, *The Rise and Crisis of Psychoanalysis in the United States*, 337–338.

72 Kim Stanley Robinson, *The Novels of Philip K. Dick* (Ann Arbor, MI: UMI Research Press, 1984), 21.

73 Dick, *Time Out of Joint*, 40–41.

74 For the original statement of this thesis see: Darko Suvin, "The Opus: Artifice as Refuge and World View (Introductory Reflections)," in *On Philip K. Dick*, 2–15.

75 As Rollo May writes in his contribution to the volume: "The distinctive character of existential analysis is, thus, that it is concerned with *ontology*, the science of being." Rollo May, "Contributions of Existential Psychotherapy," in *Existence: A New Dimension in Psychiatry and Psychology*, ed. Rollo May, Ernest Angel, and Henry F. Ellenberger (New York: Basic, 1958), 37.

76 Dick, *Martian Time-Slip*, 175; and Ludwig Binswanger, "The Case of Ellen West: An Anthropological-Clinical Study," trans. Werner M. Mendel and Joseph Lyons, in *Existence*, 277. The term "tomb world" appears in a number of Dick's novels.

77 Dick, *Martian Time-Slip*, 76.

78 Suvin, "The Opus," 2.

79 Ibid., 2 and 10.

80 It is no coincidence that *Dr. Bloodmoney*, of all of Dick's novels, also invests most in collective over individual agency. See Jameson's "After Armageddon" for the classic reading of the novel in this respect. Jameson, "After Armageddon: Character Systems in *Dr. Bloodmoney*," in *On Philip K. Dick*, 26-36.

81 I offer a more in-depth discussion of structural and generic aspects of what I call 'paranoid narrative' in chapter 5.

82 Dick, *Eye in the Sky*, 13.

83 Dick, *Time Out of Joint*, 97.

84 Dick, "The Android and the Human," in *Shifting Realities*, 208.

85 Dick, "Drugs, Hallucination, and the Quest for Reality," in *Shifting Realities*, 169.

86 Dick, *Clans of the Alphane Moon*, 77–78

87 Ibid.

88 See below for my discussion of the role played by narrative structure and voice in deconstructing distinctions between reason and unreason.

89 "Drugs, Hallucination, and the Quest for Reality," in *Shifting Realities*, 171.

90 See note 118; but also for a similar evaluation: Carl Freedman, "Towards a Theory of Paranoia: The Science Fiction of Philip K. Dick," in *On Philip K. Dick*, 7–17.

91 Michel Foucault, *The Birth of Biopolitics: Lectures at the Collège de France, 1978–79*. ed. Michel Senellart, trans. Graham Burchell (Basingstoke: Palgrave, 2008), 188.

92 Hale, *The Rise and Crisis of Psychoanalysis in the United States*, 303.

93 Dick, *A Scanner Darkly*, 11.

94 Ibid., 42.

95 Dick, *A Scanner Darkly*, 83–88. This turn toward neurology does not mean that Dick's earlier perspectives on psychosis are completely absent, but they are clearly overshadowed. A brief scene in which Arctor seems to hallucinate shows up later on the video footage he records in his own house; once again the distinction between reality and hallucination, subjective and objective, breaks down, but an earlier antipsychiatric impetus is missing. And despite the novel's dependence on brain research, the character's behavior is occasionally still explained with the help of psychoanalytic concepts.

96 Sutin, *Divine Invasions*, 204.

97 Foucault first speaks of bio-power in volume one of *The History of Sexuality*, and then develops the term in several Collège de France lectures. Michel Foucault, *The History of Sexuality: An Introduction*, trans. Robert Hurley (London: Penguin, 1990), 139–144. For Dick's use of economic language in *A Scanner Darkly* see 18–19 and 23–24.

98 Philip K. Dick, *VALIS* (London: Gollancz, 2001), 60 and 32.

99 Jason P. Vest, *The Postmodern Humanism of Philip K. Dick* (Lanham, MD: Scarecrow, 2009).

100 Jonathan Lethem and Pamela Jackson, introduction to *The Exegesis of Philip K. Dick*, by Philip K. Dick, xv.

101 Erik Davis, "How I Learned to Love the Exegesis." Paper presented at the conference "Worlds Out of Joint: Re-Imagining Philip K. Dick," Dortmund, Germany, November 2012.

102 Dick, *Exegesis*, 371.

103 Dick, *Exegesis*, 611.

104 Philip K. Dick, *The Selected Letters of Philip K. Dick, 1938–1971* (Grass Valley, CA: Underwood, 1996), 58.

105 Dick, *Exegesis*, 149.

106 Ibid., 835.

107 Ibid.

108 Ibid., 491.

109 Ibid., 167–168.

110 Leslie Marmon Silko, *Ceremony* (New York: Penguin, 1986), 125–6.

111 Ibid., 246.

112 Ibid., 18.

113 Ibid., 246.

5 Paranoid Narrative

Writing the Secret History of the Cold War

In a little-noticed aside in *The Paranoid Style*, Richard Hofstadter refers to Harold Lasswell as "one of the first in the country" to have turned "to the study of the emotional and symbolic side of political life."[1] Although he has faded into obscurity today, to the student of modern American conspiracy theories Lasswell should play a role rivaled only by Hofstadter himself. Lasswell opened up a whole new field of study by examining politics as the projection, in his words, of "private motives upon public objects in the name of collective values."[2] Scholars could now psychoanalyze political rhetoric they found dangerous or simply displeasing as the emanation of pathological minds. Following in the footsteps of Lasswell and *The Authoritarian Personality*, Hofstadter attributed the 'paranoid style' to the common man and right-wing politicians. Their rhetoric was characterized by an excessive coherence that ignored contradictory evidence and the construction of a totalizing narrative that imagined history as conspiracy. Its adherents struck him as "absolutist," marked by "feeling[s] of persecution," and "paranoid leap[s] into fantasy."[3] By definition, such conspiratorial fantasies were limited to those standing outside the increasingly narrow frame of mainstream politics. Hofstadter construed conspiracy theories as a popular sentiment only ever accommodated by the establishment or carried into the mainstream by populist demagogues who themselves lacked the rationality and sophistication distinctive of the true politician. The paranoid style, he wrote in a letter to a friend, afflicted only those out of power, and by definition exempted the moderate liberals of the 1950s and early '60s.[4] Having cut themselves off from their popular and radical roots, liberals were increasingly coming under attack from conservatives, on the one hand, and a new participatory politics headed by the Civil Rights and students movements, on the other. Declaring them both irrational, even paranoid, and discrediting their historical record as well as their mass base, left the political arena to those who already inhabited center stage.

This intellectual background, which I described in detail in chapter 2, explains a curious aspect of US discussions of conspiracy theory: why, we might ask, are they almost always seen as emanating from the fringes of society, the poor and various subcultures, to the exclusion of mainstream culture, as well as social elites? And, in turn, why are narratives about secret political machinations so rarely understood as conspiratorial when they issue from the centers of power? As Bernhard Bailyn argued in *The Ideological Origins of the American Revolution*, both proponents and opponents of independence from the British crown presented themselves as victims of a conspiracy, a belief Bailyn identified as a dominant intellectual pattern of the revolution.[5] Or to point to one of many examples from the Cold War: what should we make of Ronald Reagan's claims that the tiny Caribbean island of Grenada (population: 91.000) and its co-operation with Cuba posed an imminent threat to US security—a contention deployed for its military invasion in 1983? In a recent study, which spends considerable time reviewing Americanist research, Matthew Gray repeatedly states that the US government does not engage in conspiracy narratives.[6] This is all the more remarkable given that Gray systematically broadens our view of who engages in conspiratorial rhetoric: "the state, political elites, political leaderships, social forces, and marginalized or disenfranchised individuals and groups, among others."[7] Gray writes about the Middle East but his list impels us to ask how state and mainstream actors have been systematically exempted from such diagnoses in a US context.

Research on conspiracy theories has not only blossomed since the late 1990s—a trend that owes as much to millenarian fears as to the attacks on New York's World Trade Center on September 11, 2001—but has undergone considerable revision. Distancing themselves from the calculatedly ambiguous yet vehement pathologization of dissent initiated by Hofstadter, these studies eschew overt pathologization and insist, by varying degrees, on thinking conspiracy theories at a remove from psychopathology. Seen as distinct from paranoia, conspiracy theories are now understood as worthy of serious academic investigation but are still viewed with a heavy dose of ambivalence as to their political and epistemological value.[8] This positive reevaluation of conspiracy theories depends, however, on the continued demonization of paranoia and gives rise to a ceaseless policing of the borders between sanity and madness. As a consequence, these authors persevere with a research program that locates paranoid narratives at the margins, privileges texts that seemingly distance themselves from paranoia, and remains blind to a systematic pathologization of madness employed to stifle political opposition. Despite their best intentions, these revisions adhere to an intellectual tradition they routinely reject, and reject what does not adhere to it.

Such complex ideological operations are not overcome by grand gestures. While quite understandable as a reaction to its long-standing demonization, the countercultural investment of paranoia with progressive potential remains caught in the binary it strives to rebuff. Rather than repeat efforts to dissociate the two terms, or drop discussion of paranoia altogether, in what follows I think about their distinctiveness as part of their inseparability. That is to say, what is commonly referred to as conspiracy theories will be understood as paranoid narratives, a form of story-telling structured by a paranoid epistemology. Such a conception allows me to go beyond the static antitheses of conspiracy theories seen as either flawed and meaningless, or illuminating and subversive, and move toward an understanding of their structure and logic, strengths and weaknesses. Ultimately, rethinking conspiratorial fictions necessitates rewriting paranoia not as a madness outside reason but the madness *of* reason: to conceive it not solely as a paranoia about the state, but as part and parcel of state reason.[9] Throughout, my comments will be guided by Lacanian psychoanalysis and especially the radical revision of Jacques Lacan's thought in the mid-1970s. Arguing against the routine dismissal of their claims, Lacan asserted that the sometimes abstruse conclusions of conspiracy theories in no way negate a central element of truth. As he writes, "to misrecognize presupposes recognition."[10]

Following this reconsideration of paranoia, I discuss the relationship between what I call 'paranoid narrative' and the Cold War: a historical epoch that often reduced the globe to an imagined bipolarity between the United States and the Soviet Union, capitalism and communism, friend and foe, patriot and traitor, self and other.[11] Like all dualisms, or binary oppositions, this one was highly unstable: exhibiting a tendency toward sudden collapse and frequently in need of a dose of paranoia to reestablish clear divisions. My introduction to paranoid narrative discusses its major characteristics and surveys of some of the most canonical conspiracy fictions in postwar American literature, from William Burroughs's *Nova Trilogy* (1961–64) to Thomas Pynchon's *The Crying of Lot 49* (1966), and from Ishmael Reed's *Mumbo Jumbo* (1972) to Robert Coover's *The Public Burning* (1977). The main part of the chapter then traces the historical development of conspiracy culture from the early years of the Cold War onward and turns to Hollywood thrillers, in particular Elia Kazan's *Panic in the Streets* (1950) and John Frankenheimer's *The Manchurian Candidate* (1962). My analysis of these films centers on the complex interaction in them between closure and disclosure. Here, the ideological frames of nation, reason, heteronormativtiy, and democracy give way to a much more diverse reality: of migration and global capitalism, madness and mental illness, queer and homosexuality, power politics and media manipulation. My point is not to deny the pressure exerted by institutional and ideological containment but to show how paranoid narratives, by dint of their dualistic epistemology, reveal as much as they conceal about life during the early Cold War.

This section also analyses a number of 'conspiracy films,' a sub-genre of the crime thriller that emerges as part of the so-called Hollywood Renaissance in the early 1970s. This was a time of economic crisis for the film industry and a period of creative experimentation for filmmakers who keenly analyzed the social and economic transformations emerging from the 1960s. Surveying the extraordinary flourishing of conspiracy thrillers at the time, films such as *Klute* (1971), *The Conversation* (1974), and *The*

Parallax View (1974) are understood as instances of an emerging 'paranoia of circulation'—a term that emphasizes both their keen investigation of a now increasingly financial capitalism and their reaction to the failure of a liberal consensus. The certainty of paranoia always reacts to a threatening circulation of signifiers, which it aims to imbue with meaning. What distinguishes these conspiracy films from the Hollywood thrillers of the 1950s and early '60s is their inability to provide the reassurance of stable signification in the face of conflict and contradiction.

Finally, in section three my discussion of Don DeLillo's *Libra* (1988) and Thomas Pynchon's *Vineland* (1990) suggests a third mutation in the logic of paranoia, and madness more generally: what I term 'ordinary paranoia' corresponds to the increasing breakdown of internalized authority and a multiplication of social norms that subverts distinctions between reason and unreason. Whereas, in *Libra*, Lee Harvey Oswald's quotidian psychosis runs afoul of Cold War power politics, in *Vineland* paranoia has morphed into a general state of mind married to irony and cynicism, and the privatization of mental health care has returned the mad to the streets. DeLillo and Pynchon self-consciously appropriate the epistemology of paranoid narrative for wide-ranging counter-histories of the Cold War. In so doing, they question the privileging of political and diplomatic registers over the economy in mainstream accounts of the era and reconfigure the Cold War as a US project aimed at global capitalist expansion and the oppression of domestic opposition. Thus, this chapter traces a historical trajectory from the early 1950s to the '80s in order to describe the socio-cultural and discursive shift toward what I call 'ordinary paranoia,' and thus to an understanding of madness that works to overcome its long-standing pathologization.

5.1 From Conspiracy Theory to Paranoid Narrative

Hofstadter's identification of conspiracy theories with a dangerous insanity was rarely challenged until the late 1990s, when literary scholars began to analyze a wave of popular conspiracy narratives that had attracted large audiences and garnered positive reviews. In most of these recent monographs, the authors reject Hofstadter's more overt pathologizations. As Mark Fenster argues, Hofstadter's "understanding of it [conspiracy theory] as paranoid was confused and confusing in his own work, and has only become more simplistic and useless as it has been taken up by others."[12] Peter Knight holds that "[i]n recent decades [. . .] the images and rhetoric of conspiracy are no longer the exclusive house-style of the terminally paranoid."[13] Such differentiation between conspiracy theory and paranoia opens up two paths. In both, the recognition accorded conspiracy theories mirrors a continued demonization of paranoia. In the more traditional approach, essentially a successor to Cold War liberalism, conspiracy theories still correspond to Hofstadter's understanding. Fenster writes that they "frequently lack substantive proof, rely on dizzying leaps of logic, and oversimplify the political, economic, and social structures of power." Conspiracy theories are now acknowledged as an important if ultimately unsound element of US culture and seen as a "longstanding populist strain in American political culture." All along, a distance is maintained between conspiracy theories and the "madness of paranoia."[14] In all these cases, Hofstadter's charged diagnoses—a cultural pathology wielded as an intellectual weapon in the struggle for political influence—have sedimented into supposedly factual characteristics of conspiracy theories. A paranoid political tradition comprising both establishment and oppositional actors continues to be written as a populist strain. Meanwhile Hofstadter's twin diagnoses of rigidity and totalization have become the smallest common denominator of conspiracy theories. They are "wonderfully unified accounts of all the data at hand," characterized by "symmetrical totalities," and "rigid convictions."[15] The habitual rejection of Hofstadter's more unpalatable denigrations of paranoia therefore retains the pathologizing logic inherent in his understanding of conspiracy theory. Overt criticism goes hand in hand with the implicit continuation of what Michael Paul Rogin called the "countersubversive tradition."[16] Aided as much by an isolated reading of Hofstadter's essay on the "paranoid style," which disregards an intellectual tradition that sought to discredit political opponents by associating them with insanity, as by an absence of interest in contemporary reconsiderations of paranoia, such scholarship reinforces rationality's long-standing power over madness.

The second, more strongly revisionist, approach may equally lack any consideration of this tradition, but its close textual analyses have considerably altered the way we look at conspiracy theories. Knight has argued that they are frequently complex and self-reflexive, eschewing the rigidity and totalizing intent of which they are accused. Yet like more traditional approaches, these studies balance their partial reevaluation of conspiracy theories by the pathologization of paranoia. In Knight's case this takes the form of a historical argument that pits today's "more insecure version of conspiracy-infused anxiety" against an older "paradoxically secure form of paranoia" described flippantly as "the exclusive house-style of the terminally paranoid."[17] Jodi Dean endorses alien abduction narratives as a legitimate element of US politics, only to accuse their critics of "irresponsible paranoia."[18] The binary opposition of the two terms privileges some narratives as sane and insists on the insanity of those it labels paranoid. Or, as the philosopher Brian Keeley admits with admirable frankness: it allows "us clearly to distinguish between our 'good' and their 'bad' ones."[19] What unites both versions is the continuous reassertion of the boundaries between reason and unreason.

This presents a recurrent problem for any study of conspiracy theories, for the lesson of any ideological binary, the ultimate inseparability of privileged and repressed terms, also holds true in this particular case. As Keeley establishes in his essay, "[t]here is no criterion or set of criteria that provide a priori grounds for distinguishing warranted conspiracy theories from UCTs [unwarranted conspiracy theories]." In the end, the only argument to distinguish reason from unreason is the subversion of the distinction itself: the threat conspiracy theories pose to a narrowly defined rationality. "It is this pervasive skepticism of people and public institutions entailed by some conspiracy theories," writes Keeley, "which ultimately provides us with the grounds with which to identify them as unwarranted."[20]

Adapting Hofstadter's description of conspiracy theories as a product of society's margins, recent studies tend to focus on such subcultures as Alien abductees and right-wing extremism. Even when the analyzed texts form part of mainstream culture, such as the TV-series *The X-Files*, the dominant impulse is to read them as popular opposition. Such an interpretive thrust may be justified in some cases. But it uncritically adopts postwar liberalism's deflection from the use and instigation of paranoia as part of US establishment politics. What is overlooked is the prominent use of paranoia as the circumscription rather than the expression of dissent. The participation of paranoid thought in mainstream thought goes unexamined, whether it takes the form of official government policy, political rhetoric, or popular culture. As a consequence, Hofstadter and his brand of elitist Cold War liberalism are handed a lasting ideological victory. Attempts to overcome the binary logic of such accounts and redirect its central assumptions are rare. In general, they have remained at a stage of tentative suggestion, such as Martin Parker and Claire Birchall's proposition that the humanities and conspiracy theories share a common discursive structure.[21] Lacanian approaches to the nexus of conspiracy and paranoia remain scarce. Most of these engagements have come from critics who apply them to the concrete analysis of individual texts rather than a rethinking of conspiracy theories.

Despite this lack of engagement, Lacan's writings on paranoia arguably constitute a privileged discourse for an attempt at rethinking America's culture of conspiracy. They equally resist the pathologization and naïve idealization inherent in other approaches and combine clinical insight with theoretical acumen. Lacan fundamentally questions traditional assumptions about knowledge and the distinction between reason and unreason. At the center of his thought lies the famous conception of the imaginary relation, man's identification of himself with an other, initiated by the "mirror stage."[22] This misrecognition of ourselves as our own image simultaneously creates the ego and the understanding of an opposite object. Lacan also defines the imaginary relation as constitutively paranoid, as it involves a process in which any object is defined solely by virtue of its reflection in the ego, and vice versa. Lacan speaks of the "paranoiac structure of the ego," and identifies paranoia as the most general structure of human knowledge.[23] Paranoia becomes neither a logic radically distinct from sanity nor its excess—not a lack of insight but the very mechanism of knowledge. Rather than constituting an entity that can be neatly distinguished from scientific understandings of the object world, paranoia is "constitutive of human reality."[24]

For much of Lacan's writings of the 1950s–'60s, an imaginary paranoia could be controlled by man's integration into the symbolic register, the world of intersubjective speech and internalized authority. Correcting the strictly dyadic logic of the imaginary, the differential play of the signifier establishes a symbolic knowledge that dispels the objectifications of imaginary reality.[25] Lacan's classic writings on psychosis do not define paranoia exclusively as a logic common to all humanity. Paranoia applies to the general structure of knowledge *and* its special case paranoid psychosis—seen from the privileged perspective of a hegemonic neurosis as an inability to advance beyond it. Having failed to internalize social authority, a submission to its conventions that allows for a certain leeway within these rules, the paranoid psychotic is shackled all the more tightly to authority's unmediated power—to which delusion provides a personalized response.

Following this very brief introduction to Lacan's thought, we are in a position to clarify the central preconceptions about paranoia in discussions of America's conspiracy culture. As we have seen, conspiracy theories are routinely accused of over-coherence, rigid convictions, and totalization: arguments that can be traced to postwar liberalism's praise of irony and doubt and its pathologization of the political commitments of left and right. With Lacan we can argue that such a description of paranoia conflates two elements. On the one hand, paranoia's dyadic logic leads to absolute certainty. But this certainty only concerns the existence of the object in question. Its meaning remains highly volatile as the imaginary knowledge of paranoia is not stabilized by symbolic signification. As Lacan writes, "any purely imaginary equilibrium with the other always bears the mark of a fundamental instability."[26] As a consequence, the paranoid narrative "varies, whether it has been disturbed or not," and the paranoiac "seeks, over the course of his delusion's evolution, to incorporate these elements [external stimuli or changes] into the composition of the delusion."[27] Common descriptions of paranoid narratives as rigid thus conflate the existence of an object, frequently represented by the conspirator or persecutor in narrative, with a certainty of meaning.

A similar argument can be made in the case of so-called 'totalization.' Two elements come together in this accusation: first, what we have discussed in terms of rigidity or over-coherence, the rejection of contradictory data in favor of establishing a unified narrative; secondly, the imposition of this narrative on others. Two remarks seem pertinent here. As Freud already noted in his study of Schreber, paranoia is a partial rather than total delusion. Visitors were often surprised to find that the German judge talked affably about politics and literature but did not mention his paranoid cosmology in conversation.[28] While the exclusive presence of two terms, the opposition of self and other, means that the paranoid narrative is highly personalized, in the sense that its object relates directly to the self, such a truth is therefore also radically subjective, not the assumption of an objective reality to be imposed on others. This is not to argue that no conspiracy theories espouse comprehensive worldviews but that their total quality is not to be

taken as a characteristic of paranoia. Lacan's reflections on paranoia arguably describe conspiracy theories more accurately than existing studies that
largely derive from Cold War appropriations of psychology, yet refuse to
engage with contemporary critiques of such thought. A more internally consistent understanding of paranoia as an epistemological structure, at once
broader and more precise than previous conceptions, should encourage us
to question what we often take to be the undisputed qualities of conspiracy
theories, and to reexamine a cultural and political history that has been
written according to these supposedly objective criteria.

The reversals of Lacan's later work on psychosis are summarized in the
proposition that the Other does not exist.[29] The Other as the subject's personal relation to the symbolic world is in itself lacking: that is to say, it
is without the fullness that the subject seeks in it. The subject's acquiescence to existing reality thus depends on an element of choice, precisely
the subject's participation in, or withdrawal from, society. For the Lacan of
the 1950s, the social imposition of authority (the so-called 'Name-of-the-
Father') provided an anchor for symbolic knowledge and joined it to the
imaginary and the real. Once Lacan's increasing distance from structuralism
leads to the insight into the *in*consistency of the Other, the 'Name-of-the-
Father' becomes a fourth term that knots three radically distinct orders—a
no longer privileged symbolic, the imaginary, and the real—into common-
sense reality. As the product of such a fourth term, the social conventions of
neurotic normality are similar in structure to the delusions of the psychotic
and become only one of many impositions of contingent meaning on a baffling world.

What distinguishes neurosis and psychosis is not their inherently rational
or irrational nature. Psychosis is "not an irredeemable deficiency but rather
another form of subjective organization."[30] Both are delusions in the strict
sense of the word, but neurosis is a shared delusion as it institutes a socially
accepted limit to meaning and behavior. In contrast, psychotics must construct this limit one by one. Accordingly, both neurosis and psychosis have
to be understood as contingent attempts at interpretation, bridging a gap
between a meaningless real and a meaningful structure whose passage is
guaranteed by nothing but its practice. Lacan here exposes the supposed
epistemological privilege of sanity as a form of shared belief: precisely the
subject's conviction in an inherent structural or logical difference of a supposedly sane organization of reality, its internal consistency. It is thus that
Miller can write that "[e]veryone is crazy. It is only then that it becomes
interesting to make distinctions."[31] Such a conception of psychosis leads not,
as one might assume, to a conceptual conflation. Sanity is not denied existence as a category but defined precisely as a sub-category of madness distinguished by its hegemonic status—the one madness accepted as rational.
As the symbolic loses the status of a cure, a privilege extended to it under
the presupposition of its fullness, the delusional act of reality-production
now includes symbolic knowledge. The emphasis on sanity as hegemonic

madness also introduces, more strongly than before, the potential for historical change and the possibility of making new distinctions.

Lacan's late writings also entail a redefinition of paranoia. The paranoiac is said to imagine that "the Other enjoys [him] in his passivized being."[32] This refinement of Lacan's analysis adds an important aspect to our understanding. While earlier we noted the characteristic personalization inherent in paranoia, this final definition emphasizes the centrality of jouissance (or enjoyment) and its attribution to figures or structures of authority in situations in which the subject is unable to become an active, enjoying participant in society. Therefore, we can say that what lies at the center of paranoia is the imagination of a consistent authority, frequently portrayed as all-powerful, and the attribution to this authority of jouissance, of which the subject feels itself robbed. Herein also lies the essential truth of paranoia, without which it is difficult to imagine why conspiracy theories should exert such fascination. Its detection of a structure of authority or oppression speaks the truth of society—its structural responsibility, or the unbroken interrelation between all constituents of the symbolic universe—and transforms it into the existence of conspiracy. Yet in the meaning instituted by their portrayal of power, conspiracy theories also strengthen the belief in an authority whose potential disintegration is exposed by the need for such paranoid certainty in the first place. In other words, the paradox of paranoid narrative lies in its exposure of social antagonisms it may want to repress and the reinforcement of a status quo it may wish to subvert.

This structural ambivalence sheds light not only on the wildly divergent interpretations elicited by conspiratorial fictions, which range from outright condemnation to being hailed for their emancipatory potential. It also allows us to situate them with regard to Alan Nadel's influential postulation of a Cold War "containment culture."[33] Unlike some of the work that followed in its vein, Nadel's book was at pains to emphasize the inherent instability of containment. In this chapter, I go further in arguing that paranoid narratives reveal as much as they contain. This narrative instability may seem to contradict the bipolarity of Cold War culture, the sense shared by many authors that the world lay frozen in existential paralysis. Oedipa Maas in Pynchon's *The Crying of Lot 49*, or the Oswald of DeLillo's *Libra*, yearn to escape this paralysis. Yet the choice between a ruthless Soviet communism and America's rapacious capitalism doesn't offer much hope to them. A novel that features a female protagonist in a literature often dominated by male characters, *The Crying of Lot 49* connects its paranoia to another feature of the Cold War, a conservative model of femininity. It is here that Maas's lack of choice proves most pressing. Oedipa's wish to escape this drabness, "the absence of surprise," turns conspiracy rather than communism into the only available escape.[34] Pynchon's heroine may also be taken as exemplary for the clarity with which she faces the essential epistemological dilemma of paranoid narrative and possibly of the Cold War as a whole.

The institutionalized secrecy of the national security state, and the predominance of psychological warfare in a conflict that relegated armed combat to the global South, introduced an ever widening gap between available and necessary knowledge. In the final pages of the novel, Oedipa must decide between her belief in a conspiracy that might promise a different America and a reality devoid of any promise for a woman straining against the confines of restrictive gender norms. Oedipa's reasoning reveals that the alternative offered to her is ultimately no such thing and that paranoia remains her best option, either as a desire for knowledge, or as diversion from its impossibility: "For there either was some Tristero beyond the appearance of the legacy America, or there was just America and if there was just America then it seemed the only way she could continue [. . .] was an [. . .] assumed full circle into some paranoia."[35]

This radical skepticism about truth and falsehood engulfed not only literary culture. As Tobin Siebers has argued, much of the coherence of postmodern and poststructuralist thought must be sought against the background of Cold War secrecy, an argument that constitutes one of the starting points for my engagement with postwar literary criticism in the final chapter.[36] In the process, what remained unknown provided space for the imagination and was often transformed into the unknowable, with narrative morphing into a reflection on the possibility of storytelling. *The Crying of Lot 49* proves informative here in the way it refuses to reveal its central mystery, the existence of the postal network Tristero. Instead, the novel hovers over the central process of its narrative epistemology, the identification of the object of Oedipa's paranoia. Terms like revelation and grace abound as Tristero takes on a luminous quality, the halo of paranoid signification. Yet despite seeing it as her duty to bring Pierce Inverarity's estate "into pulsing stelliferous Meaning," her paranoia yields no definitive content.[37] Oedipa's quest for truth epitomizes the fundamental instability of imaginary knowledge noted by Lacan and the incorporation of ever new data that never settles for a final answer.

What this deferral of paranoid epiphany allows for in its stead proves to be of much higher significance. The mysterious halo of the paranoid signifier, the interpellation of the subject by the signifier's simultaneous import and *in*definition, powers an investigative process that draws in the symbolic universe with its chains of relation and responsibility. Pynchon's counter-history of US capitalism spreads out from the fictional company Yoyodyne, part-owned by the late Inverarity, to draw connections with the military-industrial complex that grew exponentially under president Truman in the 1950s. In the process, Inverarity comes to stand in for America itself: its "need to possess, to alter the land, to bring new skylines, personal antagonisms, growth rates into being."[38] Pynchon's interest in the capitalist economy may be exceptional, his geopolitical imagination is not. The bipolarity that structures Cold War conspiracy fictions forced even narratives heavily focused on the United States to imagine its participation in a global system. *Mumbo Jumbo*, Ishmael Reed's satire of the psychic epidemic Jes Grew, takes in Western Europe, Haiti, and Egypt. Coover's *The Public Burning* refracts the Rosenberg case, the quintessential spy story of Cold War America, through the mind of a paranoid Richard Nixon. Yet even this novel opposes its embodiment of authority, an allegorical Uncle Sam, with the "Phantom," a figure of worldwide communism that haunts Americans across the globe.

As Oliver Harris has said of Burroughs' *Nova Trilogy*, paranoid narratives frequently function as geo-political allegories.[39] If the USSR barely features in the inter-galactic skirmishes between the Nova Mob and the Nova police, this is due to a science-fictional estrangement of the Cold War as a sexual and drug conflict that leads Burroughs to conflate US control regimes with Soviet authoritarianism. Burroughs found himself a keen witness of the domestic repression of the late 1940s and early '50s, commenting on the removal of homosexuals from the State Department and fictionalizing Harry J. Anslinger's campaigns against drug addition in his role as first commissioner of the Federal Bureau of Narcotics.[40] In his fiction and letters, Burroughs argues repeatedly that automatic obedience represents a specifically "Russian dream" that is finding imitators in his home country. "The bureaucrats of both countries," he writes, "want the same thing: Control."[41] Burroughs at times subsumes American capitalism under a notion of totalitarianism that equates the United States and the Soviet Union with a global conspiracy against individuality, and specifically, a denial of the pleasures of sex and drugs. Such potentially subversive practices as drug use and homosexuality became highly politicized as America entered a standoff with communism and anyone suspected of unpatriotic acts or thought was in danger of being branded insane.

Unlike academic appropriations, conspiratorial narratives do not usually feature lengthy commentaries on psychopathology. However, most authors situate their paranoid epistemology within dominant conceptions of madness, from psychoanalysis to neurology. These fictions also feature a wide range of mad characters, from the hobby paranoiac to the hallucinating protagonist. Oedipa Maas compares the onset of her paranoid epiphanies to an epileptic seizure, and Burroughs, an ardent proponent of physiological accounts of mental illness, combines theories of drug addiction and psychosis. In response to Allen Ginsberg reporting a temporary improvement of his mother Naomi's condition, who spent most of her later years in mental institutions with a diagnosis of paranoid schizophrenia, Burroughs theorizes her illness as the consequence of a metabolic dysfunction. He then proposes hooking the mentally ill on heroine based on his observation "that there are no psychotic junkies, at least not when on the junk."[42] More frequent than such homegrown advice were various critiques of psychiatry. *Mumbo Jumbo* ridicules the Eurocentric bias of psychoanalysis and imagines an alternative to Western medicine that bears the imprint of an antipsychiatric thought become prominent with Laing and Szasz: "Paranoia and the like were clinical [. . .] words invented by people who [. . .] lost the knowledge [. . .] Formerly the people could go the temple and get away from it all through the guidance of a priest; now they were tortured."[43]

At times, the border between paranoid fiction and everyday life blurred for these authors, as it did for Philip K. Dick. In the letter I just quoted, Burroughs comments that he has already written twice to Ginsberg's "ship address." Most likely Burroughs was referring to the USNS Sgt. Jack Pendleton, which Ginsberg had joined as a yeoman storekeeper and which took him up the West Coast to the Arctic. Burroughs's next sentence adds: "Hope the FBI didn't intercept."[44] In another letter, again to Ginsberg who shared a history of institutionalization with his mother, Burroughs reports the conviction of his second wife, Joan Vollmer, that low-level nuclear radiation is exerting psychic control over Americans. Burroughs not only accedes that Vollmer's paranoia "contains a solid core of reality." Her theory also parallels a recurrent hallucination suffered by Naomi Ginsberg. As her son relates it in "Kaddish": "and you covered your nose with motheaten fur collar, gas mask against poison sneaked into downtown atmosphere."[45] For the Russian Jew Naomi Ginsberg, poison gas was apt to remain a lifelong presence. And after her son's trip to the Arctic, the USNS Pendleton made a long career transporting weapons for the US Navy to Korea and Vietnam, finally being abandoned after striking a reef in the South China Sea in 1973.[46] This seeming inevitability of paranoia amid nuclear fear and global confrontation no doubt contributed to the rise of conspiracy culture in the postwar era.

In the introduction to this chapter, I argued that paranoid narratives are distinguished by their construction of a paranoid Other, a persecutory object perceived as a danger to the imagined community for which the narrative constructs a cultural fantasy. The radical instability of the paranoid Other, its purported jouissance, and the threat it represents are frequently translated into its depiction as mad. As I have also maintained, the specific feature of such narratives lies in their simultaneous exposure of social contradiction and their provision of imaginary scaffolding for the norms and conventions of that community. In this sense, the recourse to conspiracy theories also played into the hands of a political and cultural establishment set to benefit from a paranoid view of its supposed and real enemies, both foreign and domestic.

5.2 Closure and Disclosure in the Cold War Thriller

In Elia Kazan's *Panic in the Streets*, released to cinemas three months after Joseph McCarthy's famous speech at the Republican Women's Club of Wheeling, West Virginia, in February 1950, an illegal alien is found murdered in the back alleys of New Orleans. When a physician for the US Health Service discovers that the victim had carried pneumonic plague, his desperate attempt to contain the virus is kept secret from a population suspected of an irresponsible reaction to the threat.[47] Kazan was a self-made American born of Greek Orthodox parents in Istanbul. In 1934 he briefly joined the Communist Party and later testified twice before the House Un-American Activities Committee (HUAC) in 1952, naming several people he knew to be or suspected of being communists.[48] In an advertisement that Kazan paid to accompany the *New York Times* article about his appearance in the House of Representatives, Kazan spoke of communism as "a dangerous and alien conspiracy."[49] Kazan did not mention the main reason for his testimony, the looming threat to his career as a film director. Declaring that it was his duty to speak out, Kazan took recourse to psychopathology to distance himself from conservative anti-communists and the left alike. In a passage that recalls Hofstadter's contemporaneous writings, he advanced that the power of reason alone could bring clarity. Opposing his own rational stance with the irrationality of others, he wrote: "Whatever hysteria exists—and there is some, particularly in Hollywood—is inflamed by mystery, suspicion and secrecy. Hard and exact facts will cool it."[50] Kazan's testimony meant that he remained persona non grata to many Hollywood liberals for the rest of his life. Yet even in his autobiography, Kazan insisted that he'd done the right thing because he had acted rationally.[51]

Kazan's film led its audience from the nuclear family of its hero, played by Richard Widmark, into the underworld of the New Orleans port: to its seedy bars and smugglers, to its dock workers unloading bananas from the Caribbean, its Chinese ship cooks, and the Union hiring hall where masses of white and black unemployed wait for jobs that might never arrive. In Widmark's passionate defense of secrecy, the national security state rears its head, and in a thrilling chase the physician shoots the infected murderer before he can join the continuous circulation of goods that is establishing a global empire. Where *Panic in the Streets* attains closure, it also exposes what its paranoid premise of contamination and containment wants to hide. Released amid nuclear confrontation and economic expansion, the film's central paradox lies in its presentation of the antagonisms it seeks to repress, and the elaboration of the contradictions it wants to deny. Underneath the narrative's defense against alien invasion glimmer the contradictions of postwar America: racial and class division at home, imperialist exploitation and violence abroad. In so doing, paranoid narrative gives voice to society's trans-individual unconscious, exposing a partial failure of social authority. These fictions speak of internal conflict and *real* impasse at the same time that their paranoid imagination displaces the truth they uncover. As Lacan writes: "For to misrecognize presupposes recognition, [. . .] in which case we must certainly admit that what is denied is in some way recognized."[52] By emphasizing what they wish to contain, paranoid narratives represent a failure of the law at the same time that they attempt to reinforce it. As I argued earlier, paranoia may be traced to the incomplete internalization of authority, the norms and conventions that regulate social interaction.

Paranoid narratives, in their perception of such a failure of the law, shore up authority by imagining a persecutor or conspirator—a solution that frequently remains highly volatile. Such narratives can thus be described as paranoid in a more precise sense than in discussions of conspiracy theories that describe a literary motif or a character's fears by that term.

Panic in the Streets constitutes a particularly apt realization of paranoia's paradoxical logic of exposure and containment. The debates between Health Service physician Clinton Reed and New Orleans officials and Reed's repeated warnings against the virus's spread to the whole nation take up a seemingly disproportionate part of the film but are key to its development. Their conflict is presented as a struggle between national authority and local ignorance, mirroring Hofstadter's disregard for the common man's intellect. The debates also form a parallel narrative to the search for the carriers of the alien virus, a gang of thugs led by Jack Palance. The criminals are apprehended and the plague contained only after Reed convinces the mayor to trust his superior understanding. National unity is reestablished in opposition to the external threat. What distinguishes the film beyond this basic plot is Kazan's careful attention to the underlying contradictions exposed in the successful containment. The bird's-eye shot of black and white workers collectively waiting in the National Union hiring hall, their deep suspicion of authority, and the film's dramatic finale in the New Orleans docks—amid the continuous exchange of goods that belongs to a distinctly transnational capitalism—all lend a deeply ambiguous quality to *Panic in the Streets*. This ambiguity finds its starkest expression in the final police hunt for Palance. His near supernatural will to survive, sheer defiance, and escape after he has been shot and surrounded, reveals him as the narrative's *objet a*, the imaginary representation of the real object cause of desire. Palance's capture as he is about to climb onto a ship and escape his pursuers precisely marks the film's point of ideological closure: the concealment of social impasse, and the assertion of a national frame of containment in a narrative that cannot but wonder about America's increasingly global reach and responsibility.

Postwar paranoid narratives like *Panic in the Streets* reverse the disintegration of the law they ponder. In the same way that the title of *Panic in the Streets* warns of a breakdown of order that it sets out to foreclose, the science-fictional invasion films of the 1950s repel the contamination of the body politic by rejecting the blurring of self and other they imagine. This holds true in such diverse films as *Invaders from Mars* (1953), *Invasion of the Body Snatchers* (1956), or *It Came from Outer Space* (1953). This formal consistency should warn us against the overemphasis on character or plot in the interpretation of these films, but also of the search for an ultimate signified of their alien invaders.[53] For the function of the paranoid object, whether it is represented as an extraterrestrial or evil conspirator, is structural. Its alien invaders refer less to a deeper meaning as they produce such meaning in order to construct an ethical binary. As Peter Biskind argues, the references to communism in many 1950s films constituted a red herring

Figure 5.1 Jack Palance attempts to escape from the police in the film *Panic in the Streets* (1950), directed by Elia Kazan.

that veiled "a domestic power struggle." Such a reading should extend to an analysis of the paranoid object: the threatening Other or enemy imagined by the narrative becomes a site of struggle over meaning as such.[54]

The Manchurian Candidate (1962) is a case in point.[55] John Frankenheimer's black comedy attacks McCarthy's media populism to advance its own brand of Cold War politics. A company of American soldiers, including the senator's stepson, Raymond Shaw, are captured in Korea. They are then 'brainwashed' by a scientist from the "Pavlov Institute in Moscow," and Shaw is chosen to carry out the plans of the communist conspirators. Later, the film reveals Shaw's mother as the mastermind of a communist plot to assassinate the presidential candidate in order to bring Iselin, his running mate, the presidency. Shaw, the film's central focus, may be understood as what Fredric Jameson calls, following Algirdas Greimas, an "actant," a structural agent of narrative development.[56] In turn, the conspiracy thriller can be seen as a generic mutation based on the detective story and, more particularly, the film noir. As Jameson observes, the key development lies in a partial unification and reduction of its agents from three to two: no longer a detective, a victim, and a villain but rather the collectivization of the detective, who may now also double as the victim, and is opposed to the villain. As I argue in my discussion of *Klute* and *The Conversation* below, what seems at first to be the film's detective is transformed into the paranoid object, or villain. In turn, popular scrutiny becomes the dangerous irrationality of the conspiracy theorist. This reduction to an essential but unstable dualism represents a version of the bipolarity of Cold War culture: an opposition between friend and foe, communism and capitalism, that is beset by the essential transitivity of the paranoid imaginary.

In *The Manchurian Candidate*, the role of the detective falls to Major Bennett Marco—played as a troubled all-American hero by Frank Sinatra—who serves in Korea alongside war hero Shaw. Marco becomes the representative of paranoid desire, whose quest for knowledge propels the narrative to its conclusion. This opposition will reveal its instability with the disclosure of Shaw's brainwashing by the Soviets and his assignment to kill the candidate for the presidency. This turns Shaw into the object of Marco's paranoid desire. The media attention garnered by Sinatra at the time added another layer to this complex narrative. Known for his activism on behalf of progressive causes and his staunch opposition to HUAC, Sinatra joined the cast only because he had to drop a film written by Albert Maltz, the blacklisted screenwriter and member of the Hollywood Ten, after sustained pressure from the press.[57] Frankenheimer's satire of anti-communism held obvious appeal to Sinatra in this situation.

In a basic metaphorical use that would become much more widespread later, the film presents us with a portrait of US society in which a mad disintegration of social order (read: communism) is an ever-present threat. Even before the film's explicit discussion of Shaw in these terms, a soldier brainwashed during the Korean War fears for his sanity. This scene is repeated in a farcical vein when Senator Iselin is afraid of going mad because his wife repeatedly changes the number of communist infiltrators in the State Department that he keeps announcing on TV. Shaw, in turn, is a man without a father, who is dominated by his manipulative mother, and the film readily portrays the incestuous relationship between the two. Lacking in his integration into social, or paternal, authority—a fact emphasized by his awkwardness and lack of humor—the film portrays Shaw as psychotic. It is no coincidence that Shaw's conditioning is activated by the Red Queen of Diamonds card, the imaginary relation to his mother. In turn, his behavior when under the sway is presented as a mad trance, a diagnosis reinforced by the reference to Shaw's conditioning as mental illness.

The ideological import of Shaw's psychosis is revealed by Yen Lo, the Pavlovian scientist, whose manipulations are explained by a pop psychology that wildly mixes behaviorism with Freud. As Yen Lo reveals to another conspirator, Shaw's conditioning has removed any trace of unconscious guilt or fear, traits he describes as specifically American—thereby marking Shaw's induced madness as un-American. But the emphasis on Shaw's psychosis suggests that he could only be 'brainwashed' into becoming a communist pawn due to an underlying illness that made him un-American all along. Shaw's portrayal inscribes a double metaphorical usage: A general emphasis on madness as a perceived disintegration of social order, widely applied to the film's characters, is matched by psychosis as an indicator of pure irrationality, an inaccessibility to reason. In its latter meaning, *The Manchurian Candidate* reproduces what became part of US foreign policy with the beginning of the Cold War: the equation of Soviet communism with an insane irrationality, a system of beliefs that remained, and should remain, inaccessible to the American mind.[58] Whereas the more literal understanding of madness as the schizophrenic splitting of the psyche frequently can be observed in cultural self-diagnoses, such as in Dick's imagination of a dystopian America, its conception as the complete absence of reason is usually reserved for political opponents, whether they are Hofstadter's right-wing extremists, or communists.

The Manchurian Candidate's portrayal of its paranoid object as mad indicates liberal Hollywood's increasing skepticism toward the state and its citizens. In contrast to *Panic in the Streets*, Shaw is characterized less by being assigned a specific meaning as by the failure of its inscription. While the film revolves around Shaw with imaginary certainty, his identification as either a communist traitor or a true patriot, never seems secure. What we are returned to is the importance of our earlier distinction between paranoid certainty and meaning: whereas the first is never in doubt, and the film is in fact built around it, the latter remains radically unstable. This instability provides the film both with its anxiety and narrative impetus. The finale, in which Shaw assassinates Senator Iselin and his mother (instead of shooting the presidential nominee as intended by the conspirators) and then commits suicide, should be understood in sharp contrast to the ideological validation of Shaw's status as a true war hero, which the last scene suggests. Rather, such aggression marks the outer limit of postwar paranoid narrative: unable to secure stable meaning, the film can only achieve narrative closure in the violent annihilation of Shaw, a form of what Lacan calls acting out.[59]

The Manchurian Candidate's portrayal of a long-range assassination attempt a year before John F. Kennedy's death has made discussion of its uncanny prescience inevitable ever since. Yet the film also indicates a deep-seated problem with the automatic identification of JFK's assassination as the starting point of a qualitatively different conspiracy culture. The problem lies not so much in the assassination's undoubted repercussions as in the tendency of such convenient classification to mask the subtle continuities of cultural history that run deeper than even the most spectacular political events. Studies of America's conspiracy culture frequently attribute an ontological shift to the Kennedy assassination that leads to a questioning of the possibility of knowledge.[60] *The Manchurian Candidate*'s inability to assign meaning *before* Kennedy's death suggests that we are confronted not so much with a punctual reversal but a gradual development. Cultural responses to November 22, 1963, integrate the events of that day into already existing narrative structures—negotiating the increasing disintegration of a hegemonic symbolic order by modifying an available, rather than creating a substantially new, fictional form. The abiding resonance of

Kennedy's death may be better understood as retrospectively crystallizing the gradual death of the Lacanian Name-of-the-Father and the dispersal of social authority.

In a gradual fragmentation of paranoid meaning, the conspiracy films of the 1970s, to which I now turn, concern that which escapes them, that which makes closure impossible. Perhaps most visibly, these films are distinguished by the emergence of the detective as a central cultural figure of his era.[61] This reappearance is not surprising given the detective's status as a simultaneous representative of social conflict and its resolution. Two characteristics of these detective figures are noteworthy: his or her frequent guise as a journalist indicates that the detective's role is less narrative resolution—in which a murder is solved, a villain apprehended, and the case closed—than the detection of the crime itself. Investigative reporters and private eyes function as social detectives, collective agents whose function it becomes to identify a conspiracy. The detective acts as the figure of a paranoid desire that identifies one signifier among the endless web of signifiers as a crime or clue and relates it back to her- or himself. In this simple gesture lies hidden the paranoid source of conspiracy theory: the election of an event or clue as personalized meaning speaks the truth of society.

In the conspiracy thrillers of the 1950s and early '60s, the paranoid object was often present from the beginning, visible as villain or alien and thereby only ever posed in a frame in which it was already contained. Two decades later, the search for this object necessitates considerable effort, and takes two distinct forms. First, and more straightforwardly, the narrative may revolve around the detective's on-going investigation of a conspiracy. These efforts focus on detecting the perpetrators of the conspiracy, a structure found in Sidney Lumet's *Three Days of the Condor* (1975), as well as *The Parallax View* (1974) and *All the President's Men* (1976). A more complicated narrative system surfaces in *Klute* (1971) and Francis Ford Coppola's *The Conversation* (1974). Both films eschew more obviously political investigations for a rotation of actantial poles in which what looks like the film's detective turns out to be its fundamental paranoid object.[62] Thus, neither *Klute*'s Bree Daniels, played by Jane Fonda, nor Gene Hackman's surveillance expert Harry Caul, are quite what they seem. This is perhaps more immediately obvious in *Klute*, Pakula's vehemently anti-feminist thriller.[63] The film begins with Peter Cable's (Charles Cioffi) assignment of private eye John Klute (Donald Sutherland) to find a mutual friend, who is said to have written obscene letters to New York prostitute Bree Daniels before his disappearance. Thus, initially Daniels is identified as the detective's object of investigation, but this changes when they become lovers and join forces to find Bree's stalker. At first glance, Pakula would appear to subjectivize Daniels in the repeated scenes of her conversations with a female psychotherapist and a recording in which she puts forward her liberated views on sexuality and self-expression. This is undercut by her visual objectification in the gaze of Klute and her stalker, who the film reveals to be no one but Klute's client, Cable. The parallels between both men are pronounced, as both spy on Daniels and reject what the film portrays as her decadent countercultural lifestyle.

Christine Gledhill sees the two characters as different facets of patriarchal authority, split between Cable as the self-proclaimed avenger of a threatened masculinity and Klute as the understanding but dominant lover intent on rescuing her from her supposedly demeaning occupation.[64] Rather than centering on an opposition between the terrified Bree and her persecutor Cable, as Pakula claimed in an interview, the film's paranoia is concerned with the threat posed to patriarchy by second-wave feminism.[65] The free-spirited Daniels, rather than representing the film's endorsement of women's liberation, stands in for the paranoid Other's enjoyment of herself, which is mirrored in Cable's felt emasculation and passivity. Daniels's rescue from the hands of Cable offers not freedom but domination under threat of a violent annihilation akin to Raymond Shaw's death in *The Manchurian Candidate*. In contrast to earlier films, *Klute*'s attempt to mask social contradiction is complicated by the paranoid object's location within America and the portrayal of widespread social decadence. Even in its reassertion of authority, *Klute* lays bare its advanced disintegration. What closure is achieved remains ambiguous as to its effect and limited to Cable's death despite the social nature of the conflict that the film exposes.

Figure 5.2 Jane Fonda visits her psychotherapist in *Klute* (1971), directed by Alan J. Pakula.

In contrast to Pakula who depicts Klute's surveillance of Daniels without investigating its relation to social control, *The Conversation* makes surveillance's disciplinary apparatus its guiding concern.[66] Cultural paranoia has become intimately associated with surveillance, of course, and rare is the conspiracy film that does not touch on the theme. This ubiquity warns us of assuming any simple referent. On a basic level, cinematic images of surveillance are probably nothing more than indicators of genre affiliation, whose singular but decisive function is to receive the assent of its viewers to the narrative premise of conspiracy.[67] Only slightly more interesting are uses of surveillance as translations of paranoia's logic of personalization, a frequently needless and sometimes obtrusive reminder of the name of the game. Of a completely different order, if not as yet the final mutation of this theme, is Coppola's approach. Harry Caul is a San Francisco surveillance expert assigned by the director of a large corporation to spy on his wife and her lover. Reassembling their conversation from the multiple tapes used for the surveillance, each of which on its own remains blurred, Harry comes to believe that the couple will be murdered by his client. Thus, the film sets up Caul as a detective identifying a conspiracy in the meaningless static of sound recordings. But despite his pursuit of the conspiracy, Harry never shows any discernible interest in the couple whose lives seem in danger or their relationship to the company's director. Harry's lack of empathy is equaled by his misunderstanding of the conversation from which his suspicion derives. As he listens to the surveillance tapes, he understands the young man to say, "He'd *kill* us if he got the chance," meaning the betrayed husband. Only later do we learn that the accent had been on the word 'us,' turning the sentence into the justification of the lovers' plot to murder the director: "He'd kill *us* if he got the chance." Dennis Turner writes that Harry fails "to understand the position of the speaker, or enunciator, [. . .] he reads things as if they had been articulated as pure denotation, devoid of the shadings and nuance of discourse."[68]

Harry's misunderstanding is never accompanied by any doubt as to the actual significance of the tape. The initially meaningless static returns to him not as a reconstruction of symbolic knowledge but as an answer from the real of sound. As he emphasizes to his assistant Stan: "I don't care what they talk about. All I want is a nice, fat recording." Harry's emphasis on the bodily quality of the sound suggests its imaginary rather than symbolic status, a fact underscored later when he insists that "I don't know anything about curiosity." On one level, Harry's discovery of the conspiracy and its pursuit could be read as a tale of sin and redemption, with the conversation triggering his unconscious guilt about an earlier murder committed under his watch. But Harry's disconnection from the Other also entails the absence of a functioning unconscious and the repressed knowledge of the neurotic. As he says to his nosy landlady, "I don't have anything personal." In a nuanced understanding of madness, Harry's later psychotic break, pictured in the violent dismantling of his apartment, follows from his inability to fully integrate into the symbolic. Even his fervent Catholicism, the attempted stabilization of his psychological structure with the help of an imaginary semblant of the Other, proves unsuccessful.

With Harry's psychotic break, triggered by his discovery of the director's murder, the film undergoes the rotation of its actantial structure mentioned above. The erstwhile detective is placed under surveillance by the director's assistant, himself in league with the young couple. This rotation of Harry's position from detective to paranoid object is foreshadowed when a competitor in the surveillance business plays a prank on him and secretly records Harry's conversations at a party. The process also transforms the detective into the victim, and the supposed victims into villains and detectives all at once, exemplifying the dramatic instability of paranoid narrative and its dualistic logic. Coppola's abandonment of the more straightforward conspiracy theory for the surveillance of Harry Caul is telling in another respect: what captures his attention is not the politically charged question of the corporation and the development of American capitalism, but rather the more narrow issue of its consequences for social cohesion.

The central occupation of the film becomes what it perceives to be a failure of social authority. This disintegration of belief culminates in Harry's destruction of a small figurine of the Madonna, which he smashes after he has dismantled his apartment in search of a wiretap. Coppola's implementation of this problematic, and therefore the true detective of the film, is the camera itself, or rather, its subtle emulation of a surveillance camera's static position and slow, limited movement.[69] What the camera records is not the power of this disciplinary mechanism but its essential failure to fully capture its object Caul, who repeatedly can be seen leaving the frame, the camera now filming nothing but empty space. Ultimately, *The Conversation* enforces the logic of that which it believes itself to be criticizing. It is not surveillance that poses the threat (in the cautionary tale of an all-powerful technology that comes to haunt the individual whose grasp its escapes) but rather Caul's distance from internalized authority, to which the film reacts by mimicking the disciplinary technologies of surveillance. As in *The Manchurian Candidate*, the film's paranoid object is portrayed as mad. At the same time, the comparison between the two thrillers reveals the absence of any political closure in the resolution of its narrative. Despite Coppola's ostentatious disinterest, what lurks behind this ideological exhaustion is an awareness of larger changes within capitalism, its increasing financialization and the rise of the international corporation, which will transform US society.

Pakula's *The Parallax View* marks a decisive moment in this regard.[70] Paranoia no longer fears what might escape its grasp, but suspects that all escape routes are now closed off. We are thus catapulted into a novel form of paranoia in Hollywood cinema. Two clusters of conspiracy film can be distinguished on this basis. The first group, of which we have discussed *The*

Conversation and *Klute* but to which we could add *Three Days of the Condor* and *All the President's Men*, includes films in which the conspiracy is successfully resolved. Some of these narratives, *The Manchurian Candidate* among them, offer a redemptive tale of power's self-purification, in which imaginary aggressivity is redirected from potentially more damaging aims and onto a part of the government apparatus to be symbolically sacrificed. In *Three Days of the Condor*, this aim is achieved by Joe Turner (Robert Redford), a reader of detective fiction for the CIA, whose transformation into undercover agent and single-handed defeat of a conspiracy of renegade officers redeems the myth of the good spy at a time of intense disillusionment with the US government. Similarly, Pakula's *All the President's Men* offers only surface criticism. Deriving its suspense from the opposition between the rationality of *Washington Post* reporters Woodward and Bernstein and the dark power of the Nixon administration, Pakula removes Nixon so far from its tale of establishment renaissance that he is only pictured in the blurry news images of a fallen past.

The second group of films, which extends from the early JFK-assassination thriller *Executive Action* (1973), to *Parallax View*, *The Domino Principle* and *Twilight's Last Gleaming* (both 1978), is characterized by the imagination of uncontainable conspiracies and thus more directly prefigures the representative paranoid narrative of the 1990s, *The X-Files*. What unites these films is not simply, as in the standard account of post-Kennedy paranoia, their increased skepticism, even if this is understood to include radical doubt as to the possibility of knowledge. Rather, such uncertainty issues from their insight into a fundamental mutation in the logic of capitalist society and its demand *for* and exploitation *of* jouissance. This novel threat constitutes the central dilemma of *Parallax View*. The film begins with the murder of another presidential candidate, this time at the top of Seattle's Space Needle. Although the opening scene clearly shows two assassins, the first falling to his death and the second fleeing unnoticed, an official inquiry finds no evidence of a conspiracy. Instead, the murder is attributed to the dead assassin's "psychotic desire for public recognition." Madness therefore enters *Parallax View* early on, and attention to this element reveals a key difference to other paranoid narratives. The film's social detective is Joe Frady (Warren Beatty), an investigative reporter for a local newspaper in Portland, Oregon, with a reputation as a social misfit. Frady returns to the case when his ex-girlfriend becomes the most recent witness to the senator's death to join his fate. Frady's investigation leads him to the powerful assassination service of the Parallax Corporation. To gain access, he takes its recruitment exam, a psychological test that identifies men with homicidal tendencies. As Jameson observes, the same traits that make Frady rebel against the establishment qualify him as a professional assassin—both for the Parallax Corporation and in the eyes of any police investigation ready to blame a lone gunman.[71]

Frady's employment spells his inevitable end: on following a Parallax assassin into a convention hall he finds himself framed as a patsy when another senator is shot; the same fate awaits him as soon as he flees from the scene. Once more we are returned to the dyadic logic of the paranoid narrative, its reduction to a collective or social detective who is also the victim, and the corporation which functions as its paranoid object. Frady's rebelliousness is appropriated by a system against which his freedom and individuality might have once marshaled resistance. Herein lies the source of the film's paranoia: it observes a modification within capitalist logic, which no longer places strict limits on the subject's jouissance in the interest of Fordist productivity but exploits that enjoyment directly even where it is seemingly directed against it. *Parallax* turns paranoia's attention not to the state or an external enemy but to an analysis of capital itself, exercising a critique that refuses the comfort of individual agency.

Jameson's casual qualification of Frady as psychotic overlooks what seems most interesting about the film and prevents him from further investigating its fundamental insight. For Frady is not a paranoid psychotic, the madman disconnected from his social surroundings, but a thrill-seeker of the most extreme kind. Always ready to initiate a pub brawl, Frady can be understood as a Lacanian pervert. Frady's perversion becomes instrumental in his self-understanding as the cause of the Other's jouissance, a subject position that simultaneously achieves and regulates its own enjoyment by attributing it to the Other.[72] Perversion therefore plays into contemporary capitalism's incitement to constantly enjoy and reinforces a belief in its values, joining paranoia in what become, with the absence of an overarching structure of repression, pragmatic "defenses against the real" and any excess of jouissance this entails.[73] In return, the real against which this paranoia defends itself is no longer that of a punctual failure of symbolization, and the classic paranoid psychosis that contained it. As Lacan's late theorization of the real as intimately bound up with language and the circulation of knowledge indicates—a real not solely experienced by the psychotic but ever-present in a symbolic become porous—the form of paranoia whose rise is marked by *The Parallax View* can be understood as a paranoia of the real's constant circulation.[74] Cultural paranoia no longer masks isolated experiences of the real but confronts a real from which there is no escape. What appears most threatening in *Parallax View* is not the corporation's disciplinary control over Frady but its appropriation of Frady's affects for profit; not simply Parallax's infiltration of the state for its own means but the ceaseless flow of information between state and economy for mutual benefit.

5.3 Ordinary Paranoia: *Libra, Vineland,* and Neoliberalism

In "American Blood," written for *Rolling Stone* five years before the publication of *Libra*, DeLillo described Kennedy's violent death "as a natural disaster in the heartland of the real, the comprehensible, the plausible."

The essay's musings about the assassination find their way, almost verbatim in parts, into the novel. There they are presented as the thoughts of Nicholas Branch, a retired agent hired by the CIA to write the secret history of the event, and become "an aberration in the heartland of the real."[75] Both descriptions decipher Kennedy's death as a disruption of continuity, the regular ebb and flow of postwar American life. Phrased differently, we could say that the description embraces or produces one continuity, the consistency of American reality, while it rejects another: a history of the United States as the site of continuous violence, whether in the repeated murders of its leaders, class and racial struggle, or an imperialist foreign politics. As a narrative, *Libra* becomes possible from its inscription of JFK's death as an event that reifies the history of the present into a before and after, an ideological binary and a tale of rise and decline. This decision transforms the moment of the assassination, "seven seconds that broke the back of the American century," into the gleaming mediator between two eras.[76]

Yet DeLillo is far from uncritically embracing the ideological valuations that usually come with this binary: the nostalgia of the 1950s and the mythical glorification of Kennedy that mars Oliver Stone's *JFK*.[77] Once *Libra* has made its historiographic choice, the novel seems determined to minimize or even reverse its possible consequences. A retrospective investigation of America's cultural paranoia written from the perspective of the Reagan years, *Libra* almost completely confines itself to the assassination's pre-history, and DeLillo situates his novel in the domestic Cold War as visibly as possible. Within the first few pages, a passing woman hands Oswald a leaflet defending Julius and Ethel Rosenberg; he is told to worry about China, not Korea where Oswald's brother is stationed as a marine. Mary Frances Everett, the wife of one of the conspirators, listens to a radio commentary that urges vigilance against the enemy. At times it seems as if DeLillo recycles stock images of the 1950s. However, his account comes to life when he follows his characters to their global outposts and dreams of future assignments—to the Soviet Union and Japan, Cuba and Vietnam. *Libra* invokes workers unloading bananas from Latin America, pictures sugar cane cutters in Cuba and factory workers in Minsk, imagining a truly global framework for understanding a conflict whose settings extend beyond the hearts and minds of US citizens. With Pynchon's novels *Libra* shares a view of the Cold War's primary motivation: expanding capitalism into every corner of the world. This perspective also provides a prescient outlook on the continuities of the national security state between the Cold War and the war on terror: "This is the future of the Agency [. . .] Keeping track of world currencies. Moving and hiding money. Building reserves of money. Financing vast operations with complex networks of money."[78]

As I have noted, the novel attributes the phrase "aberration in the heartland of the real" to Branch, who, although he becomes DeLillo's author figure, is also distinguished from him by virtue of his failure to write the history of the assassination by *Libra*'s end. DeLillo's first version of the sentence, in the format of the literary essay, specified the shift in reality as a "natural disaster," a turn of phrase that seemed to absolve both Lee Harvey Oswald and American society of their responsibility. Branch's "aberration" equally signals an outside agent, but its reference to nature has moved underground, so to speak, into history. Perhaps it is telling given DeLillo's fascination with etymology that both disaster and aberration refer to astronomy, the negation of a star in the first case, the apparent displacement of a heavenly body in the second. For what causes the disaster of Kennedy's death, America's greatest political star of the last century, what tips his presidency in one direction rather than another, is the Libran Lee Oswald. Oswald, of course, represents the novel's greatest aberration, its foremost deviation from reason. DeLillo has acknowledged the Warren Commission Report as his major inspiration, and its characterization of Oswald as a mentally troubled loner weighs heavily on the novel.[79] As Peter Boxall has written, "[i]t is the Warren report that allows DeLillo to invent Oswald."[80] What does this tell us about DeLillo's Oswald? Oswald is "a fatherless boy" and madness an ever-present threat from his childhood onward when a policeman sends "him downtown to a building where the nut doctors pick at him."[81] Almost from the first page to the last, DeLillo invokes the standard tropes of splitting and fragmentation to indicate Oswald's psychological state. All the usual images are collected in *Libra*: the lack of a father, hints at incestuous desire, and a specific awkwardness that speaks of a failed integration into the Other.

DeLillo's portrait isn't just a standard description of madness, however. During the greater part of the novel he paints the picture of a veiled, or ordinary, psychosis.[82] Unlike a classic case of paranoid schizophrenia, *Libra*'s Oswald does not suffer from hallucinations and evinces no delusions of grandeur before his participation in JFK's murder. What distinguishes him from neurotic normality is his disconnection from himself and society, an invisible but seemingly insurmountable barrier. "He was not connected to anything here," thinks Oswald, "and not quite connected to himself."[83] His repeated attempts to integrate into the symbolic world by studying history, overcoming his dyslexia, and learning Russian are to no avail: "The more he spoke, the more he felt he was softly split in two."[84] Oswald's perspective remains that of an external observer who cannot bridge the gap that separates him from the world. Unable to participate as one among countless others, he imagines history and politics as a merger with a symbolic authority that always remains alien to him, and tries to bolster his fragile sense of self with the bric-a-brac that clutters an average existence. Shortly before the assassination, Oswald imagines once more what he has attempted all his life, to find a place for himself, to slot into anonymous normality: "They'd get an apartment with a balcony, their own furniture for a change, modern pieces, sleek and clean. These are standard ways to stop being lonely."[85]

Oswald's psychosis becomes an authoritative explanation for his actions in *Libra*. What accompanies this understanding is a psychologization of politics, a conception of the latter as "just the thinnest outer crust."[86] DeLillo's characters suggest a number of deeper layers for their own and other people's actions, among them astrology, but it seems fair to say that psychology remains a privileged method of interpretation for a novel filled with psychoanalytic terminology and implicit references to the unconscious mind. DeLillo has insisted in an interview that "Oswald's attempt on Kennedy was more complicated. I think it was based on elements outside politics and, as someone in the novel says, outside history."[87] Without Oswald's final run-in with history, his selection by the novel's conspirators as an assassin and patsy all at once, he may have escaped the fate that soon awaits him and the transformation of his ordinary into florid psychosis. Like Wright's protagonist Cross Damon in *The Outsider*, the Cold War intervenes and drives those mad who find themselves in its crosshairs.

As we near a new era post-JFK, Oswald's psychosis becomes more pronounced. DeLillo now depicts him as clinically paranoid: Oswald detects subliminal messages buried in the articles of a left-wing magazine and imagines that a film about 1930s Cuba is shown on television for his sake. Persecuted and megalomaniac, Oswald appears truly external to society: "a distorted figure in some darkness outside ordinary night."[88] In the end, rogue CIA personnel turns the agency's logic of secrecy and treason against itself, and Oswald's ordinary turns into extraordinary madness. Lacking a phantasmatic image of himself, he presents an easy target for the CIA operatives that plan the assassination. "[W]e'll help him select a fantasy," one of them says early on. As Oswald lies in his cell after Kennedy's death, his own awaiting him, he adopts such a fantasy in the head rush of delusional grandeur: "He and Kennedy were partners. The figure of the gunman in the window was inextricable from the victim and his history. This sustained Oswald in his cell. It gave him what he needed to live."[89] In contrast to the narratives of Hollywood cinema, Oswald does not conform to the imagination of a paranoid Other. He lacks the threatening agency of a brainwashed Raymond Shaw in *Manchurian Candidate*; nor does he express Bree Daniels' provocative jouissance in *Klute*. When Oswald crosses the boundaries of the novel's two narrative streams, which have kept his biography and the conspirator's plot separate up to that point, DeLillo imagines Oswald's psychosis as a radical loss of subjectivity. DeLillo's perspective on madness reveals a logic contrary to countercultural celebrations of madness and a view much closer to Jameson's neo-Marxism, whose essays on schizophrenic postmodernity I analyze in the next chapter. As Frank Lentricchia writes: "The disturbing strength of *Libra* [. . .] is its refusal to offer its readers a comfortable place outside of Oswald."[90] Oswald's paranoia is ultimately shared by every major character. The conspirators Ferrie and Guy Banister, Oswald's mother Marguerite and his murderer Jack Ruby—all are depicted as paranoid in their everyday interactions, while the renegade CIA agents Win Everett and Larry Parmenter show a similar pattern in their hatred of Cuba's newly communist regime. Even Nicholas Branch, researching the past in the novel's present, succumbs to paranoia.

What distinguishes DeLillo's novel from many earlier paranoid narratives is perhaps as simple as this: in *Libra* there is no secure place outside madness, outside delusion. This generalization of psychosis extends to *Vineland*, which also shares with the former the look back at Cold War America and the publication in its dying years. Pynchon's most overtly political novel adds to this retrospective evaluation an account of psychiatric de-institutionalization and a far more ironic stance on paranoia. The privatization of mental health care, one of Ronald Reagan's neoliberal innovations during his tenure as governor of California from 1967–75, also led to a change in the status of madness, forcing many mentally ill people into homelessness and expanding the need for halfway houses and community care. Pynchon picks up on these institutional changes by introducing *Vineland*'s protagonist, Zoyd Wheeler, as certified insane. Wheeler's status as the outpatient of a local health care center means that "unless he did something publicly crazy before a date now less than a week away, he would no longer qualify for benefits."[91] As the reader learns over the course of the novel, the protagonist's monthly mental disability check forms part of a deal he strikes with a police officer variously engaged in the infiltration of left-wing organizations and the war on drugs.

Vineland thus draws a direct connection between Cold War domestic oppression and the politicization of madness. As in *The Crying of Lot 49*, this association owes less to the narrative's paranoid epistemology than to the wider investigation of social responsibility set in motion by its initial identification of conspiracy—in this case, the complicity of Zoyd's ex-wife in undercover police operations. This is not to say that Pynchon's narrative does not engage in conspiratorial story-telling: in contrast to *The Crying of Lot 49*, and its exploration of the paranoid epiphany, in *Vineland* there is no doubting the conspiracy or its consequences for old and new left. The cynicism of Pynchon's characters, the world-weary acceptance of their own government's secrets and lies, accurately reflects most of Americans' distrust of national politics. It marks the historical divide between the immediate postwar era and the final years of the century but also presents a telling evolution of cultural paranoia. As with madness, which haunts this as it had DeLillo's novel, the extraordinary has turned ordinary: the mystery of conspiracy has sedimented into a paranoia that has become part of everyday reality, one among many defenses against the real of neoliberal capitalism. Rather than counting as evidence for paranoia's slow demise in a "post-paranoid" era, as Michael Wood has claimed, this contemporary reality could be seen as illustrating paranoia's explosive dissemination.[92] What Jameson has said of postmodern culture can be adapted to include conspiracy culture, namely that the dissolution of hegemonic normality has led to its "prodigious expansion [. . .] throughout the social realm."[93] In the process, conspiracy culture splinters from a clearly identifiable structure into a basic sub-atomic particle of US society and remains with us today, long after the Cold War ended.

Notes

1 Richard Hofstadter, introduction to *The Paranoid Style in American Politics and Other Essays* (London: Cape, 1966), ix.
2 Harold D. Lasswell and Dorothy Blumenstock, *World Revolutionary Propaganda: A Chicago Study* (Freeport, NY: Books for Libraries, 1970), 296.
3 Hofstadter, "The Paranoid Style in American Politics," in *The Paranoid Style*, 4 and 11.
4 Cited in David S. Brown, *Richard Hofstadter: An Intellectual Biography* (Chicago: University of Chicago Press, 2006), 159–160.
5 Bernard Bailyn, *The Ideological Origins of the American Revolution* (Cambridge, MA: Belknap Press of Harvard University Press, 1992).
6 Matthew Gray, *Conspiracy Theories in the Arab World: Sources and Politics* (London: Routledge, 2010), 168–169.
7 Ibid., 6.
8 Among the most influential studies within such a revisionist approach are Mark Fenster, *Conspiracy Theories: Secrecy and Power in American Culture* (Minneapolis: University of Minnesota Press, 2008) and Peter Knight, *Conspiracy Culture: From the Kennedy Assassination to "The X-Files"* (London: Routledge, 2000).
9 For a recent article that emphasizes paranoia's function as a dispositif of state power see: Jonathan Bach, "Power, Secrecy, Paranoia: Technologies of Governance and the Structure of Rule," *Cultural Politics* 6 (2010): 287–302.
10 Jacques Lacan, "Presentation on Psychical Causality," in *Écrits: The First Complete Edition in English*, trans. Bruce Fink (New York: Norton, 2006), 135.
11 Insofar as it implied that the United States and the Soviet Union possessed equal power, bipolarity was highly misleading, even more so after the emergence of China as a major power in the 1970s. This reality did not necessarily blunt the ideological force that the term possessed.
12 Fenster, *Conspiracy Theories*, 36.
13 Knight, *Conspiracy Culture*, 3.
14 Fenster, *Conspiracy Theories*, 194.
15 Brian Keeley, "Of Conspiracy Theories," *Journal of Philosophy* 96, no. 3 (1999): 119; Ray Pratt, *Projecting Paranoia: Conspiratorial Visions in American Film* (Lawrence, KA: University of Kansas Press, 2001), 17; and Knight, *Conspiracy Culture*, 3.
16 Michael Paul Rogin, *Ronald Reagan, the Movie, and Other Episodes in Political Demonology* (Berkeley, CA: University of California Press, 1987), xiii.
17 Knight, *Conspiracy Culture*, 3–4.
18 Jodi Dean, *Aliens in America: Conspiracy Cultures from Outerspace to Cyberspace* (Ithaca, NY: Cornell University Press, 1998), 136.
19 Keeley, "Of Conspiracy Theories," 126.
20 Ibid., 123.
21 Martin Parker, "Human Science as Conspiracy Theory," in *The Age of Anxiety: Conspiracy Theory and the Human Sciences*, ed. Jane Parish and Martin Parker (Oxford: Wiley, 2001), 191–207; Clare Birchall, "The Commodification of Conspiracy Theory," in *The Age of Anxiety*, 249.
22 Jacques Lacan, "The Mirror Stage as Formative of the I Function as Revealed in Psychoanalytic Experience," in *Écrits: The First Complete Edition in English*, 75–81.
23 Jacques Lacan, "Aggressiveness in Psychoanalysis," in *Écrits: The First Complete Edition in English*, 82–101.
24 Jacques Lacan, *The Seminar of Jacques Lacan. Book III: The Psychoses 1955–1956*, ed. Jacques-Alain Miller, trans. Russell Grigg (New York: Norton, 1997), 120.

25 Importantly, symbolic knowledge is defined by Lacan as unconscious and as such confronts the resistance of modern reason, which seeks absolute mastery over it.
26 Lacan, *The Psychoses*, 93.
27 Lacan, *The Psychoses*, 18.
28 Sigmund Freud, "Psycho-Analytical Notes on an Autobiographical Account of a Case of Paranoia (Dementia Paranoides)," in *The Standard Edition of the Complete Psychological Works of Sigmund Freud*, vol. 12., trans. and ed. J. Strachey (London: Hogarth, 1981), 15–16.
29 Jacques Lacan, "The Subversion of the Subject and the Dialectic of Desire," in *Écrits: The First Complete Edition in English*, 688.
30 Véronique Voruz and Bogdan Wolf, preface to *The Later Lacan: An Introduction* (Albany, NY: SUNY Press, 2007), viii–xviii.
31 Jacques-Alain Miller, "A Contribution of the Schizophrenic to the Psychoanalytic Clinic," trans. and ed. Ellie Ragland and Anne Pulis, *The Symptom* 2 (2002), accessed November 29, 2010, http://www.lacan.com/contributionf.htm.
32 Jacques Lacan, "Présentation des Mémoires d'un névropathe," in *Autres Écrits* (Paris: Seuil, 2001), 214.
33 Alan Nadel, *Containment Culture: American Narratives, Postmodernism, and the Atomic Age* (Durham, NC: Duke University Press, 1995).
34 Thomas Pynchon, *The Crying of Lot 49* (New York: Vintage, 1996), 118.
35 Ibid., 126.
36 Tobin Siebers, *Cold War Criticism and the Politics of Skepticism* (New York: Oxford University Press, 1993).
37 Pynchon, *The Crying of Lot 49*, 56.
38 Pynchon, *The Crying of Lot 49*, 123.
39 Oliver Harris, "Can You See a Virus? The Queer Cold War of William Burroughs," *Journal of American Studies* 33, no. 2 (August 1999): 261.
40 William S. Burroughs, *Queer* (New York: Viking, 1985), 100–1; and see, for instance: William Burroughs, *The Soft Machine* (London: Calder and Boyars, 1968), 20.
41 William S. Burroughs, "Letter to Allen Ginsberg (5. 3. 1952)," in *The Letters of William S. Burroughs, 1945–1959*, ed. Oliver Harris (New York: Viking, 1993), 104.
42 Burroughs, "Letter to Allen Ginsberg (18. 6. 1956)," in *The Letters of William S. Burroughs*, 321–322.
43 Ishmael Reed, *Mumbo Jumbo* (New York: Scribner, 1996), 169.
44 Burroughs, "Letter to Allen Ginsberg (18.6.1956)," 320.
45 Burroughs, "Letter to Allen Ginsberg (1.5.1950)," 70; and Allen Ginsberg, "Kaddish," in: *Collected Poems, 1947–1997* (New York: Harper, 2006), 220.
46 "Sgt. Jack J. Pendleton," accessed July 20, 2015, http://web.archive.org/web/20121026115402/http://www.history.navy.mil/danfs/s10/sgt_jack_j_pendleton.htm.
47 Elia Kazan, *Panic in the Streets* (1950; Munich: Universum, 2008), DVD.
48 Richard Schickel, *Elia Kazan: A Biography* (New York: Harper, 2005), 270.
49 Elia Kazan, "A Statement," *New York Times*, April 12, 1952, 2.
50 Ibid.
51 Elia Kazan, *A Life* (New York: Da Capo, 1997), 468.
52 Jacques Lacan, "Presentation on Psychical Causality," in *Écrits: The First Complete Edition in English*, 166.
53 For two contrasting and informative studies, which rely heavily on such aspects of alien invasion films, see: Mark Jancovich, *Rational Fears: American Horror in the 1950s* (Manchester: Manchester University Press, 1996); and Peter Biskind,

Seeing Is Believing: How Hollywood Taught us to Stop Worrying and Love the Fifties (London: Bloomsbury, 2001).

54 Biskind, *Seeing Is Believing*, 111.

55 John Frankenheimer, *The Manchurian Candidate* (1962; Los Angeles: Twentieth Century Fox, 2004), DVD.

56 Fredric Jameson, *The Political Unconscious: Narrative as a Socially Symbolic Act* (London: Methuen, 1981), 112; and see for a discussion in reference to conspiracy films: "Totality as Conspiracy," in *The Geopolitical Aesthetic: Cinema and Space in the World System* (Bloomington, IN: Indiana University Press, 1992), 34–38.

57 For a detailed account see: Matthew Frye Jacobson and Gaspar González, *What Have They Built You to Do? The Manchurian Candidate and Cold War America* (Minneapolis and London: University of Minnesota Press, 2006).

58 See my discussion of George Kennan's "Long Telegram" and "Sources of Soviet Conduct" in chapter 2.

59 For Lacan's elaboration of acting out: Jacques Lacan, *Le Séminaire de Jacques Lacan: Livre X: L'angoisse*, texte établi Jacques-Alain Miller (Paris: Seuil, 2004), 135–153.

60 For an argument that theorizes the Kennedy assassination as a shift from an accessible truth to its postmodern questioning see: Eva Horn, *Der Geheime Krieg: Verrat, Spionage und moderne* Fiktion (Frankfurt: Fischer, 2007), 420–421.

61 David A. Cook, *Lost Illusions: American Cinema in the Shadow of Watergate and Vietnam, 1970–1979, History of the American Cinema*, vol. 9 (New York: Scribner, 2002), 188.

62 Jameson, *The Geopolitical Aesthetic*, 33.

63 Alan J. Pakula, *Klute* (1971; Burbank, CA: Warner Home Video, 2006), DVD.

64 Christine Gledhill, "*Klute* 2: Feminism and *Klute*," in *Women in Film Noir*, ed. E. Ann Kaplan (London: BFI, 1980), 112–128.

65 Richard Thompson, "Mr. Pakula goes to Washington: Alan J. Pakula on *All the President's Men*," *Film Comment* 12, no. 5 (1976): 19.

66 Francis Ford Coppola, *The Conversation* (1974; Los Angeles: Paramount, 2000), DVD.

67 Michael Ryan and Douglas Kellner, *Camera Politica: The Politics and Ideology of Contemporary Hollywood Film* (Bloomington, IN: Indiana University Press, 1990), 98.

68 Dennis Turner, "The Subject of *The Conversation*," *Cinema Journal* 24, no. 4 (1985): 12.

69 Coppola talks about this feature of camera work at length in his audio commentary on the film. Francis Ford Coppola, "Commentary," *The Conversation* (1974; Los Angeles: Paramount, 2000), DVD.

70 Alan J. Pakula, *The Parallax View* (1974; Burbank; CA: Warner Bros., 1999), DVD.

71 Jameson, *The Geopolitical Aesthetic*, 59.

72 For a definition of perversion that summarizes Lacan's thought on the topic see: Dylan Evans, *An Introductory Dictionary of Lacanian Psychoanalysis* (London: Routledge, 1996), 138–140.

73 Miller, "A Contribution of the Schizophrenic to the Psychoanalytic Clinic."

74 For a summary see, for instance: Voruz and Wolf, *The Later Lacan*, ix–x.

75 Don DeLillo, "American Blood," *Rolling Stone*, December 9, 1983, 22; and Don DeLillo, *Libra* (London: Penguin, 1989), 15.

76 Ibid., 181.

77 Although it is difficult today to comprehend the widespread damnation of Stone's film at the time of its release, its failures are also clearly visible. For one,

Stone transforms Kennedy into a martyr against the military and political establishment. Oliver Stone, *JFK* (1991; Burbank, CA: Warner Home Video, 1991), DVD; and see for an even-handed analysis: Christopher Sharrett, "Conspiracy Theory and Political Murder in America: Oliver Stone's *JFK* and the Facts of the Matter," in *The New American Cinema*, ed. John Lewis (Durham, NC: Duke University Press, 1998), 217–247.
78 DeLillo, *Libra*, 361.
79 Kevin Connolly, "An Interview with Don DeLillo," in *Conversations with Don DeLillo*, ed. Thomas DePietro (Jackson, MS: University Press of Mississippi, 2005), 25; and President's Commission on the Assassination of President Kennedy, *Report of the President's Commission on the Assassination of President Kennedy* (Washington, DC: United States Government Printing Office, 1964), 375–424; and 669–740.
80 Peter Boxall, *Don DeLillo: The Possibility of Fiction* (London: Routledge, 2006), 142.
81 DeLillo, *Libra*, 11.
82 My use of this term is somewhat broader than in Lacanian clinical practice, and takes seriously Jacques-Alain's Miller's suggestion that it also applies to cases where a psychotic break might later occur. See Miller, "Ordinary Psychosis Revisited," *Psychoanalytical Notebooks* 19 (2009): 139–167.
83 De Lillo, *Libra*, 89.
84 Ibid., 90.
85 Ibid., 371.
86 Ibid., 320.
87 Anthony DeCurtis, "'An Outsider in This Society': An Interview with Don DeLillo," in *Conversations with Don DeLillo*, 59.
88 De Lillo, *Libra*, 424.
89 Ibid., 435
90 Frank Lentricchia, "*Libra* as Postmodern Critique," in *Introducing Don DeLillo*, ed. Frank Lentricchia (Durham, NC: Duke University Press, 1991), 204.
91 Thomas Pynchon, *Vineland* (London: Minerva, 1990).
92 Michael Wood, "Post-Paranoid," *London Review of Books*, February 5, 1998, accessed April 9, 2015, http://www.lrb.co.uk/v20/n03/michael-wood/post-paranoid.
93 Fredric Jameson, "Postmodernism, or the Cultural Logic of Late Capitalism," *New Left Review* I/146 (1984): 53–92.

6 A Schizophrenic Postmodernity

Literary Studies and the Politics of Critique

In *The Liberal Imagination* (1950), perhaps the decisive text of postwar criticism, Lionel Trilling observed a curious reversal in attitudes toward mental illness. Increasingly, psychological vocabulary was used not only by those who sought to discredit artists but, quite to the contrary, functioned as an honorific. These cultural diagnoses, Trilling noted, accepted the artist's essential madness as a fact and made it a condition of his or her power to speak the truth. Far from condemning such statements as naïve, or dismissing them as a return to romantic notions of genius, Trilling offered a series of characteristically level-headed observations. Neurotic and psychotic patients were often more aware of their unconscious thoughts and feelings than supposedly sane people, and their perception of reality was undoubtedly more intense. Then Trilling went a step further, somewhat undermining the distinction between sanity and insanity that he had just established. One could argue, he added, that *"[w]e are all ill"*—a statement whose implications of "understanding the totality of human nature in the terms of disease—are vast."[1]

Since making his name as a literary critic for *Partisan Review* in the late 1930s, Trilling had steadily distanced himself from his earlier communist sympathies and embraced a self-styled liberal center that had become weary of political commitment and guided by an awareness of the subtle power of sentiment in the expression of ideas. Trilling's remarks on mental illness extended an earlier discussion in the same volume that noted the great value of psychoanalysis for criticism, specifically a renewed sense of literature's "latent und ambiguous meanings."[2] This emphasis on latency pointed toward the unconscious as the well-spring of culture, and it was there that the critic should go to discover literature's ultimate significance. Trilling's method was aptly summarized in the title of his essay: "Freud and Literature." By necessity, this embrace of Freudianism was deeply entangled with the historical conjuncture in which it intervened: Trilling portrayed the founder of psychoanalysis as an arch-rationalist, a thinker who was distrustful of emotions and argued for the control of the irrational. Such a reading unequivocally understood Freud's famous injunction "Where id was, there ego shall be" to mean that id should become ego, rather than discovering in his words a call to free the unconscious from repression.

The complex relationship between ego and id also came to the fore in the preface to *The Liberal Imagination*, which declared liberalism to be the "sole intellectual tradition" in the United States after World War II.[3] Trilling's statement was brazen but it did not lack a certain programmatic truth. Published in the same year as Schlesinger's *The Vital Center* and three years prior to Reinhold Niebuhr's *The Irony of American History*, Trilling's essays signaled the emergence of postwar liberalism and the arrival of a distinctively Cold War literary criticism. One of the defining gestures of the former was to slander the left and right with equal gusto, and in typical fashion Trilling did so by denying that liberalism's rivals possessed any ideas at all. Leaving behind his Marxist past, and in the knowledge that progressive politics was already on the defensive, it was the right that drew his ire. It couldn't be doubted, Trilling wrote, that conservative and reactionary impulses were strong in the United States, perhaps much stronger than most people acknowledged. Yet these did not "express themselves in ideas but only in action or in irritable mental gestures which seek to resemble ideas."[4] In the emphasis on the irrationality of the right, and the portrayal of its proponents as cranks, *The Liberal Imagination* joins the ranks of liberal psychopathology.

At stake for much literature and literary criticism in the postwar era was the development of a new relation between politics and art after the disillusionment with Marxism—a series of disappointments marked most dramatically by Nikita Khrushchev's disclosures about the crimes of Stalinism in 1956.[5] Trilling, as so many scholars in his wake, found himself moving toward a liberal skepticism that countered the enthusiasm of (his own) youth with a critical distance from emotions seen that he now saw as potentially dangerous. This was coupled with an emphasis on small-scale reform rather than revolution. Frequently, such a strategy of small steps began by educating those very emotions, and thus entailed a novel definition of what constituted politics. Trilling writes:

> It is the wide sense of the word that is nowadays forced upon us, for clearly it is no longer possible to think of politics except as the politics of culture, the organization of human life toward some end or other, toward the modification of sentiments[6]

Such an understanding of politics and literary scholarship had the advantage of retaining their intimate bond while limiting what either could legitimately engage in. If politics as the "organization of human life" was to be located in the cultural arena rather than in wholesale economic transformation, Trilling now saw the goal of literature and its criticism in the "modification of sentiments." Here, the distance to Marxist views seemed less pronounced but any potential misunderstanding was clarified by Trilling's thoughts on method. For if the meaning of literature was "latent and ambiguous," as he had written in "Freud and Literature," neither literature nor literary criticism should seek a modification of sentiments by outright pedagogy. To make latency manifest and deny ambiguity in exchange for political partisanship, as most left-wing authors and critics had done until World War II, was to do violence to essential characteristics of literature—specifically ambiguity and paradox, soon to become central to the ideology of literary studies.

The liberal critic's distrust of emotions also carried risks, and Trilling was well aware of them. Liberalism's goal, the "rational direction of human life," placed limits on the emotions: only certain sentiments were admissible, they were rationally justified only under certain circumstances—and in practice this often meant that they were justifiably felt only by certain people.[7] An illiberal vein ran through liberalism, and this presented particular problems for the study of culture, for the denial of certain emotions also put limits on the imagination and the critic's appreciation thereof. The relation between "Art and Neurosis" thus presented a test case for the method Trilling was putting forward. A Freudian depth model of reading, in which literature offered up its latent meaning to a critic schooled in probing those very depths, could not easily dismiss the abyss of madness. After all, psychoanalysis derived its major insights into supposed normality from studying what counted as abnormal. Against this stood the need many critics felt for moral evaluation: of writers and their writing, of US society, its literature and culture. Trilling's solution to this conundrum was seemingly to brush it aside. "[T]he belief in the artist's neuroticism allows the philistine to shut his ears to what the artist says. But on the other hand it allows him to listen [. . .] If he did not want to listen at all, he would say 'insane.'"[8] In the end, not only philistines felt the need to condemn the madness of culture—unless one considered most literary critics philistines. Nor did Trilling, no different in this respect from most postwar intellectuals, keep to the distinction between neurosis and psychosis when it suited his needs. But his seeming dismissal was otherwise straight to the point. Throughout the Cold War era, literary critics would return time and again to the relation between art and madness. Most of them kept one ear shut, branding some literature schizophrenic and selected authors insane, while keeping the other close to the ground, analyzing cultural change with the help of a sophisticated understanding of that very same psychopathology.

After *The Liberal Imagination*, psychopathology would rarely be absent from the core vocabulary of literary studies during the Cold War. The debates around postmodernism that slowly gained traction after 1960 and occupied much of the terrain in the 1970s and '80s made schizophrenia and paranoia central to a phenomenon whose rejection or celebration often depended on, or went hand in hand with, the position taken on these two concepts. Critics and philosophers, like Sylvère Lotringer, who disseminated the writings of Gilles Deleuze and Félix Guattari in the United States, or the Egyptian-born Ihab Hassan, celebrated a revolutionizing schizophrenia alongside postmodern art and literature. Most critics, particularly those who situated themselves on the left or had started out as Marxists, remained wary. Two reasons, not always easily separated, motivated their skepticism. The first was the moral rejection of a youth and counterculture that violated the particularly narrow Cold War version of social mores. The second, which motivates Fredric Jameson's cultural pathology, shares a similar preference for rational over affective politics and advances a measured critique of an at times depoliticized counterculture. Jameson's analysis of a schizophrenic subjectivity is not primarily motivated by ethical judgment. But his appropriation of psychopathology expresses a skepticism that shares more with liberalism's retreat from mass politics than it dare admit.

Part one of this chapter looks at a number of prominent critics who were faced with the evident decline and arrival into middle-class respectability of modernism and the rise of a movement that appeared equally amorphous if much less dignified. The names they gave to this novel phenomenon reflected their struggle to grasp it: the post-modern, post-modernism, and with increasing use, postmodernism. In the writings of Irving Howe, Leslie Fiedler, and Hassan, the difficulty of understanding a new phenomenon at times combined with a philistine unwillingness to listen to insanity. What constituted postmodernism? Was it a literary style? A Foucauldian episteme? Did it merely mark a modernism in decline, or the arrival of something excitingly new? What seemed clearer to these critics, if perhaps too obvious to warrant much discussion, was the political and cultural background against which they wrote. As Fiedler notes, his *Collected Essays* (1971) "record impressions and responses [. . .] to a period bounded by two Cold Wars: the first between the two great powers on either pole of Europe, [. . .] the second between the old and the young."[9] Writing at the tail end of the Sixties, the generation gap was at the forefront of Fiedler's mind but the showdown between East and West overshadowed even that conflict. The existential threat of the Cold War meant that critics frequently proposed periodizing notions such as "the Atomic Age" as alternatives to postmodernism.[10] Yet the impact of the Cold War went much further than terminological discussions. The destruction of parties, unions, and left publications; the blacklisting of artists, teachers, and academics; and the public backlash against progressive ideas forced many into silence, and drove untold others into hiding or switching their political allegiance.[11]

Once again, Trilling pointed the way when he redefined the relation between scholarship and politics. The prominence of psychological vocabulary was itself evidence of postwar criticism's moral impetus. Increasingly, politics shrank to an ethics of the self and an aesthetics of abstract ideals, mass action met with disdain. As literary criticism turned into an academic exercise, and literary critics became isolated from the tastes of ordinary readers, this sentiment only gained in strength. In *The Postmodern Turn* (1987), which collected two decades of thinking about the topic, Ihab Hassan writes: "politics can overcrowd our responses to art and life. For what is politics [. . .] again? An excuse to bully or shout in public."[12] Literature and literary figures that failed to keep their distance from politics, or violated the ideals of respectable behavior, were increasingly classified as insane.

Postmodern literature and theory, Ann Douglas and others contend, remain inexplicable outside of their Cold War context.[13] This book has argued that psychopathology provided America with a set of tropes that became central for thinking through its politics and culture, and nowhere was this more pronounced than in a literary criticism that made their intersection its very foundation. Examining this psychological vocabulary enables us to comprehend the intellectual culture of the Cold War more accurately than we have been able to so far. Douglas and Siebers lay out a general framework for understanding Cold War criticism, but their polemics do not engage in the analysis of individual writers or intellectual movements that would allow us to specify these interconnections. Following my reading of prominent postwar critics in part one of this chapter, the next section focuses on the European philosophies of madness that spread through academic and artistic circles in the 1970s and '80s. If the writings of Fiedler and Hassan were already awash in references to Michel Foucault and R.D. Laing, a succeeding generation of critics based much of their thinking on the imported goods of Jacques Derrida, Deleuze, Jean Baudrillard, Jacques Lacan, and others. Yet, the dominance of fashionable French terminology has tended to obscure the continued impact of earlier intellectual traditions and specifically Cold War debates. This chapter aims to recover some of these continuities.

One of the signal events of the importation of European psychopathology was the "Schizo-Culture" conference, held at Columbia University in New York in 1975. Three years later, it was followed by an eponymous issue of the journal *Sémiotexte* that reprinted some of the talks given at the conference and added artwork that engaged with its theme. While "Schizo-Culture" remains far less known than the famous symposium on "The Language of Criticism and the Sciences of Man" that took place in 1966 at Johns Hopkins University and has since figured as a convenient birth date for 'French theory' in the United States, the later occasion illustrates the unique crossover between community activism, psychology, philosophy, and literature that characterized Cold War psychopolitics. Despite the huge potential of such a gathering, which took Deleuze to America on his only visit there and brought him together with William Burroughs, its impact on US culture is too diffuse to specify concretely. The remainder of the chapter thus turns to the work of Jameson, America's most influential theorist of postmodernism. My discussion of Jameson's writings functions as a case study of the transfer and translation of European psychopathology to Cold War America. Jameson's shift from a euphoric Deleuzian schizophrenia to Lacan's tragic account of psychosis exemplifies a much wider movement from revolutionary enthusiasm to political retreat that begins soon after the

"Schizo-Culture" conference and culminates in a dystopian portrayal of US culture during the Reagan years.

Despite Jameson's ostentatious Marxism, his work continues to pose many of the questions that animated Trilling's liberal criticism. Where Trilling formulated the relationship between culture and politics anew for the postwar era, half a century later Jameson seeks an exit from the limitations of Cold War culture. Yet his starting point—and some of the contradictions inherent in his undertaking—owe much to postwar criticism. Like Trilling, Jameson's tethers politics to the psyche and tends to restrict political action to the cultural sphere, more specifically to the expertise of the academic intellectual. It is far from coincidental, then, that one of his best-known works recalls Trilling's emphasis on the "latent and ambiguous" meaning of literature. *The Political Unconscious* (1981) initiates the most productive time of Jameson's career, a decade capped by the publication of *Postmodernism, or, the Cultural Logic of Late Capitalism* (1991). The next section looks at the first discussions of that phenomenon in the United States.

6.1 Literary Criticism and Cultural Pathology since Modernism

When literary scholars began to analyze the cultural formations emerging in the wake of modernism, diagnoses of madness often featured prominently in their writing. Schooled in a Freudian criticism that sought to decipher unconscious traces and latent meanings, they were intimately familiar with psychological concepts and the writings of leading European and US psychoanalysts. As they negotiated a mixture of fascination and dread for a literature that refused to yield to established categories, critics tended to understand these works and their authors as an assault on reason. In their hands, psychopathology became central to defining postwar culture, and their lay diagnoses have shaped our understanding of it ever since.

Irving Howe's essay on "Mass Society and Postmodern Fiction" (1959) may not have been the first North American mention of the term, an honor that seems to belong to the poet Charles Olson.[14] Yet Howe established what might be the most important feature of US discussions of postmodernism, namely their essential ambivalence. Where Olson had spoken of the postmodern affirmatively, linking poetic innovation to a utopian future, and C. Wright Mills compared the postmodern period to the dark ages, Howe seesawed between positive and negative evaluations in a manner later critics would never shake off.[15] Howe spoke approvingly of the postmodern novel as representing the "interesting minority" of literature published in the 1940s and '50s, counting among them Ralph Ellison's *Invisible Man* and Saul Bellow's *The Adventures of Augie March*. By contrast, "the young men in San Francisco," as he referred to the Beats and other West Coast writers, were judged very differently.[16] Ellison's and Bellow's achievement was to make sense of an incoherent epoch, a mass society threatened by dehumanization. Unlike these writers, the Beats rejected metaphysical reflection for a literature in which Howe could only detect an "incoherence of feeling and statement."[17] Such perceived incoherence signaled a lack of reason to a critic who diagnosed countercultural authors with "psychic and social disturbance."[18] Ultimately, Howe preferred to read literature that strayed from established criteria as symptoms of an underlying disorder, and the minds who produced such work as mad.

Half a decade later, Leslie Fiedler's "The New Mutants" continued this vein of literary symptomology. Describing himself as a former Marxist and rationalist humanist, Fiedler portrayed the counterculture as a radical break with earlier models of a centered self: authors such as Ken Kesey, Norman Mailer, and Burroughs could only be described as schizoid, schizophrenic, and psychotic—the terminology varied and was, in fact, used interchangeably. Fiedler also highlighted the role of drugs in moving toward a madness that epitomized creativity and freedom and replaced rational judgment with hallucinatory vision. Not only did these authors see insanity as a honorific, as Trilling had already noted, but these "new irrationalists" sought to live a life modeled on madness.[19] Far more so than Howe before him, Fiedler positioned psychopathology at the center of a new postmodern era. It was, he wrote, "a hallmark of our times."[20] In specifying this new era, Fiedler introduced a theme that would come to play a dominant role in Jameson's later writing on postmodernism: to writers emulating catatonia, the past and even the present meant very little. As a consequence, history itself stood on the verge of disappearing. Fiedler's position on his subject was aptly captured by the negative implications of his essay title, but this was to change considerably in his later statements on this topic. Early appraisals of postmodernism consistently failed to judge the new era on its own terms. Both the method and language of critics remained indebted to a now defunct modernism, charged Fiedler in "Cross the Border—Close the Gap." Thus, they were unable to see what contemporary literature had to offer. His solution was to call for a postmodernist criticism appropriate to its subject, a form of reading that was radically contextual and eschewed moral judgment. Striking out in a new direction, Fiedler embraced the current rage of pop art as subversive, despite or because of its apparent lack of political content.

This conception of postmodernism as innovative and rebellious, yet safely apolitical, constituted the main thrust of Ihab Hassan's essays—easily the most insightful critic of postmodernism in the United States before Jameson, and one of its most prolonged interlocutors. Hassan presented a much more sophisticated conception of postmodern literature and would have a profound impact on later writers. Howe and Fiedler's early essays had evaluated the new literature against the standard of an increasingly canonized modernism, but Hassan observed postmodernism's emergence from distinct strands within the former. Samuel Beckett, Dada, even Ernest Hemingway, represented a "literature of exhaustion" that approached silence and heralded the fragmentation of the bourgeois subject.[21] If silence was the logical consequence of this process of fragmentation, then within it lurked an escape route for literature: the mystic pain and ecstasy of madness. For Hassan, modernity had discovered "the postmodern at its center" and its foremost representatives were writers and philosophers that appropriated madness as vocabulary or method: Friedrich Nietzsche, Michel Foucault, Norman O. Brown, R.D. Laing, and once again, Burroughs.[22]

The lineage of postmodern literature sketched by Hassan not only offered a plausible historical and intellectual trajectory—as Hassan was well aware, Burroughs had inherited his cut-up method from the French Dadaist Tristan Tzara. Hassan also explicitly linked what he saw as the schizophrenic language of postmodernism to "the growing insanity of the cold war."[23] This acknowledgment did not lead to an explicitly sociopolitical conception, however. From time to time, Hassan toyed with the possibility that postmodernism represented not just an artistic tendency but constituted part of a larger economic and political conjuncture. Such ideas were never fully developed because they ran up against what he admitted to be a deep personal ambivalence toward politics, a suspicion that sustained political reflection would somehow damage literary criticism. This did not mean that Hassan refrained from ideological evaluation: if modernism was deeply elitist, it successor was portrayed as a natural ally of Cold War liberalism and applauded for its inherent anti-authoritarianism.[24]

The question that emerged most forcefully from the historicizing focus of Hassan's criticism, whether postmodernism was part of, or a break with, modernism, could not be satisfactorily answered in this way. In the absence of an account that squared culture, politics, and socio-economic change, new essays included an ever-increasing number of characteristic features. Postmodernism was "a number of related cultural tendencies, a constellation of values, a repertoire of procedures and attitudes."[25] Hassan's most famous contribution to the debate, two long, opposing lists of modernist and postmodernist traits illustrate the achievements and failures of his approach. Wildly mixing stylistic terms with literary movements and philosophical abstractions, this tally offered a grab bag of concepts, from which critics and students could—and did—take what suited their needs. Conjunctural analysis it certainly was not. Nevertheless, Hassan's list proved decisive. About two-thirds down, two terms added to a cluster of psychological vocabulary that opposed modernist symptom to postmodern desire, and genital/phallic to polymorphous/androgynous. In the left column paranoia was yoked together with modernism, on the right stood schizophrenia—cipher for the literature and lifestyle of a mad counterculture.[26] Hassan's pairing of the two terms was not the first time that these psychiatric diagnoses were associated with modernism and postmodernism, respectively. But their stark opposition, easily remembered and frequently reproduced alongside the rest of the table, entered literary studies thereafter. It finds a distinct echo, for instance, in Jameson's theory of postmodern schizophrenia and its modernist remedy, a paranoid cognitive mapping.

Hassan's table also presented the most comprehensive liberal reappraisal yet of postmodern literature. Howe and Fiedler, both former Marxists who remained on the liberal left, largely identified postmodernism with authors that had attracted as much attention for their supposedly immoral life-styles in the 1950s as for their writing. Jack Kerouac, Allen Ginsberg, John Barth, Mailer, and Burroughs were some of the authors they contrasted with their modernist forbears, or more palatable contemporaries. The charge of insanity leveled at the Beats and other counterculture icons was usually a straightforward moral indictment by critics who valued reason above all. Various forms of insanity were a common motif in countercultural writing, of course, and the positive spin authors put on madness, including their own mental troubles, made them an easy target. Beyond such thematic concerns, hardly any literary analysis was involved in labeling postmodern literature mad. Consequently, the psychological vocabulary varied widely from text to text, and sometimes from one paragraph to the next. Instead, psychopathology summarized succinctly what was most threatening about the 1950s counterculture to liberal critics: the flaunting of a promiscuous, often gay, sexuality; the exploration of drugs and altered states of being; bohemian attitudes toward work and family—in short, everything that could undermine early Cold War values shared by wide sections of the establishment.

Writing on postmodernism in the early 1970s offered a somewhat different perspective. The Beats, to the extent that the term still applied, no longer seemed quite as threatening. Neither did some of the more recent postmodern fiction, from Ken Kesey to Thomas Pynchon and the then fashionable French *nouveau roman*.[27] The scope of acceptable behavior was changing rapidly, particularly for younger critics like Hassan, and the Cold War rivals themselves showed signs of fatigue as political détente approached. In any case, Hassan now focused as much on the visual and performing arts as on literature. A whole new roster joined the ranks of the postmodern in his essays: painters Andy Warhol and Robert Rauschenberg, the architects Robert Venturi and Charles Jencks, composer John Cage, the dancer and choreographer Merce Cunningham. Considering this diverse group, Hassan shifted emphasis from postmodern decline and dispersal to willful play and process. Pop art, hailed earlier by Fiedler, undoubtedly played a role in this redefinition, as did a decorative architecture, and a more tongue-in-cheek literature.

In the process, the postmodern was made safe for liberalism. Or rather, postmodernism itself became an example of anti-communist values. Postmodernism's "anti-authoritarianism," which Hassan saw as one of its distinguishing virtues, found numerous stylistic equivalents on his list. Thus, in an overt parallel to American democracy, postmodernism was open and participatory in form. In contrast to the heavy baggage carried by modernism, it was all about surface, while rejecting *grande* for *petite histoire*.[28]

Finally, this new epitome of liberal culture—soon to be promoted to friend and foe abroad as the expression of American freedom and ingenuity—left behind metaphysics to enjoy irony and immanence. By association, the psychological vocabulary included in the table could be more concretely defined as part of a playful postmodern style. Whereas paranoia stood for a closed form that was potentially elitist and totalitarian, schizophrenia was open and anarchic. As we will see, these associations functioned in various combinations, turning schizophrenia into an effective tool for literary criticism. No longer merely a cipher for immorality, the term could now perform critical work in the analysis of politics and culture, without thereby losing its considerable ethical charge.

In the next section, Jameson's writings on postmodernism will be read for their appropriation of a specifically French psychopathology. But looking back at postwar criticism from Trilling to Hassan, it's worth emphasizing how many of the characteristics that Jameson assembled into a 'cultural logic' had already been established. I have mentioned Trilling as the precursor of a method seeking to decipher literature's political unconscious. A decade later, Fiedler pinpointed a distinct lack of historicity, one of Jameson's main arguments. Harry Levin, writing a year after Fiedler, set postmodernism against the canonization of modernism in universities and museums.[29] More comprehensively than either of them, Hassan spoke of postmodernism's new temporality, postmodern patchwork and parody, and its fable for simulation and simulacra. Jameson picks up on all of these characteristics, and his debt to US literary criticism contradicts a tendency to read him as a critical theorist whose work almost exclusively builds on European thought. His close relationship to a distinctively American intellectual culture also makes it imperative to read his reflections on postmodernism in the context of the renewed Cold War of the 1980s.

6.2 Translating French Philosophies of Madness

Warhol and Rauschenberg, Cage and Cunningham, Ginsberg and Burroughs were all declared representatives of a new postmodern culture by critics during the 1960s and early '70s. They also shared another characteristic: they were all prominent members of a New York art scene that had long served as a gateway for intellectual currents crossing the Atlantic in both directions. Surrealism, Dada, phenomenology, and existentialism were just some of the intellectual movements that had made an impression in the United States, and they were soon to be joined by a new influx of ideas from France. Foucault, whose *Folie et Déraison* (1961) was translated in a heavily abridged version as *Madness and Civilization*, already featured in Fiedler and Hassan. The same was true for Laing, who edited the book series in which *Madness and Civilization* appeared, and whose *The Divided Self* (1960) became a bestseller across the Atlantic. This interest in new ideas was anything but one-sided. Foucault shared a deep interest in US literature with Deleuze and Guattari (whose *Anti-Oedipus* would sing the praises of the Beats, Melville, Henry Miller, and Fitzgerald), as well as Jean Baudrillard, soon to become the darling of avantgarde art. Foucault's prominence as a radical thinker was rivaled by the reception of Roland Barthes and, increasingly, Jacques Derrida.

In his history of their American reception, Francois Cusset links the enthusiastic welcome French thinkers received upon their arrival to the gradual disappearance of the New York Intellectuals, prominently among them Trilling. Their political reversals and McCarthyist repression left "a void at the heart of American public space," to be filled by French theory.[30] Cusset's metaphor ignores the continuing influence of liberal ideas, not to mention more dissident intellectual traditions, which made a decisive impact on the reception of European thought. The invention of 'French theory' out of a disparate, sometimes bitterly opposed, group of philosophers makes sense only within the force field of the Cold War humanities: an intellectual scene that prized politics as rhetoric but kept political action at bay; that valued ambiguity, irony, paradox, and conceptual abstraction in literature but sidelined issues of economy and class. This story is a much larger one than can be written here, and considerable parts of it are yet to be told. As far as the US reception of French psychopathology is concerned, however, major strands intersected at the aforementioned "Schizo-Culture" conference, held from 13–16 November 1975 in Manhattan. Bringing together philosophers, critical psychiatrists, activists within the mental patients' liberation movement, literary authors, and an unruly audience drawn from the city's art and bohemian scene, this event proved to be conflict-laden and chaotic. As organizer Sylvère Lotringer recalls, the publication of the *Anti-Oedipus* two years earlier provided the inspiration for this meeting of different radical currents. Speakers included Deleuze and Guattari, Foucault, Laing, Jean-Francois Lyotard, and the ever-present Burroughs. To this were added a number of workshops on issues such as "Feminism and Therapy," led by British analyst Susie Orbach, and the "Politics of Psycho-Surgery." After the *Village Voice* advertised the conference as its 'pick of the week,' 2,000 visitors flooded the venue at Columbia University. In the end, they participated more actively than many of the keynote speakers were comfortable with: Guattari was booed off stage and Foucault accused of being a CIA stooge by an audience member.

The chaos and conflict at "Schizo-Culture" could be read as an instance of a non-hierarchical schizophrenic politics, as Lotringer does, at least in retrospect.[31] The talks collected in the volume, and the absences from it, highlight a different aspect. Politically and intellectually, the mid-1970s represented a breaking point for radical politics in the United States: after the withdrawal of troops from Vietnam, the anti-war movement's rallying cause disappeared and progressive forces rapidly splintered into different factions and issues. At "Schizo-Culture," the vocal protests against Guattari's autocratic handling of a panel chaired by him—he proposed to cut

Semiotext(e)

sponsors a colloquium on

schizo culture

13-16 november 1975
columbia university

"One does not desire revolution, desire is revolutionary"
—G. DELEUZE and F. GUATTARI

"The power to punish is not essentially different from the power to cure or to educate"
—M. FOUCAULT

Thursday, November 13

2:30 p.m. (Harkness):

Sylvère Lotringer, John Rajchman
Introduction

James Fessenden
Transversality and Style

7:30 p.m. (Harkness):

Arthur Danto
Freudian Explanation

Jean-François Lyotard
La Force des Faibles

Friday, November 14

9:30 a.m.

Workshops: **Psychiatry and Social Control. — Radical Therapy. — Schizo-City [Harlem]; Cinema: Representation and Energetics. — Ontologico-hysterical theatre.**

2:30 p.m. (Harkness):

Robert Fine
Psychiatry and Materialism

Joel Kovel
Therapy in Late Capitalism

François Péraldi
A Schizo and the Institution

Panel with Félix Guattari

8:00 p.m. (S.I.A.):

William Burroughs
The Impasses of Control

Michel Foucault
Nous ne sommes pas Réprimés

Saturday, November 15

10 a.m. (A-B Law)

Panel on Prisons/Asylums
Judy Clark, Michel Foucault, Robert Michels, David Rothman

2:30 p.m. (A-B Law)

John Cage
Empty Words

Gilles Deleuze
Le Régime des Signes

8:00 p.m. (A-B Law)

Ti Grace Atkinson
The Psyche of Social Movements

Félix Guattari
Politique et Signification

Sunday, November 16

9:30 a.m.

Meetings will be held at the Maison Française of the French Department, 560 W. 113 St.
Workshops: **Feminism and Therapy.—Psychoanalysis and Politics.— Gay Liberation—Mental Patients' Liberation**

2:30 p.m.

Workshops: **Prison Politics — Lincoln Detox. — Mass Culture. — Psychoanalysis and Schizoanalysis**

9:00 p.m. (John Jay):

Schizo-Party

Information: Write to Semiotext(e), 522 Philosophy Hall, Columbia University, N.Y.C. 10027
Contribution: Six dollars (students), twelve dollars (others). Checks or money orders payable to Semiotext(e), Inc. Register early if you wish to receive abstracts in advance. Fee includes a copy of the proceedings of the Schizo-Culture colloquium in Semiotext(e). Subscriptions to Semiotext(e): $7.00 (individual), $12.00 (institution).

Figure 6.1 A poster advertising a conference on "Schizo-Culture," held at New York's Columbia University from November 13–16, 1975. Courtesy of Semiotexte

everyone's presentation short mid-way through the first paper—exposed basic conflicts about leadership and organizational democracy. The accusations against Foucault came from right-wing provocateurs, who had been infiltrating the movement for years. The media theorist Mark Poster recalls "a feeling of things falling apart," and the volume not only documents Deleuze and Foucault's well-known rejection of Freudianism and the Frankfurt School but sharp attacks on Laing and mental patients' liberation by the psychiatrist Joel Kovel.[32] Whereas the main stage was shared almost exclusively by male academics and writers, feminist and grassroots issues found themselves relegated to parallel workshops and are not recorded in the book.

"Schizo-Culture" also had more productive outcomes. Deleuze's only visit to the United States sparked meetings with Burroughs and Ginsberg, and a trip in search of California's counterculture with Guattari. Burroughs's remarks at the conference, which inspired Deleuze's later essay on societies of control, marked a new inflection of schizophrenia.[33] As Burroughs notes, the conference title refers not to "clinical schizophrenia but to the fact that the culture is divided up into all sorts of classes and groups, etc., and that some of the old lines are breaking down, and that this is a healthy sign."[34] Burroughs certainly had not read *Anti-Oedipus*. His comments nevertheless presented an Americanized take on Deleuze and Guattari's machine of schizophrenic desire. The notion that desire could become a revolutionizing force that broke down norms and hierarchies carried obvious appeal to an anti-establishment libertarian. Burroughs's prestige also served as an entrance point into the New York arts scene for the French expatriate Lotringer.

In 1978 Lotringer edited an issue of the journal *Sémiotexte* that printed some of the talks from the conference three years earlier, among them Burroughs's comments on social control, and advanced schizophrenia as an artistic style and experimental method. In addition to speakers present at the conference, the journal issue included poems by Kathy Acker, reprinted the lyrics of the Ramones song "Teenage Lobotomy," and featured interviews with composer Philip Glass, dancer Douglas Dunn, and stage director Robert Wilson. The topic of schizophrenia played a role in all of these texts, but a group of artists around Kathryn Bigelow also sought to incorporate notions of dispersal, delirium, and non-hierarchical collaboration visually. They interspersed magazine advertisements for anti-psychotic medication with images of violence and sadomasochism and divided pages into columns of varying sizes in order to induce a kind of "experimental delirium" in readers.[35] The guiding idea, in Lotringer's words, was that "it is impossible to understand anything about schizophrenia if one doesn't participate in it in some way."[36] Certain elements of *Sémiotexte*'s design appear rather literal-minded, advancing little beyond the inherited notion of schizophrenia as splitting. Nonetheless the emphasis on the creative force of schizophrenia, its introduction as an aesthetic formula derived from contemporary philosophy, left an impression on an arts scene that was rapidly becoming more conceptual and would soon immerse itself in French theory.

Acker's novels, in particular, fuse a philosophical understanding of madness with the avant garde sensibility of New York's conceptual art scene and Burroughs's science-fictional dystopias. In a later interview, Acker described her interest in schizophrenia as an aesthetic model. Basing her writing on the "idea that you don't need to have a central identity, that a split identity was a more viable way in the world," she combined explicit sex scenes and sometimes fake autobiographical strands with material lifted from other authors.[37] The result was a frequently non-linear pastiche that attempted to induce an experience of schizophrenia in readers, presenting them with narrative fragments and characters whose identities were equally dispersed and whose gender and sexuality approached complete fluidity.[38] Acker's method self-consciously appropriated what she observed in the work of contemporary artists. Indeed, Sol Lewitt quickly became one of Acker's mentors, subsidizing the publication of her early books. Different pieces of writing would be created following a set of guidelines established in advance to counter any notion of literary inspiration. Acker's fascination with schizophrenia had initially been piqued by antipsychiatry, specifically Laing and Cooper. Lotringer and the Schizo-Culture conference introduced Acker to Foucault, as well as to Deleuze and Guattari, supplying her with additional philosophical vocabulary.

All these influences are present in *Empire of the Senseless* (1988), one of her later novels. Set in the near future in Paris, the book aims to deconstruct on the nuclear family, part of an explicitly anti-Freudian attack on patriarchal violence, as well as the Cold War nexus of psychiatry and political oppression. Specifically, Acker picks up on military uses of psychiatry and returns to lobotomy as a metaphor for mind control. For Acker all these avenues lead to the subversion of reason. Echoes of the *Anti-Oedipus* can be heard in theoretical statements that occasionally intersperse the narrative. "Reason is always in the service of the political and economic masters," writes Acker. "It is here that literature strikes [. . .] Literature is that which denounces and slashes apart the repressing machine."[39] In keeping with this pronouncement, Acker's politics amounts to a schizophrenic dispersal of libinous energy, the darkly carnivalesque abandonment of the self. Thus, although the novel's ruminations on state power follow in Burroughs's footsteps, Acker rejects the paranoid desire for knowledge that drive the former's fiction. As she argued, using Watergate as an example for the machinations of American politicians: "Everybody now knows that's happening. [. . .] they just don't give a damn. The society's totally disintegrated."[40] Rather than countering this disintegration, Acker aims at the opposite. In her Deleuzian transvaluation, schizophrenia appears as liberation from identity.

Acker's friend and mentor Lotringer, then teaching at Columbia, was only one among a number of scholars who were starting to apply Deleuze and Guattari's writings. None of them should have a greater impact than Jameson. Perhaps the most influential cultural critic writing in the 1980s and '90s, Jameson authored a series of essays that blended psychopathology and postmodernism more closely than before or after. Jameson's appropriation of the term schizophrenia needs to be seen in the context of his continuous concern with subjectivity and, more particularly, modernity's defining split between subject and object. From his first published essay onward, Jameson consistently described this split as a two-fold disintegration of subject and object that he would call schizophrenic from the mid-1970s onward. As elsewhere, schizophrenia functions not as a medical diagnosis but a cultural metaphor. Jameson translates psychopathology into a figuration of structural crisis—the destruction of the Marxist Left, leaving behind only isolated splinters incapable of sustained or coordinated action. This experience of fragmentation concerns not so much the Sixties for Jameson, about which he proved strikingly fatalistic, but rather the repression of the postwar years. Born in 1934, Jameson has said very little in public about growing up in the early Cold War but described himself as a "person of the 1950s rather than the 1960s" in an interview.[41] The term Cold War appears quite rarely and in off-hand remarks in his writing, which was concerned with contemporary culture at a time when the term seemed of little relevance to literary critics. Throughout, Jameson's use of schizophrenia gives expression to a structural ambivalence, a feature he inherits from earlier critics but that is further magnified in his work. Jameson formulates a left politics that seeks an exit from the straightjacket of the Cold War but is also heir to its essentially conservative pathologization of madness. Such ambivalence may not surprise, but its consequences are severe. For the understanding of a dominant subjectivity as schizophrenic, defined as the disintegration of rational insight, leads to an equally bleak view of social change, an overestimation of the power of the status quo, and ultimately prevents the construction of a coherent alternative.

In a footnote appended to the title chapter of *Postmodernism*, Jameson names two sources for his understanding of schizophrenia: Lacan's classic theory of psychosis as summarized in "On a Question Prior to Any Possible Treatment of Psychosis," and the *Anti-Oedipus*.[42] It is mostly Lacan who guides Jameson's seminal account of postmodernism, but Deleuze and Guattari have an interesting role to play. As we will see, Jameson's view of the postmodern subject is deeply pessimistic, positing a loss of autonomy, historical understanding, and intellectual capacity that draws on his reading of Lacan. At the same time, he keeps returning to Deleuze and Guattari's figure of the heroic schizophrenic and his or her deterritorializing desire. Between these two sources, psychosis becomes Jameson's central trope for the status of the contemporary subject for almost two decades. Consider the following enumeration in "Postmodernism, or the Cultural Logic of Late Capitalism," the peak of Jameson's cultural pathology:

> a new depthlessness, which finds its prolongation both in contemporary 'theory' and in a whole new culture of the image or the simulacrum; a consequent weakening of historicity, both in our relationship to public History and in the new forms of our private temporality, whose 'schizophrenic' structure (following Lacan) will determine new types of syntax or syntagmatic relationships in the more temporal arts; a whole new type of emotional ground tone—what I will call intensities [. . .] the deep constitutive relationship of all this to a whole new technology, which is itself a figure for a whole new economic world system[43]

This passage summarizes the main properties identified by Jameson as postmodern. Within it, the diagnosis of a schizophrenic structure arguably determines postmodernism's key features: the inability to structure past and present leads to a failure to map global capitalism—symbolized in paranoid narratives and the unnavigable spaces of a building like John Portman's Bonaventure Hotel. The postmodern subject experiences not genuine feelings but the "intensities" and "waning of affect" Jameson deduces from the autobiography of a schizophrenic girl.[44] Lacking in personal identity and historical continuity, this subject falls for the simulacra of mass culture and produces art without personal style that is characterized by pastiche and nostalgia.[45] Jameson's debt to earlier critics becomes apparent in his emphasis on simulacra and postmodernism's lack of historical understanding— features already analyzed by Fiedler and Hassan. Yet, these are due to changes in lived experience, a distinct subjectivity that forms the gravitational center of Jameson's account.

Jameson first discusses the term schizophrenia at length in an essay on modernism in 1975, the same year as the "Schizo-Culture" conference. Here, Jameson uses the term in strikingly different ways from the later evocation of loss and fragmentation.[46] What proved attractive in the 1970s were rather the interpretative possibilities he detected in the *Anti-Oedipus*. Like its co-authors, Jameson sees schizophrenia as a figure for "decoded flux" and the book plays a central role in *Fables of Aggression* (1979) and *The Political Unconscious* (1981).[47] In the first, the prose of Wyndham Lewis heralds "the emergence of some new, properly postmodernist or schizophrenic conception of the cultural artifact" and is rewritten as the literary coding and decoding of libidinal energies.[48] *The Political Unconscious*, in turn, explicitly aligns its hermeneutic method with that of Deleuze and Guattari. Jameson's cooption of the *Anti-Oedipus* is all the more striking given their considerable political differences but provides evidence of its impact on his thought.

The Political Unconscious proves interesting for other reasons as well. Its neo-Marxist theory of interpretation made Jameson an academic celebrity, and his reflections on method and modernism still dazzle. Yet as Tobin Siebers has argued, postmodern criticism derives much of its coherence from the Cold War lurking in its shadows.⁴⁹ This becomes clearest in the vocabulary literary critics use to describe their epistemology. As I noted in my earlier discussion of paranoid narrative, one major consequence of Cold War politics was to destabilize judgment: to induce a profound skepticism about truth and falsehood, so that interpretation was to remain constantly aware of ambiguity and double meaning. From the very beginning, the *Political Unconscious* sets out to reject the ideological restrictions of liberal critique. As Jameson writes, the book's aim is to "demonstrate the structural limitations of [. . .] [its] 'strategies of containment.' " In turn, Jameson contains liberal criticism by his recourse to what he sees as a superior Marxism.⁵⁰ Jameson critiques a Cold War strategy only to repeat it and remains caught in its vocabulary. Postmodernism appears as a "complex and mushrooming cultural superstructure" that spreads like nuclear radiation. Its political meaning appears secret, driven underground, and must be unearthed by the author and critic.⁵¹

Deleuze and Guattari may be the more prominent references in the *Political Unconscious* but this changes drastically with Jameson's first foray into postmodernism. Perry Anderson has christened Jameson's 1982 lecture at New York's Whitney Museum "a prodigious inaugural gesture that has commanded the field ever since."⁵² In contrast to the essays of the 1970s, a broadly Lacanian conception of psychosis, and thus a perspective on schizophrenia that stresses not an unbound flow of intensities but the subject's fragmentation, dominates from the first version of "Postmodernism and Consumer Society" onward. But where psychosis leads to the constitution of a qualitatively different subject for Lacan, Jameson decrees a fragmentation of subjectivity per se. As he writes a year later: "[W]hen the links of the signifying chain snap, then we have schizophrenia in the form of a rubble of distinct and unrelated signifiers."⁵³ Lacan's broken signifying chain is transformed from an accident that triggers the psychotic break into the structure of psychosis as such.⁵⁴ In contrast, Lacan consistently speaks of the psychotic as a subject, and is at pains to sketch her or his different subjective logic rather than simple disintegration.⁵⁵ Despite appearances, then, Jameson's aim in using the term schizophrenia is not primarily a critique of contemporary structures of subjectivity (not to speak of its clinical forms) but a pathology of culture. So why did Jameson move from Deleuze and Guattari to a simplified Lacanian conception of schizophrenia?

It's important to stress that Jameson's interest in the *Anti-Oedipus* always lay in the interpretative possibilities opened up by schizoanalysis rather than Deleuzian schizophrenia as such. Quite rightly, schizophrenia never functioned as the harbinger of a possible revolution for Jameson but provided a critical tool for literary interpretation. As a consequence, he always kept his distance from the "glorification of schizophrenia (and of the schizophrenic as the 'true hero of desire') to be found in Deleuze and Guattari's *Anti-Oedipus*."[56] Even in *The Political Unconscious*, which explicitly sought them as methodological allies, the evaluation of Deleuzian politics was unambiguously negative.[57] By the time Jameson turned from modernist literature to the postmodern present, the two founders of schizoanalysis had themselves moved away from their original celebration of schizophrenia.[58] More decisively, perhaps, Jameson's work on postmodernism called for analyzing an era that resembled not so much the alienation of modernist culture but seemed entirely "isolated, disconnected, discontinuous."[59] His adaptation of Lacanian psychosis would furnish him with exactly such a description.

The proximity of Jameson's schizophrenic subject to its so-called 'poststructuralist' deconstructions seems obvious. This has led commentators to describe Jameson's account of subjective fragmentation as "quasi-poststructuralist."[60] However, Jameson arrives at his analysis not via a widespread disillusionment with Marxism that followed the defeat of the left in 1968 but rather by way of a unique reading of Western Marxism that leads to a partial alignment with strands of contemporary French philosophy. The overwhelming influence of the work of Georg Lukács on Jameson sheds light on Jameson's understanding of subjectivity.[61] In the central chapter of *History and Class Consciousness*, Lukács elevates the concept of reification to the central force of a mature capitalism, under which he summarizes not only Marx's alienation and objectivation but Max Weber's concept of rationalization. Reification becomes the single most important process of capitalist society and tears asunder the objective and the subjective. Lukács writes: "The rational breaking-apart of the work process destroys the organic necessity with which inter-related processes are unified [. . .] Secondly, this fragmentation of the object of production necessarily entails the fragmentation of the subject."[62]

Lukács's understanding of reification and its consequences for the capitalist subject are evident throughout Jameson's work. He already refers to capitalism as a disintegration of the subjective and objective in his first published article. Slightly later, he describes the reduction of the subject, in terms reminiscent of Lukács's account of industrial work, "to a mere component part," and this conception remains at the center of his analysis of culture.[63] As Jameson writes in 1984, the postmodern "shift in the dynamics of cultural pathology can be characterized as one in which the alienation of the subject is displaced by the fragmentation of the subject."[64] Jameson's exact repetition of Lukács's phrase of the "fragmentation of the subject" also explains his emphasis on the breakdown of the signifying chain before all other elements of Lacanian schizophrenia. His foregrounding of this aspect of schizophrenia results less from a casual adaptation, or even a misunderstanding, of Lacan but owes to Lukács's Marxism.

Jameson's cultural pathology should be understood as motivated by two main considerations. The Deleuzian and Lacanian vocabulary allows him to reframe long-standing Marxist concerns with a loss of subjective agency. To put it differently: the term schizophrenia gives such traditional debates a broader appeal in an Anglo-American academia in thrall to French philosophy. The agent in question is not individual, but the working class as Marxism's revolutionary subject. Ultimately, the conception of a schizophrenic postmodernism attempts to think the absence of a revolutionary class at the end of the twentieth century. This does not mean that psychopathology merely acts as superficial sheen for an essentially unreconstructed Marxism. Standing in a long tradition of Marxist appropriations of psychoanalysis, Lacan's work allows Jameson to think the consequences of contemporary capitalism on psychological structure. But the potential of this conjunction is severely undermined by Jameson's conception of psychosis as a fragmentation of subjective agency, rather than changes within subjective organization. In other words, schizophrenia and reification are seen as one-way streets. For Jameson, these social processes can only lead to a loss of agency—and in line with such an understanding he at various points speaks of psychosis as a disease.[65] Despite the absence of overt moral judgments of the kind found in Hassan and Fiedler, Jameson's work remains part of a pathologizing politics of madness, and is characterized by the constitutive ambivalence toward the psychoanalytical vocabulary it employs. In contrast to its liberal version, however, Jameson's cultural pathology is not so much directed at an ideological enemy but functions as an inward-looking explanation of defeat, a defensive Marxism concerned less with political gain than with the mourning of loss.

6.3 Reaganism as Dystopia, or, Fredric Jameson's Postmodernity

The reference to Lukács is important for reasons that go beyond the details of Jameson's conception of schizophrenia. It returns us to my stated intention to connect Jamesonian schizophrenia to the politics of postmodernism. As I argued earlier, Jameson's bleak view of the postmodern subject as dispersed, fragmented, and disconnected from itself and society can help account for many of the contradictions and gaps in his cultural politics. Jameson's reliance on Lukács's reification as his central link between economy and culture has been amply criticized.[66] As Lambert Zuidervaart notes, Jameson portrays postmodernity as an era in which "reification has become nearly total both on the side of the subject and on the side of the object."[67] Zuidervaart's characterization of a "nearly total" split between subject and object indicates that Jameson also retains a residual if highly problematized space for counter-hegemonic practice.

This extreme rift between the object and the subject is given its most dystopian expression in Jameson's writings of the mid- and late 1980s. Against a background of cultural and economic reaction under Ronald Reagan postmodernism appears at its most overwhelming and total.[68] In an interview in 1987, Jameson describes postmodernism as "a situation where subjects and objects have been dissolved, hyperspace is the ultimate of the object-pole, intensity the ultimate of the subject-pole, though we no longer have subjects and objects."[69] Given the extreme effects of psychotic fragmentation Jameson detected and the absence of a working class subject, any radical politics was thrown in doubt. The political impetus of Jameson's thought meant that the theorization of emancipatory practice was never absent from his work for long. But as I want to argue over the next few pages, Jameson's endeavors in this field remain riddled by serious contradictions as long as they are conceived within the force field of schizophrenia and reification.

We have seen how Jameson conceived of the postmodern subject as fragmented, depthless or even, as in the excerpt above, as non-existent. Added to this were the results of reification on the object world—a view that informs the references to simulation and hyperspace. Indeed, Baudrillard's anti-utopian vision of a world of simulacra disconnected from reality and a society caught in the hyperreal had been the dominant influence on Jameson's account of postmodern image culture.[70] At times, Jameson seems to side outright with a Baudrillardean anti-utopianism:

> What we now begin to feel, therefore—and what begins to emerge as some deeper and more fundamental constitution of postmodernity itself, at least its temporal dimension—is henceforth, where everything now submits to the perpetual change of fashion and the media image, that nothing can change any longer.[71]

If nothing were able to change any longer in postmodernity, the system would by definition be total. Although Jameson conceives of postmodernism as a cultural dominant that coexists with resistant and heterogeneous elements, there is a tendency in his work to conceive of it as all-encompassing.[72] As he writes with reference to the related pessimism of Theodor Adorno: "Here at length [the 1980s], in this decade which has just ended but is still ours, Adorno's prophecies of the 'total system' finally came true."[73] Despite Jameson's doubts about the social movements of the 1960s and '70s, his views still reflected a renewed sense of defeat after two terms under Ronald Reagan from 1981–89. Reagan's attempt to rekindle anti-communism, and the constant lurch of US politics to the right during his time in office, reinforced the view that even the remaining pockets of progress were now on the wane. As Jameson writes in his major statement on the decade, the essay "Periodizing the 60s": the sense of universal freedom that then had felt like a realistic possibility now seemed "a historical illusion."[74]

Yet even as Jameson presented his readers with such a bleak outlook, he aimed at alternatives. Three paths toward an emancipatory politics emerge from his work on postmodernism. Most famous is the notion of "cognitive mapping."[75] The second, increasingly prominent from the 1990s onward, is utopia.[76] Thirdly, and in lesser detail, Jameson has written on what he calls homeopathy.[77] Jameson defines "cognitive mapping" as a modernist project and a code word for class consciousness.[78] More specifically, cognitive mapping is conceived as a reaction to a spatial problematic: the spatiality of postmodernism that Jameson traces to the fragmentation of subject and object, the first unable to recount its history and situate itself in a narrative, the second transformed into a surface of identical copies and unnavigable spaces. Cognitive mapping can be understood as a striving for totality, which allows the individual to critically apprehend global capitalism. If Jameson tends to imagine postmodernism as all-encompassing, cognitive mapping can be seen as a logical reaction to it: an attempt to think such an outside—the system named and conceived in its totality—from the *inside* of postmodern culture, be it cyberpunk literature or conspiracy film.[79] The Cold War is never explicitly discussed and rarely mentioned in these essays. However, Jameson tends to discuss genres that are intimately concerned with Cold War politics. Whether in his reading of Dick's science fiction novel *Time Out of Joint*, or the crime thriller *Three Days of the Condor*, in which Robert Redford plays a CIA researcher pursued by his superiors, these texts examine the manifestations of the national security state at the same time as they mimic its hermeneutics of suspicion. Jameson's analysis of the films *Salvador* and *Under Fire* shows a keen appreciation of US imperialism in the Third World and continues his remarkable history of the Sixties as a global conjuncture in "Periodizing the 60s." And unlike many analyses of Cold War culture in the 1990s, which overemphasized the domestic influence of containment, Jameson also stresses the productive power of modernization and interstate rivalry, from the space race to the newest blessings of consumer culture and its image worlds.

From all this, organized politics remains absent, at times bafflingly so. Jameson's luxurious prose glides over representations of political actors and events to plant his writing ever so firmly in its twin anchors of the economy and its cultural logic, or the objective versus the subjective. With the perceived absence of a revolutionary subject in the postmodern present, cognitive mapping takes on an essentially utopian quality—class consciousness awaiting its class subject.[80] The problem lies not solely in the absence of class in Jameson's writing, or more precisely, in his disinterest in the progressive potential of existing class formations. Cognitive mapping, while undeniably important, comes to play such a prominent role only because Jameson denies postmodernism any subversive potential.[81] Usually, Jameson identifies subversive impulses as belonging to that which projects an outside, the future society of utopia. This utopian impulse is part of the political unconscious of postmodernism, hidden under a surface conceived as so homogeneous as to have repressed its own yearnings for a different future. Driven underground and pointing to a time utterly different from the postmodern present, utopia is both inside and outside but importantly allows Jameson to retain the largely self-identical character of postmodernism. At other times, Jameson designates political art in the postmodern as essentially modernist, that, is as being part of another outside, the past seen as more effectively critical. Jameson's bias, whether justified or not, recalls the preference of earlier critics like Howe and Fiedler for modernist reason against a postmodernism deemed irrational. This is not to claim that utopian impulses are absent from postmodern culture, or that it does not retain modernist forms. On the contrary, Jameson's analyses of utopian or conspiratorial texts *within* the postmodern clearly shows that it not only preserves the critical power of earlier cultural forms but produces new constellations that speak of the subversive potential of postmodernism itself.

Jameson's third and final strategy of resistance, termed homeopathy, alone conceptualizes resistance to postmodernism from within. Homeopathy appears to be a reaction to an impasse Jameson perceived in his theorization of the postmodern. Writing about Hans Haacke, he notes that his oppositional yet clearly postmodern art "does not compute within the paradigm and does not seem to have been theoretically foreseen by it."[82] Jameson's solution to this exception comes 250 pages later in the conclusion to *Postmodernism*, where he conceives of a "more properly postmodern political aesthetic," which would be intent on "undermining the image by way of the image itself, and planning the implosion of the logic of the simulacrum by dint of ever greater doses of simulacra."[83] Arguably, critical contemporary culture frequently enacts such a weakening of postmodernism from within. However, this homeopathic strategy is never fully theorized and does not play any role in Jameson's later work.

Jameson's conception of homeopathy is also undermined by the association with Baudrillard's anti-utopian sociology and, in particular, his *Symbolic Exchange and Death*, on which Jameson draws.[84] Given his conviction that "the subject [. . .] has been lost," and "every reality is absorbed by the hyperreality of [. . .] simulation," Baudrillard does not seem too concerned with social change.[85] Still, Jameson conceives of simulation as a Baudrillardean repetition of sameness rather than, with that other contemporary philosopher of the simulacrum, Gilles Deleuze, as the repetition of difference: an adherence expressed in his understanding of homeopathy as ever greater doses of simulacra rather than the copy's inherent difference with itself.[86] Jameson's preference for a Baudrillardean model of repetition is understandable given his perspective on Deleuze and Guattari's politics of schizophrenia. But the foundation of homeopathy on sameness betrays its debt to a related conception of postmodernism as totality that fails to open up postmodernism to the gaps and fissures in which an oppositional politics could emerge.

Cognitive mapping, utopia, and homeopathy all seek to construct escape routes from a late Cold War culture that appears overwhelmingly homogeneous in Jameson's writings of the 1980s. As he himself warns at one point, "the more powerfully one has been able to underscore and isolate the antipolitical features of the newer cultural dominant [. . .] the more one paints oneself into a corner."[87] All three of Jameson's subversive strategies mark important challenges to a late capitalist culture, all three retain their relevance even after the Cold War officially ends, an ending with which the publication of these pessimistic essays somewhat ironically coincides. Yet every single one of these conceptions founders on a dystopian conception of the American present: a schizophrenic postmodernity that carries the traces of a postwar discourse whose moralism it ultimately cannot escape. Only on the margins of Jameson's writing at the time, far removed from the Reaganist dystopia that subtends his conception of postmodernism, can a different conception of schizophrenia emerge. In a passage that evokes antipsychiatric thought, madness sheds its pathology for a moment to imagine a future freed from the fetters of Cold War culture and neoliberal capitalism. Such a world would amount to:

a Utopia of misfits and oddballs, in which the constraints for uniformization and conformity have been removed, and human beings grow like wild plants in a state of nature [. . .] who, no longer fettered by the constraints of a now oppressive sociality, blossom into the neurotics, compulsives, obsessives, paranoids and schizophrenics, whom our society considers sick but who, in a world of true freedom, may make up the flora and the fauna of 'human nature' itself.[88]

Notes

1 Lionel Trilling, "Art and Neurosis," in *The Liberal Imagination: Essays on Literature and Society* (Oxford: Oxford University Press, 1981), 167. Italics in the original.
2 Trilling, "Freud and Literature," in *The Liberal Imagination*, 38.
3 Trilling, preface to *The Liberal Imagination*, vii.
4 Ibid.
5 For a version of this argument see: Thomas Hill Schaub, *American Fiction in the Cold War* (Madison, WI: University of Wisconsin Press, 1991).
6 Trilling, preface to *The Liberal Imagination*, ix.
7 Ibid, xi.
8 Trilling, "Art and Neurosis," in *The Liberal Imagination*, 156.
9 Leslie Fiedler, introduction to *The Collected Essays of Leslie Fiedler*, vol. II. (New York: Stein and Day, 1971), ix–x.
10 Ihab Hassan, "Culture, Indeterminacy, and Immanence: Margins of the (Postmodern) Age," in *The Postmodern Turn: Essays in Postmodern Theory and Culture* (Columbus: Ohio State University Press, 1987), 65.
11 For a detailed recent account see: Alan M. Wald, *American Night: The Literary Left in the Era of the Cold War* (Chapel Hill: The University of North Carolina Press, 2012).

12 Ihab Hassan, "Pluralism in Postmodern Perspective," in *The Postmodern Turn*, 178.
13 Ann Douglas, "Periodizing the American Century: Modernism, Postmodernism, and Postcolonialism in the Cold War Context," *Modernism/Modernity* 5, no. 3 (1998): 71–98; and Tobin Siebers, *Cold War Criticism and the Politics of Skepticism* (New York: Oxford University Press, 1993).
14 Perry Anderson, *The Origins of Postmodernity* (London: Verso, 1998), 7.
15 C. Wright Mills, *The Sociological Imagination* (Oxford: Oxford University Press, 2000), 165–166.
16 Irving Howe, "Mass Society and Postmodern Fiction," in *Decline of the New* (London: Gollancz, 1971), 205.
17 Ibid.
18 Ibid.
19 Leslie Fiedler, "The New Mutants," in *The Collected Essays of Leslie Fiedler*, vol. II (New York: Stein and Day, 1971), 384.
20 Ibid., 395.
21 The phrase "literature of exhaustion" is John Barth's. See John Barth, "The Literature of Exhaustion," in *The Friday Book: Essays and Other Non-Fiction* (Baltimore: Johns Hopkins University Press, 1984), 62–76.
22 Ihab Hassan, *The Dismemberment of Orpheus: Toward a Postmodern Literature* (New York: Oxford University Press, 1971), x.
23 Ibid., 152.
24 See Ihab Hassan, "POSTmodernISM: A Paracritical Bibliography," *New Literary History* 3, no. 1 (1971): 25.
25 Ihab Hassan, "Toward a Concept of Postmodernism," in *The Postmodern Turn*, 85.
26 Ibid., 92.
27 Hassan, "POSTmodernISM: A Paracritical Bibliography," 26.
28 Hassan, "Toward a Concept of Postmodernism," in *The Postmodern Turn*, 92.
29 Harry Levin, "What Was Modernism?" *The Massachusetts Review* 1 (Summer 1960): 609–630.
30 Francois Cusset, *French Theory: How Foucault, Derrida, Deleuze, & Co Transformed the Intellectual Life of the United States*, trans. Jeff Fort, Josephine Berganza, and Marlon Jones (Minneapolis: University of Minnesota Press, 2008), 22.
31 Sylvère Lotringer, introduction to *Schizo-Culture: The Event 1975*, ed. Sylvère Lotringer and David Morris (Los Angeles: Sémiotext, 2013), 20.
32 David Morris, "Schizo-Culture in Its Own Voice," in *Schizo-Culture: The Event 1975*, 212.
33 See Gilles Deleuze, "Control and Becoming," in *Negotiations* (New York: Columbia University Press, 1995), 169–176.
34 William Burroughs, "Q & A," in *Schizo-Culture: The Event 1975*, 161.
35 Sylvère Lotringer, "Notes on the Schizo-Culture Issue," in *Schizo-Culture: The Book*, ed. Sylvère Lotringer (Los Angeles: Sémiotexte, 2013), xxii.
36 Ibid.
37 Kathy Acker, "Devoured By Myths: An Interview with Sylvère Lotringer," in *Hannibal Lecter, My Father* (New York: Semiotexte, 1991), 7.
38 Sam McBride, "Un-Reason and the Ex-Centric Text: Methods of Madness in Kathy Acker's *Great Expectations*," *Critique: Studies in Contemporary Fiction* 40 (1999): 344.
39 Kathy Acker, *Empire of the Senseless* (New York: Grove, 1988), 12.
40 Acker, "Devoured By Myths," 17.
41 Ian Buchanan, *Fredric Jameson: Live Theory* (London: Continuum, 2006), 120.

42 Fredric Jameson, *Postmodernism, or, the Cultural Logic of Postmodernism* (Durham, NC: Duke University Press, 1991), 420; and see Jacques Lacan, "On a Question Prior to Any Possible Treatment of Psychosis," in *Ecrits: The First Complete Edition in English*, trans. Bruce Fink (New York: Norton, 2002), 445–488.

43 Fredric Jameson, "Postmodernism, or the Cultural Logic of Late Capitalism," *New Left Review* I/146: 58.

44 Ibid., 61 and 72–73.

45 Ibid., 64. For the discussion of nostalgia film see: Ibid., 66–68.

46 Fredric Jameson, "Beyond the Cave: Demystifying the Ideology of Modernism," in *The Ideologies of Theory: Essays 1971–1986*, vol. 2: *Syntax of History* (Minneapolis: University of Minnesota Press, 1989), 115–132.

47 Ibid., 123–128.

48 Fredric Jameson, *Fables of Aggression: Wyndham Lewis, the Modernist as Fascist* (Berkeley, CA: The University of California Press, 1979), 19–20.

49 Siebers, *Cold War Criticism*, 142.

50 Fredric Jameson, *The Political Unconscious: Narrative as a Socially Symbolic Act* (London: Methuen, 1981), x.

51 Ibid.

52 Anderson, *The Origins of Postmodernity*, 54.

53 Jameson, "Postmodernism, or the Cultural Logic of Late Capitalism," 72.

54 "On A Question Prior to Any Possible Treatment of Psychosis," in *Ecrits: The First Complete Edition in English*, 449 and 479.

55 Ibid., 448 and 470.

56 Jameson, "The Ideology of the Text," in *Ideologies of Theory*, vol. 1, 70.

57 Jameson, *The Political Unconscious*, 92.

58 Jameson refers to Deleuze's abandonment of ideal schizophrenia "in the face of all the tragedies and devastation of the drug culture among his [Deleuze's] students in the 1970s." Fredric Jameson, *A Singular Modernity: Essay on the Ontology of the Present* (London: Verso, 2002), 194.

59 Fredric Jameson, "Postmodernism and Consumer Society," in *The Anti-Aesthetic: Essays on Postmodern Culture*, ed. Hal Foster (Seattle: Bay Press, 1983), 119.

60 Peter Osborne, "A Marxism for the Postmodern? Jameson's Adorno," *New German Critique* 56 (1992): 186.

61 See, for instance: Terry Eagleton, "The Idealism of American Criticism," *New Left Review* I/127 (1981): 61 and 64.

62 George Lukács, *History and Class Consciousness: Studies in Marxist Dialectics*, trans. Rodney Livingstone (London: Merlin, 1971), 88–89 [Translation modified]. The literal translation of Lukács's German term for fragmentation, the verb *zerreißen*, is to tear apart, and stresses the breakdown into single, disconnected parts more forcefully than the English equivalent.

63 Fredric Jameson, *Marxism and Form: Twentieth-Century Dialectical Theories of Literature* (Princeton, NJ: Princeton University Press, 1971), 27.

64 Jameson, "Postmodernism, or the Cultural Logic of Late Capitalism," 63.

65 Jameson, "The Ideology of the Text," 244; and Fredric Jameson, "Reflections on the Brecht-Lukács Debate," in *The Ideologies of Theory*, vol. 2, 146.

66 Eagleton, "The Idealism of American Criticism," 64; Sean Homer, *Fredric Jameson: Marxism, Hermeneutics, Postmodernism* (Cambridge: Polity, 1998), 168; and Lambert Zuidervaart, "Realism, Modernism, and the Empty Chair," in *Postmodernism/Jameson/Critique*, ed. Douglas Kellner (Washington, DC: Maisonneuve Press, 1989), 220–223. However, the best critique of Jameson's use of Lukácsian reification is still Lukács's own in the 1967 preface to *History and*

168   *A Schizophrenic Postmodernity*

Class Consciousness: Georg Lukács, preface to *History and Class Consciousness: Studies in Marxist Dialectics*, ix–xlvii.

67 Zuidervaart, "Realism, Modernism, and the Empty Chair," in *Postmodernism/Jameson/Critique*, 221.

68 For a concise overview over the right's successful accession to economic and cultural hegemony in the United States in the late 1970s and '80s, often summarized in the key phrases of the rise of the New Right and Reaganomics: James T. Patterson, *Restless Giant: The United States from Watergate to Bush vs. Gore* (New York: Oxford University Press, 2005), 108–217.

69 Anders Stephanson, "Regarding Postmodernism: A Conversation with Fredric Jameson," in *Postmodernism/Jameson/Critique*, 47.

70 Jameson acknowledges his debt to Baudrillard in 1989 when he writes: "my version of all this [the concept of postmodernism] [. . .] obviously (but perhaps I haven't said so often enough) owes a great debt to Baudrillard." Fredric Jameson, "Marxism and Postmodernism," *New Left Review* I/176 (Jul–Aug 1989): 32. For a succinct summary of Baudrillard's conception of simulation and the hyperreal see: Jean Baudrillard, "The Precession of Simulacra," in *Simulacra and Simulation*, trans. Sheila Faria Glaser (Ann Arbor, MI: The University of Michigan Press, 1994), 1–42.

71 Fredric Jameson, "The Antinomies of Postmodernity," in *The Cultural Turn: Selected Writings on the Postmodern 1983–1998* (London: Verso, 1998), 59.

72 Jameson, *Postmodernism*, 159. Jameson's lack of distinction in his theoretical essays between postmodernism, postmodernity, and late or global capitalism seems to be an indicator of this, or vice versa, its result. Linda Hutcheon comments on this lack of distinction in: Linda Hutcheon, *The Politics of Postmodernism* (London: Routledge, 1989), 25.

73 Fredric Jameson, *Late Marxism: Adorno, or, the Persistence of the Dialectic* (London: Verso, 1990), 9.

74 Fredric Jameson, "Periodizing the 60s," in *The Ideologies of Theory*, vol. 2, 208.

75 Jameson, "Postmodernism, or the Cultural Logic of Late Capitalism," 89–92; Fredric Jameson, "Cognitive Mapping," in *Marxism and the Interpretation of Culture*, ed. Cary Nelson and Lawrence Grossberg (Urbana, IL: University of Illinois Press, 1988), 347–357; Jameson, *Postmodernism*, 409–418 and Fredric Jameson, "Totality as Conspiracy," in *The Geopolitical Aesthetic: Cinema and Space in the World System* (Bloomington, IN: Indiana University Press, 1992), 9–84.

76 Fredric Jameson, *The Seeds of Time* (New York: Columbia University Press, 1994), 73–128; and Fredric Jameson, *Archaeologies of the Future: The Desire Called Utopia and Other Science Fictions* (London: Verso, 2005).

77 Jameson, *Postmodernism*, 409.

78 Jameson, *Postmodernism*, 409 and 417–418.

79 For the discussion of paranoia in relation to conspiracy film, see: Jameson, "Totality as Conspiracy," 9–84. Cyberpunk is implied in the *New Left Review* article but only explicitly mentioned in a short paragraph added to the 1991 book chapter. Jameson, *Postmodernism*, 38. Jameson, "Postmodernism" [1984], 61–68.

80 Jameson, "Cognitive Mapping," 356.

81 For a related argument see Paul Maltby's critique of Jameson in: Paul Maltby, *Dissident Postmodernists: Barthelme, Coover, Pynchon* (Philadelphia: University of Pennsylvania Press, 1991), 11–13.

82 Ibid., 159.

83 Ibid., 409.

84 Jean Baudrillard, *Symbolic Exchange and Death*, trans. Iain Hamilton Grant (London: Sage, 1993), 71.
85 Ibid., 2 and 23.
86 Deleuze's theory of repetition can be found in: Gilles Deleuze, *Difference and Repetition*, trans. Paul Patton (London: Continuum, 2004).
87 Jameson, *Postmodernism*, 158–159.
88 Jameson, *Late Marxism: Adorno, or, the Persistence of the Dialectic*, 102.

Index